Hostess gift from Ellen Wooten - 4-21-96

Sam Okamoto's
INCREDIBLE VEGETABLES

Sam Okamoto's
INCREDIBLE
VEGETABLES

By Osamu Okamoto

PELICAN PUBLISHING COMPANY
Gretna 1994

The word "Pelican" and the depiction of a pelican are trademarks
of Pelican Publishing Company, Inc.,
and are registered in the U.S. Patent and Trademark Office.

Library of Congress Cataloging-in-Publication Data

Okamoto, Osamu
    Sam Okamoto's incredible vegetables / Osamu Okamoto.
      p.   cm.
    Includes bibliographical references and index.
    ISBN 1-56554-025-5
    1. Vegetarian cookery.   I. Title.
  TX837.039 1994
  641.5'636—dc20   94-8520
                                                           CIP

Manufactured in the United States of America.

Published by Pelican Publishing Company, Inc.
1101 Monroe Street, Gretna, Louisiana 70053

For my wife, Michelle;
my three children, Michael, Serena May, and Meghan;
and the countless friends and students
who supported me in completing this book.

Contents

Acknowledgments

I would like to express my gratitude to the following people who supported me in completing this project:

Tanya Wulff, M.D., Henning Wulff, and Michael Klaper, M.D., for their kind and endless effort and energy in proofreading and offering other technical advice; Lynn Powers, for advice with the computer, editing, and the technical aspects of book publishing; Betty Beltzer, who provided an endless supply of information; Megan and Gordon Holley for support and medical research material; Eric Chan and Patrick and Rosemary Ng, for Chinese ingredients research (mushrooms and fungi in particular); Graham Howard and Jeff Chilton of Northwest Reishi for mushroom research; Michael Wiener, for health food marketing information in the Northwest; Shig Amano and Wes Tsuchya for miso and soy sauce material; Peter Jeo and Diane Jong for tofu and tofu by-product information; Leslie Louie for Chinese product information; Yves Potvin, for tofu processed products and information; Bob Bellows and Marnie Dunnaway, for research material, support, and suggestions on content; and last, Carol Jong and Frank Ogden (a.k.a. Dr. Tomorrow), for making publication possible.

Sam Okamoto's
INCREDIBLE
VEGETABLES

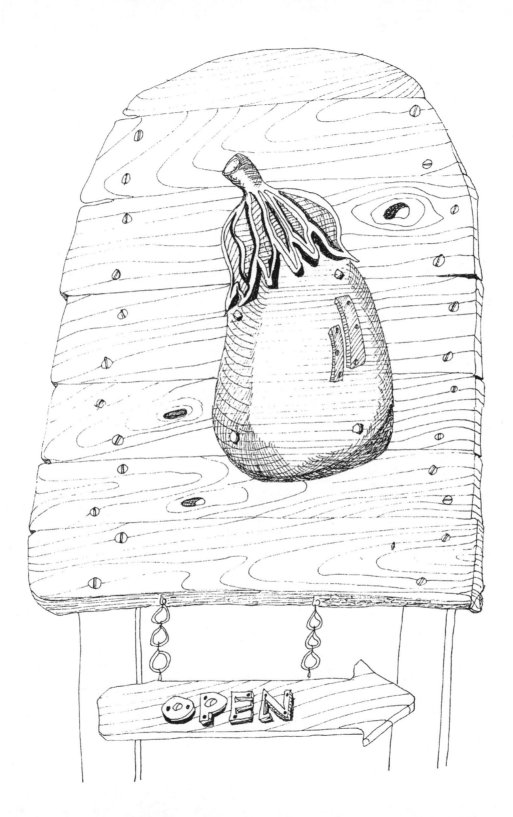

Fundamentals

At the beginning of my cooking classes, I give the students a summary of the three elements and the seven seasonings. This method works well in teaching both professionals and amateurs several decision-making processes. I challenge students to be more aware of themselves, not only while cooking, but also in their relationship with food. An awareness of yourself and the significance of food in your environment can help make you a healthier, happier individual. This awareness simplifies selecting, combining, preparing, cooking, and seasoning foods. It provides for a deeper understanding of the logic of cooking, making cooking a more enjoyable activity.

The first of the three elements is *water*. We cannot live without water, and as one of our natural resources, we must ensure its supply. The second of our three elements is *oil*—another gift of nature and an important element in cooking and in life. These are the two elements that we use and consume every day, with a little help from *fire,* the third element.

My realistic way of looking at food and cooking continues with the seven seasonings. The seven seasonings allow for variety and some, with proper use, have medicinal advantages. Also included is additional information on how to make seasonings, where to buy them, how to select them, and what to avoid.

Cooking techniques that combine the three elements, seven seasonings, and nutritional information about the ingredients follow the secrets of nature and make for a healthy and fulfilling diet. Look for little hints throughout this section; they liven up the food, its preparation, and the cook. Understanding these fundamentals will give you a surprising pleasure, instead of a headache, and will help you to develop a simple, more enjoyable cooking style. I always remember what my father said: "Do not complicate your life, keep it simple."

In this book, I've added instructions concerning important cooking methods. Each time, I will explain why I use them. You can learn how and why when the time comes.

The Three Elements

WATER

On a Rainy Day

The small hotel room was filled with seventeen young kids, all sitting quietly, cramped on folding banquet chairs. This wasn't my idea of fun, packed into a tiny room with unknown faces. We were uncomfortable, fearing the unknown, with no idea of what was going to happen next. As a rule, we were not informed. *Tsuyu,* the humid rainy season, had just begun. It was early in the month of June 1965, in Hakata City, Japan.

We were still wondering and waiting. At 8:30 A.M., two men and a young woman walked into the room. Both men, one young and the other old, wore blue suits with matching blue ties. I knew it was customary for hotel staff to wear dark blue suits in Japan. The young woman kept staring at the floor of the platform on which she stood; she also wore blue with a white blouse. The older man introduced himself, his younger assistant, and the woman briefly, but he did not mention the reason for our being there. I knew it wasn't a good idea to question authority—not for an apprentice, not in Japan.

After a moment, the older man asked the young man to sit in the chair placed on the middle of the platform. It looked more comfortable than ours. I suspected we were going to have a waiter training session. We were in an apprenticeship program that began three months before. I first worked in room service, then as a bus boy in the grill, a bell boy carrying heavy luggage, and then unloading dirty laundry. I didn't know where they would send me next.

"Try to imagine, please," the old man said, pointing at the young one, "that he is a customer, and this woman is a waitress." He waved his finger to the woman. He asked the young man to stand up and pretend that he was walking into a cocktail lounge in a hotel. The young man walked to the end of the platform and stood still. The woman had a small round serving tray in her left hand. The old man gestured to the actor to come in, but when he was halfway to the chair, the older man stopped him, looking straight at us. I saw the expression on his face change very quickly. The soft, easygoing friendly old man was no longer there. I thought he suddenly grew ten centimeters taller and he looked strong. "Think slowly and imagine, please," he sharply stated, "that this is not a man! Think of this man as water that is walking—a giant 42-kilogram tank of water."

It thrilled me to hear something different. I felt the excitement instantly. I was going to hear something different today, so I sat up and took notice of what this old man had to offer. That is how we started our first day of a two-day study of water. It was hot and humid and still raining outside.

Water Business

Hotels, restaurants, and other food service establishments are all called "water businesses" in Japan. Clearly, managing waste is an important and determining factor of their business profit. I learned timing for when to serve water or flavored liquids, when not to serve water, and the reasons. How much water used per guest on average in the hotel was detailed. From washing vegetables to cleaning pots and pans, from washing dishes to linens, a hotel's water usage per customer must be considered. I learned that a forty-two-kilogram man can waste a lot of water—and hence the hotel profits—as could hotel personnel.

I tried to absorb as much as I could about this precious gift from nature. After the two-day intensive lecture and training, I must admit, I learned a lot. It was enjoyable, exciting, and truly an experience. If you can learn the secret of managing water while cooking and have a deep understanding of the importance of quality water, I believe you'll understand the important part you play in food ecology.

Water in Foods

We use water in everyday life: for washing, bathing, drinking, and cooking. Understanding the water content of your ingredients makes cooking easy and simple. Let's start by examining the water content of food in more detail.

Different foods have different water contents. Obviously, the water content in fresh fruits and vegetables is much higher than in dried. The quality of fruits and vegetables is the result of their water content. Fresh vegetables and fruits contain plenty of water, and they look firm and fresh. On the other hand, old fruits and vegetables have a lower water content and thus, they look limp and unappetizing.

It's common sense, right? Maybe, maybe not.

Just-picked fruits or vegetables have more water than ones picked the day before. It seems simple enough, but can you tell the difference between rice stored for a year and rice stored for two years? When cooking, we will always be either removing or adding water to food. Let me give you an example.

A man, alone, walked into a French restaurant in San Francisco. He was on a business trip. His meeting of that afternoon was with an important client, and he was more than satisfied with the event. He decided to overindulge on the rich French food. He began as a 180-pound businessman. After he sat at his table, he began to search for a cocktail waitress. With luck he would get one; with more luck, maybe quickly. He ordered a drink—a beer. He finished his drink, gaining eight to ten ounces of additional weight in a short time. The alcohol in the beer reached his brain and heart within a minute, and began to take effect. He became more relaxed as alcohol circulation increased. He ordered another beer and finished this one in ten minutes. He has now gained a total of twenty ounces.

He looked at the menu briefly and ordered potato and leek soup made from potatoes, leeks, and broth (water), seasoned with salt, pepper, and cream. Consider it water with a high fat content. He ordered a bottle of chardonnay (twenty-six ounces of water with alcohol and grape flavoring) to celebrate the success of his trip. He was happy with his choice and became more relaxed. Within an hour, he finished his soup and bottle of wine and had made one trip to the bathroom. He then ordered a salad (lettuce is mostly water, the dressing made with oil and water) and a filet mignon with sautéed vegetables (meat contains blood, which contains water). If he preferred the steak well done, the chef would remove more water from the meat by cooking it longer; if he preferred his steak rare, more blood would remain in the meat due to less cooking. In a sautéed dish, when properly done, the water is sealed in the vegetables over high heat. Finally, the businessman chose a dessert. You can guess that it most likely contained water, fats, and some flavorings. This may be an unusual way of looking at food, but it helps to illustrate how important the role of water is.

Water Facts

In North America, the per capita use of water is 175 gallons of water per day. Less than one gallon is used for actual human consumption. The remaining 174 gallons are used for personal purposes such as bathing, washing clothes, or for commercial and industrial use.

Since World War II, scientists have unleashed about sixty-five thousand new chemicals into our environment. Many of them are toxic and find their way into our drinking water, vegetables, and fruits. Substances found in water can cause injury, disease, or even death under certain circumstances. Water, the "cleaner of the environment," can carry almost everything in it—cadmium, chromium, cyanide, lead, mercury, hydrocarbons, bacteria, pesticides, insecticides.

Water is the most fundamental and valuable element for the environment and human existence. Our adult bodies are composed of 71 percent water, and a three-month-old infant's body is 80 percent water. During the day, one-half of a baby's water is lost and must be replaced; otherwise the baby will dehydrate. An adult also needs to be aware of water loss and water replacement needs.

Thirst

Hunger and thirst are two very basic human instincts. Sometimes, we are unsure of whether we are thirsty or hungry. When you are unsure, drink a glass of water or a cup of tea first, and wait five minutes. If you are still hungry, then eat. Sometimes hunger goes away after having only a drink of water.

Those who live in harsh conditions, such as war, poverty, or drought, satisfy their need for food and water as best they can. To our water-abundant, wealthy, media-filled country, basic thirst and hunger have become targets for the advertising departments of large food and beverage corporations. Take your time and be cautious; remember to read about the chemical content in your foods and beverages. Almost all commercially prepared beverages are accented by some sort of substance. Caffeine, sugar, alcohol, food coloring, preservatives, and other types of chemicals hide under expensive packaging and are disguised in clever mass marketing.

Good Water

I look at the environment in a somewhat different way. Every day, I observe how chemicals get into our bodies, either by food, liquid, or air.

"If the river gets polluted, so does your liver." If the air is polluted, the rain carries chemicals with it into the soil, and the chemicals in the soil get into the plants we eat and into our water supply. If you drink polluted water, the chemicals will be taken up by the liver, which acts as a filter for your body. Therefore, pure water becomes essential to good health. It is a simple theory.

Analyzing your local water supply is the first step in obtaining information about the quality of your water. Purchasing mineral water or spring water is recommended, unless you must avoid certain minerals. A high-quality charcoal-activated water filter is another good alternative for obtaining good water. Distilled water is the safest water, recommended by many doctors and institutions.

Adding and Removing Water

In cooking, water takes a very important role. Water can be an ingredient or part of the cooking method. We add water to food for cooking and to dried food for hydration. We add seasonings to water for soups and sauces, and we freeze flavored water or liquids for frozen desserts. We remove water when we bake, deep-fry, and broil. We are constantly either removing or adding water to our food. Think about whether water is being added or removed the next time you are cooking.

When food is deep-fried in hot oil, for example, the water in the food is being removed from the food by the hot temperature of the oil. Pay special attention to the surface of the hot oil after you place battered, breaded, or flour-dusted food into the oil. Large bubbles will form on the surface of the oil. That is liquid from the food. When the food is almost done cooking, the bubbles on the surface become much smaller.

The method you choose for cooking may be deep-frying, frying, boiling, stir-frying, poaching, braising, blanching, soaking, steaming, baking, or broiling. What you are choosing is how much water is retained or removed while cooking. Remember that water is one of the three elements—one of the secrets of cooking this book is based upon.

To remove liquid from cucumbers or other vegetables, rub salt against the skin of the vegetable and leave it at room temperature for an hour. You will be amazed at the amount of liquid that comes from the vegetable. This method of removing water from vegetables is handy when cooking watery vegetables or making pickles.

As we learned earlier, water can carry almost everything with it, including nutrients from food. The longer food is soaked or cooked in water, the more nutrients are carried away or leeched from the food, especially water-soluble vitamins. Use caution to avoid cooking the vitamins out of your food.

OIL

The most frequently asked questions in my cooking classes or lectures are about fats and oils. "What kind oil should I use, and how do I use it properly?" The fats and oils in our diets come from either animal or vegetable sources. The fats and oils you choose will have a great impact on your health. As people become concerned about their health, the fats and oils they consume in everyday life will become more important.

Plenty of foods have a high fat content. High fat diets are addictive to animals and humans alike. As we are often addicted to beverages containing sugar, we are also often addicted to diets high in fat. Once you are used to a high fat diet, it's hard to change.

Animal Fat

Animal fat sources include meat, fish, eggs, and dairy products (cheese, sour cream, yogurt). Lard and butter are animal fats in a concentrated form. While some parts of fish can contain as much as 37 percent fat, the overall fat content of fish can vary depending on the season, water temperature, age, and spawning activity. Excessive consumption of animal fats is now widely regarded as a source of many health problems. Animal fats are high in saturated fat and cholesterol, causing blood and circulation problems, and are the major source of disease in North America with cardiovascular disease the most common.

Plant Oil

Vegetable oil sources include olive, peanut, palm, coconut, sunflower, safflower, flax, and other nuts and seeds. Most vegetable oils do not contain saturated fats and thus don't have the thickening effect on blood that animal fats have. Therefore, with a few exceptions, they do not cause the blood and circulation problems the animal fats cause.

Plant Fats

All living plants contain fatty acids. We eat plant stems, roots, seeds, leaves, and flowers. Most of the fats contained in green plants and fruits are found concentrated in their membranes. In plants with dark green leaves, more than half of the plant's oil is unsaturated linolenic acid (LNA) when eaten raw. The plant absorbs sunlight energy and stores it in membranes with a little help from LNA. LNA then produces sugar, protein, carbohydrates, and fats. In our bodies, the sunlight energy stored in plant membrane is released slowly by our bodies' process of oxidation—a process used by all mammals to break down food.

According to the *U.S. Department of Agriculture Handbook on the Composition of Foods,* green plants have a fat content of 0.1 to 0.8 percent; seaweeds have a fat content of 0.3 to 3.2 percent.

Grain, Legume, Seed, and Nut Oils

The oil content of grains is from 1 to 3.3 percent. Half of the oil found in grains is unsaturated linoleic acid (LA), which oxidizes quickly once crushed or milled. Modern processing techniques remove most of the unsaturated linoleic acid—a good oil—from the wheat when making flour, along with other vitamins and minerals.

The oil content in legumes varies: peanuts contain about 47.5 percent oil; soybeans, 18 percent; chickpeas 4.8 percent; lentils, 1.1 percent; ingen beans 2 percent. Of all the nuts and seeds, macadamia nuts have the highest oil content of 72 percent. Walnuts, brazil nuts, and filberts contain 55 percent oil; cashews, sesame, sunflower, and safflower seeds contain between 40 and 50 percent oil; coconuts and flax seeds contain 35 percent oil; and chestnuts contain 1.5 percent oil.

When heated, oils contained in legumes are preserved, but nutrients can be quickly destroyed.

Processed and Refined Oil

The difference between processing and refining was very confusing to me. Processed food, processed cheese, processed meat, processed fish, refined flour, refined sugar, and refined salt all sound like the foods are being improved. If someone tells me now that something is processed, I either avoid it or loose confidence in its manufacturer. The word *processed* is a bad word to me.

When processing oil, the manufacturer wants every drop of oil from the source to be cost efficient. Hand-processing oil is complicated. Seeds are first cleaned mechanically, then pressed in an expeller. When pressing, some oil is produced and bottled to be sold as cold-pressed oil.

Using another method of extracting oil, seeds are washed, then a solvent, hexane, is added to make the extraction of oil easier and the yield greater. Then the degumming process begins. Major nutrients, including polysaccharides, lecithin, chlorophyll, calcium, magnesium, iron, and copper, are removed from the oil during this process. Sodium hydroxide or a mixture of sodium carbonate is then added to the oil to remove free fatty acids before the oil goes through the bleaching process that removes leftover beta carotene and chlorophyll. The next step, deodorization, removes vitamin E and phytosterol during a high-temperature process. At this stage, oils produced are bottled and sold as a cold-pressed oil. The remaining oil has synthetic antioxidants (BHT, BHA, TBHQ, citric acid, and methysilicone) added before being bottled to replace lost true antioxidants (beta carotene and vitamin E).

Quality Oil

Good quality oil should not be processed, so necessary nutrients are maintained. Quality oil contains important nutrients such as essential fatty acids, both unsaturated linoleic acid and unsaturated linolenic acid, vitamin E, minerals, and other vitamins that protect cells, retard the aging process, and benefit the circulatory system.

Oil breaks down in the presence of light, heat, and oxygen. If the oil is extracted naturally, it will oxidize rapidly with sunlight and oxygen. Oil should be kept in a dark bottle rather than a clear bottle to protect it from sunlight. After opening, store the oil, tightly sealed, in the refrigerator to avoid oxidation. Purchase quality cold-pressed oil in small amounts and use it within a couple of weeks.

Processing and cooking at high temperatures destroys an oil's nutrients. Eating high-quality oils in salad dressings, cold sauces, nuts, seeds, and legumes will supply your body with plenty of essential fatty acids and nutrients for everyday good health. Extra virgin olive oil and unrefined sesame, sunflower, and safflower oils are all excellent oils.

There are no guidelines for how much oil to consume. Oil is available in many foods, either in beneficial form or otherwise. Even if you eliminate all the animal source fats, you will still consume a lot of oil from different types of vegetables, legumes, grains, seeds, and nuts. Be conscious of what you eat, and use oil sparingly in your kitchen.

Benefits of Oils

Wheat Germ Oil contains octacosanol, which protects and improves heart function.
Olive Oil is used for liver flushing for over-stressed livers.
Flax Seed Oil is high in LA and LNA, helps to disburse deposits of saturated fats and cholesterol from body tissues, and helps prevent hardening of the arteries.
Evening Primrose Oil contains gamma linolenic acid (GLNA), which helps in the production of special hormones (prostaglandin) to regulate cardiovascular functions and reduce inflammation like arthritis and eczema.

Types of Oil to Avoid

Avoid any type of oil that is processed, refined, cooked for a long time, or heated to a high temperature as well as foods that are prepared using these oils. For example, most fast-food restaurants deep-fry foods; the food is cooked in processed oil and, typically, heated to a high temperature.

When oil is heated for a long time or to a high temperature, not only do you risk destroying the oil, but you also risk changing its molecular structure. This new substance, called trans-fatty acids, is an unknown intruder to the body. According to Dr. Erasumasu in *Fats and Oils,* trans-fatty acids increase blood cholesterol level by 15 percent, triglyceride level by 50 percent, and the size of atherosclerotic plaques. Cancer growth rate is increased at the same rate of consumption of partially hydrogenated vegetable oil products (e.g., margarine, shortening), which contain 37 percent trans-fatty acids.

Oil in Your Kitchen

I normally stock my kitchen with three types of oil: one for cooking, one for flavoring, and one for uncooked use (e.g., salad dressings).

Cooking
Extra virgin olive oil, sesame oil.

Flavoring
Dark roasted sesame oil, tahini, gi-ma-chiang.

Dressings

Wheat germ, safflower, sunflower, rice bran, corn germ oil, flax seed oils. Cold pressed or preferably, mechanically pressed.

HEAT

We use heat to cook. Sometimes we use water or oils heated to cook our foods, or only direct heat. When cooking using water or oil, use heat to control the temperature of the water or oil, not the other way around. Pay extra attention to how heat affects oil and water (liquids). Don't let the temperature of the oil or water fool or control you.

I have had the opportunity to cook over many different heat sources. I learned to adjust to many different types of ranges and ovens—both gas and electric—as well as to different types of cooking utensils. Some, of course, were easier to use than others. Often, I check on the kitchen facilities of my classes prior to deciding upon my cooking class materials and planning my timing. Experiment in your own kitchen to learn the temperature of your stove and timing. Organize your kitchen in a way that is comfortable for you, with oils and other often-needed items in easy-to-reach places. Remember the importance of oil, water, and heat—the three elements.

Starting to Cook

When you use any type of cooking method, pan-frying, sautéing, or stir-frying, it is important to heat the cooking utensil first. Place the open palm of your hand near the pan to determine the heat. If the pan is too hot, simply add several drops of water or remove it from the heat to reduce the temperature.

Once the pan is the right temperature, add the oil. At this time, you can add many things to season the oil, but be careful not to burn the oil and prevent oxidation. Adding high water content foods will drop the temperature of the cooking utensils rapidly. Hard or root vegetables tend to release water more slowly than other vegetables.

In the next few pages, details of common cooking techniques are described; read carefully and try to master these techniques. The majority of cooking mistakes come from not understanding the connection between oil, heat, and water. Choose quality oil and water, and learn how to control the heat for controlling the temperature of heated oil and water. Observe the cooking process. For example, notice how heat changes the cooking utensil, observe the making of water vapor. Most importantly, notice the sounds of cooking.

The Seven Seasonings

Seasoned food is a luxury to human kind. You can eat food as is or raw, you can cook it, and you can season food to enjoy a wide variety of taste sensations. You can enjoy tastes every time you eat or drink. Do not confuse taste with texture or how food feels in your mouth (feelings such as chewy, crunchy, crumbly, soggy). A food's texture has nothing to do with taste.

Adults can experience seven distinct tastes: salty, sweet, sour, pungent, bitter, spicy-hot, and nutty. In this section, I'll explain what kinds of seasonings belong in each category, how to use them, how they are made, where to buy them, and the nutritional advantages of the foods that create these tastes. It is handy to supply your kitchen with quality seasonings. Get to know your seasonings well, and this knowledge will stay with you for the rest of your life.

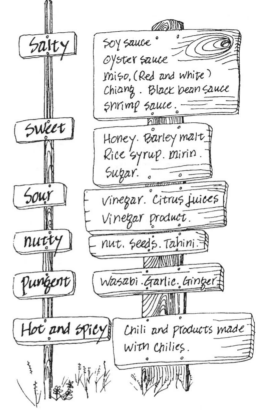

SALTY

Salty seasonings include soy sauce, miso, or chiang. Fermented tofu, fermented black beans, and black bean sauce are also popular salt-based products that you can add to your seasoning list. They are available in most Oriental markets, ethnic markets, and in some supermarkets.

Follow the recipe until you get to know salty seasonings such as miso, chiang, fermented tofu, and salted black beans. After a few experiments, try to create your own dishes using these seasonings. Add salty seasonings with caution because you can always add salt later, but it may be difficult to remove once added. Start out by adding a small amount, then decide how much salty seasoning to add before serving. Do not taste salty seasonings more than three times within a short period of time; otherwise your tongue will become numbed by the salt.

A small amount of salt in your diet will increase your appetite and aid in digestion. An excess of salt may cause migraine headaches, insomnia, hives, epilepsy, high blood pressure, debility, fluid retention, impotence, aging of the skin, hyperacidity, and inflammation. An average North American consumes about ten to fifteen grams of sodium chloride per day. When sugar is paired with excessive salt intake, it raises blood pressure faster than salt alone.

SWEET

The following sweet seasoning products are sweeteners, but because they are sugars, use them sparingly: maple syrup, sorghum, barley malt syrup, fruit juices, barley malt, corn syrup, molasses, brown rice syrup, mirin, amazake, yam, sweet vegetables, and other fresh or dried fruits. All of these sweet seasonings can usually be found in local health food stores.

Sugar provides energy, strength, and nourishment. An excess consumption of refined sugar will cause mucus, lassitude, indigestion, frequent colds, obesity, calcium loss from bones, tooth decay, and possible cross-linking of proteins through glycosalation (leading to premature aging of tissues).

SOUR

Sour seasonings include vinegar or fresh citrus fruits. There are several kinds of vinegars available including brown rice vinegar, rice vinegar, black vinegar, apple cider vinegar, and balsamic vinegar. Citrus juices such as lemon, lime, grapefruit juice, and tamarind juice are all used as sour flavorings.

Vinegar aids in digesting fats from nut products, leaving the nuts' flavor to enhance your dish. Vinegar also kills bacteria and microorganisms, including living enzymes in food. When using sour seasonings, it is best to add them just before serving. Sour flavors mellow hot, salt, and sweet flavors when a small amount is added to the food as a "hidden" taste. For example, a few drops of vinegar added to miso soup at the last minute bring out the aroma of miso, but the sour taste of vinegar is undetectable in the soup.

Vegetables and fruits that have a rapid oxidation rate—lotus root, eggplant, potatoes, cauliflower, pears, and apples—can be slowed by soaking them in a 10 to 15 percent solution of vinegar and water.

Vinegars stimulate the appetite and digestive secretions and relieve fatigue. An excess will cause fevers, inflammation, and burning sensations. For more information, see the index entry for Brown Rice Vinegar.

BITTER

Green onion, leeks, chives, Chinese chives, garlic chives, bitter melon, and other bitter vegetables or herbs add a bitter flavor to dishes. In Asian cooking, minced green onions, shallots, garlic chives, or other types of bitter vegetables are used quite often. They are either sprinkled on top of the dish or served as a condiment with a dipping sauce. This provides a refreshing sensation between each mouthful, while the enzymes in these foods aid digestion—simple Oriental wisdom.

Bitter foods help to clear the throat, sharpen the intellect, and benefit the skin and flesh, while also aiding in the digestion of protein. An excess of these foods will cause headaches and loss of strength.

NUTTY

Nutty flavors come from roasted nuts and seeds or from oil or oil-based paste products derived from nuts and seeds. Nutty seasonings are best enhanced by sour seasonings, which cut the oily taste, because all nutty products are high in oil. Tahini, *gi-ma-chiang* (Chinese ground sesame seed paste), sesame oil (roasted or unrefined), sesame seeds, and various kinds of nuts all provide a nutty flavor in cooking.

Seeds and nuts contain high concentrations of vitamin E, which is important in preventing blood from clotting, thereby protecting us from heart attacks and strokes. Vitamin E is an antioxidant and helps prevent the skin from aging and wrinkling while also protecting us from cancer by absorbing free radicals. Nuts and seeds also contain many essential minerals. Eat nuts and seeds with caution because of their high fat and calorie contents.

PUNGENT

Pungent seasonings not only give a flare and punch to your food, but also provide excellent nutritional value. Ginger, garlic, horseradish, daikon, and wasabi (green Japanese horseradish) are pungent vegetables available in local ethnic markets.

Most pungent foods, such as garlic and ginger, are stronger when grated than when chopped. When garlic and ginger are added to hot oil, vitamin E from the garlic's oil adds flavor and prevents oxidation of the hot oil.

Pungent foods aid in the assimilation of other foods, stimulate the organs, help eliminate excess water from the body, heal ulcers, soothe itching, and prevent obesity. Excesses of these pungent foods will cause fatigue, giddiness, loss of strength, and thirst.

HOT (SPICY)

Various fresh and dried hot chilies, chili products, and different varieties of peppers and peppercorns are used as hot seasonings.

Capsaicin, a compound found in chilies, is very effective for respiratory system dysfunction. The Oriental theory of therapeutics calls for *yang* (hot) to treat *yin* (cold) respiratory diseases. When chilies or chili by-products reach the stomach, they trigger a flood of liquid, relieving nose and sinus congestion and clearing bronchial tubes. Chilies are also known to increase the appetite and to relieve constipation. In India, they are used to treat ulcers and hemorrhages, as a pain killer for treating arthritis, and as a cold remedy along with vitamin C.

Warning: After touching those burning hot chilies, especially the hot oil from the skin of peppers, you will have a regrettable irritation if you then touch any sensitive skin area. Wear gloves when peeling or chopping chilies, and keep your hands away from your eyes.

COMBINING SEASONINGS

Salty & Sweet

Salty and sweet flavors work well together. The opposite of salty taste is sweet. A touch of sweet with salt increases salty flavor; a touch of salty with sweet increases sweet flavor. Mixing a salty seasoning with sweet seasoning makes an excellent combination of sweet and salty tastes as long as the seasonings are well balanced. Keep this in mind because it is a very handy thing to know.

Nutty & Sour

Sour flavor enhances nutty flavor. The expression used by professional Japanese chefs for the technique of using nutty and sour seasonings together is "kill sesame with vinegar." The oily taste from sesame oil or sesame seeds is eliminated by adding a few drops of vinegar to the dish, thus leaving only a nutty taste.

Cooking Techniques

So far, we have learned the basics: the importance of the water and oil, how to apply heat to both, cooking methods, and seasoning techniques. Remember to use your five senses and awareness for everything you do and have done. Season your food according to your own taste. Only practice, not theory, makes a good cook.

Several basic cooking techniques will help you add variety to your dishes. To create and use your own style, start out with very simple recipes. Begin experimenting with different cooking techniques and combinations of seasonings. For example, take a carrot and taste it. The carrot tastes good as is. But, you can cut the carrot in a variety of ways, choose a method of cooking, and enhance the flavor by adding a seasoning, perhaps choosing a combination of the seven seasonings. The result may be a brand new experience.

Seasoning and timing will determine the taste and flavor of your dish. Season according to personal taste; in the beginning you may want to follow the recipe until you have enough confidence and experience to experiment. When you have mastered a recipe that you like, begin to experiment with the seasonings according to your own tastes. Timing refers to changing or stopping the cooking process by adjusting cooking times. Timing is mastered by experience or testing, by following new recipes carefully, and by observing and remembering variances due to your cooking equipment and utensils.

BRAISING AND STEWING

Stewing

Used for either large cuts of vegetables or hard vegetables, stewing simmers ingredients slowly in water until they are rich, mellow, and extremely tender. A wok, dutch oven, or similar heavy utensil may be used. From the three elements, water, fire, and sometimes oils are involved in this cooking style.

Braising

Stewing as a cooking method normally requires more time to cook the food than braising, but is otherwise identical. By sealing natural flavor inside the food, braising tenderizes and adds flavor from outside the food at the same time. There are several braising techniques, including fast braising, steam braising, sauté braising, and deep-fry braising. Braising is generally used for cooking root and hard vegetables such as potatoes and carrots. Fast braising is best for cooking leaf or other soft vegetables.

The main ingredients are generally browned first in oil, then cooked, with or without the lid, in various amounts of liquid with seasonings. The amount of liquid used in braising is determined by the length of cooking time, which can be divided into three categories: *Enough water,* or the minimum amount of liquid needed for cooking; *Water to cover,* or enough liquid to cover the food; and *Plenty of water,* where the food floats in liquid while cooking.

Drop Lid (Otoshi-buta) is a cooking method using a lid smaller than the diameter of the cooking pot to keep foods from moving around and breaking while cooking. It's used mostly when braising.

BOILING

Boiling is simply cooking food in water. In a pot, combine water and the food you want to cook, and bring to a boil. Turn the heat down to a produce a gentle boil rather than a raging boil. Remove vegetables before they become tender, as the cooking process continues after the foods are removed from the water. Reserve the cooking liquid for later use; for soups, salad dressings, or sauces. The cold-to-hot boiling method is used for foods such as hard vegetables, grains or small legumes. For pasta or noodles—either fresh or dried—water should be boiled before ingredients are added.

BLANCHING

Blanching is a very fast method of cooking food—the preferred method for green vegetables. This is a simple way to cook vegetables such as green beans, spinach, broccoli, cabbage, bok choy, gai-lan, and many other soft vegetables with a minimum loss of nutrients.

Blanch foods by placing ingredients in plenty of boiling water until almost done, then remove and quickly release into very cold water to stop the cooking process and to prevent the chlorophyll from escaping; remove and drain. Serve the food immediately so the food is still piping hot.

STEAMING

Steaming is used to cook rice, buns, breads, pastries, and vegetables or to reheat various other foods. Foods cooked in their serving dishes or directly on a rack can go directly from stove to table with all their natural juices, flavors, and nutrients preserved.

In the steaming cooking process, hot steam rises from the boiling water, circulates around the food, and cooks by direct contact. Compared to boiling, steamed foods are cooked fast and efficiently, with less nutrient loss. It requires boiling water in a large container such as a large wok, skillet or pot, and a steamer with a tight-fitting lid to prevent steam from escaping too rapidly. The ingredients are then placed in a shallow dish or directly on a rack in the steamer.

In rack steaming, the rack stands two or three inches above the boiling water. As a rule, the steamer should be opened as little as possible during cooking. With dishes requiring longer cooking times, the water level should be checked from time to time, and replenished with boiling water when needed.

Steaming can follow other cooking methods. For example, tofu skin with stuffing is usually deep-fried then steamed, or fried in oil first and then steamed. By combining two or three cooking methods, you give food more flavor and texture.

STIR-FRYING

Stir-frying or sautéing is cooking foods in oil or fat over very high heat. Technically, the foods are being sautéed only if they are relatively dry and each piece has frequent contact with the bottom of the cooking utensil and hot oil.

Begin by heating the pan to high. Add oil and any pungent spices desired, such as garlic, ginger, cumin seeds, mustard seeds, or coriander, to accent the flavor of the oil. Next, add the ingredients to be cooked, tossing and stirring frequently so they don't burn, causing them to have a burnt aroma. If the ingredients are added to the pan or skillet while the temperature of the utensil is too low, then moisture in the food is released instead of being sealed inside by the high heat. The result? Soggy vegetables with no aroma.

Stir-fry Hints

Listen for the sound of water sizzling; if the oil temperature is not high enough and you have more water than oil, then you won't hear a sizzling sound. You are boiling oil with water, and the water will eventually evaporate.

When adding liquid salt seasoning (soy sauce, tamari sauce, or mushroom soy sauce) while stir-frying, pour it around the rim of the hot cooking utensil. This will ensure that it evaporates immediately, creating a slight burnt soy aroma that transfers to the food. Pouring it on top of the food while stir-frying causes the temperature to drop, and prevents the addition of the slight burnt soy aroma.

FRYING

To fry, place flat-shaped foods onto a hot, flat cooking utensil with little or no oil until the food is brown on one side, then turn to complete the cooking process. The temperature under the food rises to extremely high temperatures. Because heat will remove the moisture from the food, it is important to know that moving the food on the cooking surface continuously will prevent the food from sticking and burning. When the food  has a large cutting surface, you can lift the food and add some oil to prevent sticking and burning.

DEEP-FRYING

Tempura is a well-known Japanese deep-fried dish in which vegetables, fish, meat, or sometimes ice cream are coated with a light batter and deep-fried until crisp. It is customarily served with warm *Tuke-Dashi,* a dipping sauce to soften the crisp batter and "cut through" the oil. It is also served with a small amount of freshly grated daikon to which several drops of tamari are added.

In North America, tempura is translated to a method of cooking. It is believed that the cooking method used for tempura originated in Portugal and was brought by merchants and sailors to Nagasaki, a city on the western peninsula of Kyushu Island, decades ago during the Tokugawa period. Portuguese-style deep-fry methods used a heavy batter; that style of cooking still exists in the city of Nagasaki as *shippoku ryori*. Tempura was later refined to suit the Japanese taste.

In recent years in Japan, tempura shops have been found in almost every city. Some are very popular and expensive; others are very reasonable and specialize only in tempura. As a rule, it is not recommended to eat tempura on a regular basis. Another rule repeated often by my father is to never combine oyster, tempura, and ice cream; certain foods do not mix, no questions asked.

Tempura Hints

Most of the good tempura shops use three parts regular sunflower oil to one part light sesame oil for deep-frying. The batter is a mixture of cake or pastry flour with icy cold water. The water is mixed with the flour just before vegetables are dipped in the batter and dropped in 345 to 355-degree oil. Avoid mixing the batter too often because it will activate gluten formation in the batter, which will result in a thicker, heavier batter. Lower oil temperatures make soggy and oily tempura, and higher temperatures will cause the batter to color too quickly and burn without cooking the food completely.

Onion, carrot, sweet potatoes, lotus roots, broccoli, burdock root, potatoes, green onions, parsley, shungiku, zucchini, mushrooms, fresh shiitake, and eggplant are all good candidates for tempura. All vegetables should be washed and cut into 1/8-inch-thick slices or other various shapes, florets, rounds, or half moons. Onions are usually cut across the grain, and a toothpick is inserted into slices to prevent them from separating.

Tempura Batter I

1 cup whole wheat pastry flour
1 tbsp. arrowroot powder
1¼ cup icy cold water and ice cubes
Pinch salt
Pinch baking powder

Tempura Batter II

¾ cup whole wheat pastry flour
¼ cup corn flour
1¼ cup icy cold water with ice cubes
Pinch salt
Pinch baking powder

Tentsuyu Dipping Sauce

1 cup dashi
¼ cup tamari or soy sauce
¼ cup sake
2 tbsp. mirin
1 tsp. grated ginger

Serve tentsuyu slightly warm in small dishes.

Cooking Preparation

Preparation of foods before cooking is a time-consuming, pain-in-the-neck job, but good preparation is necessary to ensure the success of your dishes. Be patient, read the instructions carefully, and take the time you need to prepare your ingredients properly.

There are a great variety of vegetables available in North American markets—some are imported, some are grown locally. Each vegetable, fruit, nut, seed, and legume has its own flavor and character. It is important to know how to purchase them and how to handle them properly for preparation.

Sorting, washing, draining, peeling, cutting, cleaning, and sometimes soaking before cooking is necessary to prevent unpleasant

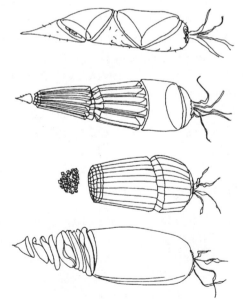

surprises in your dishes, removing sand, grit, slime, and bitter tastes from your dish. Special methods can be used for certain purposes, such as salting the food to remove unwanted flavor and water before braising or pickling, or soaking foods in vinegar to keep foods from becoming dark in color.

Begin preparation by placing all ingredients and cooking utensils that you think you need where you want them or beside the cooking pan, along with the seasonings you've chosen from the seven seasonings, serving plate, cooking tools, and whatever else you need to stop yourself from running around the kitchen once you begin to cook. Remember, stir-frying takes only a couple of minutes—you don't have time to go looking for salt or a spatula. Disconnecting the telephone may help to prevent burnt food as well.

Combining Foods

Combining a variety of foods is important to establish nutritionally balanced meals. If food lacks variety and becomes boring, people will return to their old eating habits. There are three basic things you can do to increase the variety of your foods:

1. Combine the colors of foods.
2. Blend seasonings.
3. Combine mixtures of various food textures.

COMBINING COLORS

Food should look appealing as well as taste good. Selecting vegetables by color is a simple way to choose a wide variety of vitamins and minerals. Different colored vegetables have different nutrients; combining them will provide the necessary nutrients to maintain a healthy body.

Because nature has already provided vegetables in a variety of colors, use them. When shopping in the market, select and combine vegetables of different colors—green from spinach, broccoli, and pepper; red from beets and tomato; orange from carrots; and purple from eggplant. By mixing nature's colors, you can create dishes that are not only appealing to the eyes, but are also nutritionally balanced.

COMBINING SEASONINGS

We have already learned about the seven basic seasonings. Additionally, every food has its own unique flavor. It is important to appreciate natural taste as well as seasonings done properly. Every time you eat, train your taste buds to be more discerning.

COMBINING TEXTURES

When one advances beyond a meat-based diet, certain food textures will be eliminated, leaving chewy, crunchy, smooth, flaky, and slippery. Creating the mouth feelings that you experience when you bite or swallow using vegetable sources alone becomes an art. Combining the appearance, taste, and texture of foods to satisfy the senses requires special attention. Select, cook, and present the foods with care; your efforts will be rewarded with more than just hunger satisfaction.

Begin by paying attention to the texture of your food. Your awareness of food texture will become more acute. Remember, each vegetable has a different texture in your mouth. As your awareness of taste and texture develops, it will become easier to recreate another dish by simply tasting it.

Balancing Nutrition

It was hard to learn nutrition in English when my basic nutritional knowledge came from a different culture and language, where the food is not that to which North Americans are accustomed. I was, at first, concentrating on learning to cook elaborate meals with exotic ingredients while competing with other chefs. Nutrition was the last thing on my mind. I began to learn about nutrition by translating information from English to Japanese. The more I read, the more I got confused.

The average North American has a good idea of what is bad and what is good for the body, due to the vast amount of information available in recent years. Unfortunately, *knowing* and *doing* are not the same thing. We are attracted to foods that are convenient and fast, which often have less rather than more nutritional value. Learning nutrition is a serious matter—if you don't eat well, you won't feel good. Your body will make you pay one day.

The most common concern expressed by students interested in vegetarian cooking are protein, calcium, iron, vitamin B12, vitamin D, and folic acid requirements for adults. Yes, you can obtain these nutrients from vegetable sources alone; and you can obtain the daily requirements of these nutrients with less health problems.

Daily nutritional requirements vary depending upon the source. I selected several sources that were recommended by professionals. On the following pages, I have attempted to arrange the basic daily nutritional requirements for healthy adults.

NUTRIENT REQUIREMENTS

Vitamin A

Recommended daily requirement: 5,000 iu

Vitamin A is needed in the liver to help change the protein that is consumed into a usable protein. It has a healing effect on cell membranes, works along with Vitamin E to protect cells from membrane oxidation, guards against infections through its direct stimulation of the immune system, and maintains adrenal glands for quick response to all sort of stresses.

Vitamin A Sources

Brussels sprouts, romaine lettuce, carrots, tomato, pumpkin, winter squash, sweet potatoes, kale, spinach, bok choy, apricots, green beans.

Symptoms of Vitamin A Deficiency

Weak immune system, anemia, and fatique, resulting in a vulnerability to the flu and colds.

Depleting Factors

Alcohol, tobacco, stress, and pollution.

Vitamin B1 (Thiamin)

Recommended daily requirement: 50 mg

Vitamin B1 is essential for burning sugar for energy. Not enough vitamin B1 results in an incomplete combustion collection of acidic waste, impairing the brain, heart, and lungs, as well as digestion, the immune system, and the nervous system.

Vitamin B1 Sources

Whole grains, bran, brewer's yeast, blackstrap molasses, soybeans, sunflower seeds, peas, leeks, mustard greens.

Symptoms of Vitamin B1 Deficiency

Depression, fatigue, irritability, memory loss, confusion, insomnia, anxiety, restlessness.

Depleting Factors

Alcohol, excess sugar or tobacco, stress, exercise, pregnancy, nursing, caffeine.

Vitamin B2 (Riboflavin)

Recommended daily requirement: 10 mg

Vitamin B2 is needed for red blood cell formation; the function of the nervous system; utilization of carbohydrates, fats, and proteins; healthy skin and eyes.

Vitamin B2 Sources

Whole grains, spinach, alfalfa sprouts, winter squash, turnip greens, broccoli, nutritional yeast, asparagus, avocados, wheat germ, currants.

Symptoms of Vitamin B2 Deficiency

Inflammation of mouth tissues, poor vision, fatigue, depression, trembling, cataracts, insomnia, cracks and sores on the corner of the mouth, red sore tongue, narrowing upper lips, blood-shot eyes, burning eye lids.

Depleting Factors

Excessive intake of protein, carbohydrate, alcohol, sugar, antibiotics, pregnancy, nursing.

Vitamin B3 (Niacin)

Recommended daily requirement: 20 mg

Niacin is necessary for proper utilization of nutrients by cells. Niacin is required for more than forty different biochemical reactions in the body. Niacin also prevents and relieves mild anxiety, fatigue, insomnia, depression, and other mental disturbances.

Niacin Sources

Avocados, asparagus, mushrooms, peanuts, legumes, whole grains, rice bran, brewer's yeast, alfalfa sprouts.

Symptoms of Niacin Deficiency

Scaly skin, diarrhea, canker sores, sore mouth, abdominal pain, memory loss, insomnia, indigestion, swollen gums, schizophrenic type reactions, insomnia, dermatitis, pellagra.

Depleting Factors

Stress, sugar, caffeine, antibiotics, refined carbohydrates.

Vitamin B5 (Pantothenic acid)

Recommended daily requirement: 50 mg

Pantothenic acid is required to produce protective antibodies and for all energy-requiring processes. It is in almost all foods, but processing (e.g., canning, refining, freezing) reduces its presence by thirty to fifty percent.

Vitamin B5 Sources

Brewer's yeast, peanuts, wheat germ, legumes, walnuts, whole grains, mushrooms, brown rice, broccoli, cauliflower, carrots.

Symptoms of Vitamin B5 Deficiency

Depression, fatigue, vomiting, eczema, allergies, hypoglycemia, arthritis, cramping in arm and legs, burning feet, low blood pressure.

Depleting Factors

Stress, tobacco, caffeine, eating processed foods.

Vitamin B6 (Phyriodoxine)

Recommended daily requirement: 50 mg

Vitamin B6 helps to maintain almost the entire protein and collagen structure of the body. It supports the immune system by helping to maintain the thymus gland, and it aids in the utilization of protein, carbohydrates, and fats. As one of the busiest vitamins, it helps the function of the brain, liver, pancreas, and muscles, and supports enzymes to function properly. Vitamin B6 aids a liver enzyme to metabolize estrogen, which in excess may lead to irritability, fatigue, and puffiness that occurs during menstruation.

Vitamin B6 Sources

Fruit (bananas, pears, grapes, avocados), green vegetables, alfalfa sprouts, sunflower seeds, wheat bran, broccoli, brussels sprouts, cauliflower, corn, brown rice, spinach, tomatoes, soybeans.

Symptoms of Vitamin B6 Deficiency

Irritation, depression, mental disorder, asthma, oxalate kidney stones, poor stamina, edema, anemia, numbness, tingling, joint pain, stiffness.

Depleting Factors

Stress, alcohol, birth control pills, tobacco, excess sugar, excess protein, food processing, nursing.

Vitamin B12 (Cyanocobalamine, Hydroxocobalamine)

Recommended daily requirement: 40 mcg

Vitamin B12 helps in the utilization of folic acid, in DNA and RNA synthesis, in maintaining a healthy nervous system and improving concentration, memory, and balance, and it increases energy.

Vitamin B12 Sources

Fortified nutritional yeast, miso (some exceptions), tempeh.

Symptoms of Vitamin B12 Deficiency

Fatigue, weakness, unsteadiness, paresthesia, memory loss, confusion, anemia, sore tongue, mood swings, poor memory, numbness, tingling, rapid heart beat, chest pain.

Depleting Factors

Alcohol, pregnancy, excess vitamin C, laxatives, stress.

Vitamin C (Ascorbic Acid)

Recommended daily requirement: 2,000 mg

Vitamin C is essential to the formation of collagen, a protein that supports bone, skin, teeth, tendon, and connective tissue. Vitamin C boosts the immune system, encourages rapid healing, and fertility. It also increases the blood level of high-density lipoprotein, which may help to prevent cardiovascular disease.

Vitamin C Sources

Lemons, oranges, orange juice, mangos, papayas, strawberries, parsley, green peppers, pineapple, potatoes, romaine lettuce, raw spinach, squash, rhubarb, broccoli, brussels sprouts, cabbage, cauliflower, collard greens, mustard greens, turnip greens.

Symptoms of Vitamin C Deficiency

Impaired immunity, gall stones, thrombosis, diabetes, edema, low resistance to infection, bleeding gums, rough skin, hay fever, anemia, anxiety.

Depleting Factors

Stress, tobacco, pregnancy, nursing, excessive iron, antibiotics, long-term dieting, excessive protein, processed foods, cortisone.

Vitamin D

Recommended daily requirement: 400 iu or 10 mcg

Vitamin D is a hormone essential to encourage the absorption of calcium and phosphorus from the intestines, and it controls the deposit of these minerals in bone, blood, and tissues. It is also created for the body when ultraviolet light hits the skin. Those who live in extreme northern regions are recommended to take vitamin D supplements because of limited sunlight. High doses of vitamin D can suppress the immune system and have a toxic effect.

Symptoms of Vitamin D Deficiency

Rickets, soft bones, severe tooth decay, osteoporosis.

Depleting Factors

Lack of sunlight, pollution.

Vitamin E

Recommended daily requirement: 400 iu

A well-known antioxidant that protects cells from free radicals. It discourages blood platelet aggregation and has been valuable for treating ulcers, gangrene, rheumatic fever, arthritis, diabetes, and menstrual problems.

Vitamin E Sources

Brussels sprouts, corn oil, flax seed oil, leafy greens, primrose oil, safflower oil, sesame oil, soy beans, sunflower seeds, wheat germ, whole grains.

Symptoms of Vitamin E Deficiency

Destruction of blood cells, muscle degeneration, and reproductional disorders.

Depleting Factors

Heat, oxygen, food processing, iron, chlorine.

Biotin

Recommended daily requirement: 300 mcg

Biotin is necessary for the synthesis of fatty acids and proteins and the utilization of carbohydrates. It maintains thyroid and adrenal glands and the immune and nervous systems.

Biotin Sources

Brewer's yeast, whole wheat, brown rice, chickpeas, corn, lentils, oats, barley, mushrooms, soybeans, cabbage, collard greens, cucumber, kale.

Symptoms of Biotin Deficiency

Depression, weakness, fatigue, rough skin, bleeding gums, allergies, poor digestion, low resistance to infection.

Depleting Factors

Depression, anxiety, grayish skin color, muscular pain, dry skin, chest pain.

Calcium

Recommended daily requirement: 1000 mg

Since calcium is poorly absorbed by the body, with an average of 400 grams excreted daily, it is recommended that twice that much should be taken daily to compensate for calcium loss. Poor calcium absorption can be explained by the increased ingestion of phosphorus in meat and soft drinks in recent years. It is a good idea to exercise, as it improves calcium absorption, and to avoid a high fat and meat-based diet, as they reduce calcium absorption. Some doctors recommend a magnesium-calcium supplement. The ideal mixture of the two minerals is 500 milligrams of calcium to 250 or 300 milligrams of magnesium.

Caution: Avoid excessive calcium intake if you have a history of kidney stones.

Calcium Sources

Collard greens, kale, oats, chickpeas, tofu (calcium precipitated), sea vegetables (hijiki, arame, wakame), broccoli, mustard greens, Swiss chard, almonds, peanuts, sunflower seeds, lentils, tahini, sesame seeds.

Symptoms of Calcium Deficiency

Palpitations, insomnia, muscle cramps, arm and leg numbness, tooth decay, osteoporosis, and rickets.

Depleting Factors

Large consumption of fat, oxalic acid (found in chocolate, spinach, swiss chard, parsley, and beet greens), phytic acid (found in grains), and animal protein.

Choline

Recommended daily requirement: 250 mg

Choline, a member of the B-complex family and a lipotropic (fat emulsifier), helps to control cholesterol build-up and the sending of nerve impulses—especially those in the brain used in the fomation of memory. It also assists in the production of cell membranes.

Choline Sources

Avocado, green beans, bok choy, legumes, yeast, and wheat germ.

Symptoms of Choline Deficiency

Fatty degeneration of the liver, hardening of the arteries.

Chromium

Recommended daily requirement: 400 mcg

Most of the chromium is lost in food processing. This mineral is vital to increase energy efficiency of healthy people. It also eliminates or reduces the insulin requirements of diabetics. Topsoil is easily depleted of its chromium, so unless you know that the foods you are eating come from healthy soil, a chromium supplement is recommended.

Chromium Sources

Brewer's yeast, corn oil, grains, wheat germ.

Symptoms of Chromium Deficiency

Lack of chromium is a suspected factor in arteriosclerosis and diabetes.

Depleting Factors

Consumption of food that is grown in unhealthy soil or foods that have been processed.

Folic Acid

Recommended daily requirement: 400 mcg

Folic acid is essential to the enzymes that lead to the synthesis of DNA, and thus is important for growth and reproduction. A folic acid supplement is recommended for pregnant women, early infancy, and adolescence—when rapidly growing cells are vulnerable to deficiency.

Folic Acid Sources

Almonds, peanuts, walnuts, oats, rye, wheat, mushrooms, asparagus, spinach, cabbage, legumes, broccoli, kale, yau-choy, gai-lan, brussels sprouts.

Symptoms of Folic Acid Deficiency

Anemia, malabsorption, depression, muscular and intellectual fatigue, poor memory, diarrhea, low white blood cell count.

Depleting Factors

Alcohol, caffeine, birth control pills, antibiotics, pregnancy, nursing, food processing.

Iron

Recommended daily requirement: 15 to 30 mg

Iron helps carry oxygen to cells so they can metabolize nutrients to provide energy. Iron is needed for the formation of hemoglobin. Menstruating women, newborn babies, pregnant women, and children require more iron. Vitamin C, B12, folic acid, a low protein intake, and a good calcium-to-phosphorus ratio (1:1) enhance the absorption of iron. Zinc, copper, and manganese supplements will suppress the absorption of iron. Cooking in a cast-iron pan three times a week will provide the daily requirement of iron.

Iron Sources

Brewer's yeast, blackstrap molasses, prune juice, raisins, brown rice, chickpeas, lentils, millet, spinach, tofu, whole grains, wheat germ and bran, beets, apricots, artichokes, soybeans, sesame, sunflower, pumpkin seeds, almonds, pistachio nuts.

Symptoms of Iron Deficiency

Anemia, depression, impaired learning, poor memory, sore or burning tongue, dizziness.

Depleting Factors

Caffeine, pregnancy, nursing, excessive zinc, calcium, phosphorus, antacid, high phytate diet.

Magnesium

Recommended daily requirement: 500 mg

Magnesium plays a key role in the control of cell metabolism and growth and is responsible in many enzyme reactions. Magnesium keeps us alert, strong, and balanced.

Magnesium Sources

Wheat germ and bran, almonds, cashews, blackstrap molasses, brewer's yeast, sesame, and sunflower seeds, wild rice, soybeans, orange juice, grapefruit, oats, rye, millet, barley, corn, legumes, carrots, broccoli, brussels sprouts, dates, spinach, sesame seeds.

Symptoms of Deficiency

Hypertension, anorexia, tooth loss, malabsorption, retarded dentition, muscle twitching, numbness, tingling, appetite loss, rapid pulse, kidney stones, high blood pressure.

Depleting Factors

Alcohol, excess sugar, low protein diet, birth control pills, excess protein, fat, calcium, vitamin D.

Manganese

Recommended daily requirement: 10 to 20 mg

Manganese is needed for synthesis of fatty acids, cholesterol, DNA, RNA, protein, and the use of insulin to regulate blood sugar. Calcium and phosphorus impede its absorption. Manganese content in food varies depending on the topsoil content where grown.

Manganese Sources

Coconuts, seeds, nuts, legumes, grains, spinach, raisins, blueberries, avocados, olives.

Symptoms of Manganese Deficiency

Epilepsy, uncoordination, ear noises, diabetes, backaches.

Depleting Factors

Pregnancy, nursing, excess calcium, zinc, phosphorus, soy protein, cobalt.

Potassium

Recommended daily requirement: 600 mg

Potassium supports the rhythmic beating of the heart and the strength and contraction of the muscles. Potassium counteracts the blood pressure-rising effects of sodium.

Potassium Sources

Potatoes, avocados, dried apricots, whole grains, bananas, most fruits, and vegetables.

Symptoms of Potassium Deficiency

Boredom, depression, headaches, insomnia, chronic fatigue.

Depleting Factors

Coffee, alcohol, salt, sugar, cortisone drugs, diuretics.

Protein

Recommended daily requirement: 20 to 40 grams

Mixing two ample servings of any of the below sources will provide 15 to 30 grams of high-quality protein, constituting a large measure of the daily protein requirements for a normal healthy adult. Mixing protein-rich foods will increase the nutritional value of the dish significantly.

Excessive consumption of protein can cause stress to the kidneys and result in kidney failure and may contribute to osteoporosis.

Protein Sources

Grains: Brown rice, oats, corn, millet, barley, bulgur, whole wheat pasta.
Legumes: Alfalfa sprouts, mung bean sprouts, green peas, lentils, chickpeas, peanuts,

beans of all sorts (e.g., kidney, lima, navy, and azuki), soybeans, tofu, tempeh, soy milk, and other soy products.

Nuts and Seeds: Almonds, brazil nuts, pistachios, cashews, walnuts, filberts, pecans, sunflower seeds, sesame seeds, tahini.

Selenium

Recommended daily requirement: 200 mcg

Selenium is a powerful antioxidant that stimulates the immune system. It helps to improve vision, skin, and hair. Selenium helps the special enzyme, glutathione peroxidase, in the synthesis of prostaglandins. Food processing destroys about half of the selenium content. Sulfate in fertilizer reduces the intake of selenium by plants.

Selenium Sources

Green leafy vegetables, whole grains, legumes.

Symptoms of Selenium Deficiency

Premature loss of stamina, Keshan disease.

Depleting Factors

Consumption of over-processed foods.

Zinc

Recommended daily requirement: 15 to 30 mg

Zinc plays an important role in male potency, in the creation of the male hormone, testosterone. Zinc supplements have been shown to be beneficial in treating acne and rheumatoid arthritis. Without sufficient zinc intake, the body cannot grow, reproduce, or breathe.

Zinc Sources

Whole grains, avocados, leafy green vegetables, mushrooms, nuts, sesame seeds, pumpkin seeds, tahini, legumes, miso, peas, wheat germ and bran, nutritional yeast.

Symptoms of Zinc Deficiency

Slow growth, delayed sexual development, slow healing, enlarged prostate, hair loss, learning disabilities, sore joints, eczema.

Depleting Factors

Stress, alcohol, excess calcium, excess copper, pregnancy, nursing, food processing, birth control pills, excess iron.

Vegetables, Fruits, Seasonings, Nuts, and Seeds

What you see is not what you get.

This chapter will provide you with information on foods that may not be familiar to you and information on making choices about which food remedy will help you stay healthy. Knowing about these foods and using them in your menu will help you widen your food variety and cook more appetizing dishes. You will feel great and live longer. The information includes the use of foods as folk remedies in various countries, scientific research findings, how to select and where to buy, followed by interesting recipes.

When selecting fruits and vegetables, I try to use the five senses: sight (color), smell, touch, sound (when I can), and taste.

Allspice

Allspice is produced in Jamaica, Honduras, and Mexico. It bears a resemblance to a peppercorn, and it is also known as Jamaican pepper. Most of the allspice available in North America comes from Jamaica. The name "allspice" came from the mixed flavor of cinnamon, nutmeg, and cloves. Once the nuts of allspice ripen, the fragrance is lost completely. They are picked when they are still green, and then they are dried. Once dried, allspice has a stronger flavor.

Asparagus

When the first asparagus appears in the market, everyone begins to notice the change in season. The long winter is almost over, and it is time to go light with everything.

Asparagus is a truly unique vegetable in texture, flavor, color, and appearance. Asparagus may be served in a variety of ways—add this eminent vegetable to a dish or serve it by itself—to always make for an elegant dish. For example, Japanese-style asparagus is blanched or steamed asparagus served with mustard, soy, or ginger soy sauce. It may seem plain, but you can truly taste the asparagus flavor. Asparagus served Chinese-style is quickly stir-fried with black bean sauce or garlic and soy sauce, or simply steamed and served with lemon chiang dressings. You can also wrap asparagus in phyllo pastry with pistachios or roasted pine nuts inside, then roast until flaky crisp. The possibilities are endless.

Choose asparagus that is bright green in color, from the top of the stems to one inch from the bottom. The tip should be tightly closed and purplish in color. Bend the asparagus; if it is soft and wilted or shows wrinkles on the skin, it should be avoided.

To prepare asparagus, do not bend and break off the bottoms, as many recipes recommend. Instead, cut one-half inch off from the bottom of the stems, peel the skins with a vegetable peeler, then blanch to not waste asparagus.

Benefits of Asparagus

Eating asparagus in season not only adds beauty to your dishes, but is also a good source of vitamin A, C, and B-complex along with potassium and iron. It is also a good source of protein. According to Dr. N.W. Walker, asparagus juice combined with carrot juice has been effective as a diuretic to treat kidney dysfunction and general glandular problems. He also indicates that asparagus juice is used to effectively remove the oxalic acid crystals in the kidneys and throughout the muscular system. Therefore, asparagus is valuable for conditions such as rheumatism, neuritis, and gout caused by an over-consumption of meat and meat by-products.

You can add roasted nuts or seeds to asparagus dishes for an extra touch. Use pine nuts, walnuts, pistachio nuts, or other types of nuts or seeds to compensate for nutrients that asparagus lacks when serving as a main dish.

Caution: A person on anticoagulant medication, who decides to overindulge by eating pounds of steamed asparagus at one sitting, should be aware that the vitamin K in asparagus may interfere with the effectiveness of their medication.

ASPARAGUS MARSALA

Adding Dijon-style mustard, minced tarragon, or fresh enoki mushrooms to the sauce will make this dish even more elaborate.

4 tbsp. oil
2 tbsp. unbleached flour
¼ cup Marsala wine
¾ cup soy milk or nut milk
½ cup fresh or frozen peas
salt
pepper
4 lb. fresh asparagus, remove bottoms
½ cup slivered roasted almonds

In a heavy skillet, heat oil together with flour; cook over low heat for three minutes. Mix wine and milk in a separate saucepan, heat until medium warm. Add warm soy milk and wine mixture slowly to the flour mixture, whisking the mixture to prevent curdling. After adding liquids, bring to a boil, then simmer over low heat for 5 minutes. Adjust thickness by adding more liquid. Add fresh peas to the sauce and cook for 1 more minute. Remove from heat and season with salt and pepper to taste.

While the sauce is simmering, steam asparagus to your liking; remove and place on a warm serving platter. Pour Marsala sauce over hot asparagus and sprinkle with freshly roasted almonds as a garnish. Serve piping hot.

Yield: 8 servings
Preparation Time: 10 minutes

ASPARAGUS AND WALNUT SALAD

1 to 1½ lb. young asparagus,
  prepared and cut into 1-inch lengths
¼ cup finely chopped walnuts
2 tbsp. sesame oil
1 tbsp. umeboshi vinegar or brown rice vinegar
2 tbsp. soy sauce
1 tsp. natural sweetener
1 stalk scallion, finely minced

Blanch asparagus in boiling water. Drain and quickly place into ice-cold water. Drain and dry thoroughly. Combine remaining ingredients in a bowl. Add asparagus and toss well. Cover and chill for one hour before serving.

Yield: 3 to 4 servings
Preparation Time: 3 minutes

Almond Powder

Made from almonds very finely ground into a powder, almond powder is found mainly in Chinese food stores in a bottle or a clear package. It is used mainly for dessert and medicinal purposes.

Amaranth Green

This unusual vegetable, which resembles spinach, is only available in season at select Chinese, Japanese, and Korean food stores. Amaranth comes with either green or red stems and dark green leaves. The seedling can be eaten, but more often, the tender stems and leaves are pinched or cut off for consumption as the plant grows from mid to late spring and throughout the summer. It is great sautéed, steamed then sautéed, or stir-fried with minced garlic. Amaranth's nutritional value is similar to that of spinach, yet its taste is rather distinct with a mild tart flavor.

To select amaranth greens, choose those with dark green, unwilted leaves that look fresh, are brilliant in color, and feel heavy when lifted. Avoid any amaranth greens with signs of bruises or dark spots on leaves.

AMARANTH AND TOFU POUCH IN PUNGENT SAUCE

For color contrast, chewy texture, and increased nutritional value, add ten pieces of well-cleaned and soaked wooden ear fungi at the beginning.

½ cup dashi

2 tbsp. soy sauce or tamari

2 usu-age, prepared and cut into ½ x ½-inch squares

½ tsp. sea salt

½ tbsp. sesame oil

1½ lb. amaranth, with stems and leaves, washed
   and cut into 2-inch lengths

1 tsp. ginger juice

1 tbsp. umeboshi vinegar (optional)

2 tbsp. mirin

In a medium pot, combine dashi, tamari, usu-age, sea salt, and sesame oil. Bring to a boil. When liquid starts to boil, add amaranth, cover, and cook until it becomes soft. Uncover, reduce heat, and cook over medium heat until sauce reduces to 2 to 3 tablespoons. Add ginger juice and umeboshi vinegar. Toss then add mirin at the last minute, just before serving.

Note: See index for more information on dashi, usu-age, and umeboshi vinegar.

Yield: 4 servings
Preparation Time: 9 minutes

Amazake (Sweet Sake)

Amazake is a Japanese product made with cooked sweet glutinous rice and koji starter that is fermented for a short period of time. Sweet and subtle, it is normally taken as a special drink for occasions such as a New Year's celebration or Buddhist birthday. It is also used as a natural sweetener in desserts and cooking.

Amazake contains an abundance of natural sugar and digestive enzymes that remain active as long as the product is not pasteurized using high heat. Some vegetarian chefs prefer to use amazake rather than any other sweetener to sweeten food. Amazake is found in almost all natural food stores and some Japanese food stores.

Apples

Apples are very common, are available year-round, and are relatively inexpensive to purchase. There are quite a few varieties of apples available. They are a handy fruit for sweetening sauces, soups, salad dressings, dips, and also can be used as a hidden "secret" ingredient in various dishes and desserts as well. It is true that the apple is one of the most perfect foods. It supplies numerous nutrients for a healthy adult: "An apple a day will keep the doctor away."

For medicinal use, as a secret ingredient, or just for a quick snack, keep some good quality apples handy in your kitchen at all times. If you can, choose organic apples from your local supermarket. Avoid apples that are bruised, have soft skin or brown spots, or apples that are light when lifted.

Benefits of Apples

Apples provide carbohydrates and fiber including pectin, cellulose, hemicellulose, and lignin, which are otherwise found only in vegetable stems, leaves, and skins. Fiber helps to regulate the bowel. Apples provide a small amount of vitamins A, C, and B and potassium. The pectin of the apple combined with vitamin C is effective in lowering LDL cholesterol in blood. Apples raise blood sugar slowly, which is good for diabetics and those who want to avoid rapid blood sugar increases. In the latest findings from Irish and Italian researchers, eating three apples a day for one month as a part of a regular diet made a significant change in cholesterol levels. The result was an average drop of ten percent in total cholesterol count.

APPLE AND CELERY SALAD WITH CURRY

The pungent curry and sweet tart taste of apples go very nicely together. When you make the curry dressing, you may need to adjust for the water content of your tofu brand or how long you press the tofu. Try following the recipe first, then adjust the thickness by adding more liquid or pressing the tofu longer next time. Do not freeze this dressing.

¾ cup slivered almonds
5 sticks celery, peeled and chopped
2 apples, cored, peeled, and chopped
½ cup golden saltana raisins
1 tbsp. minced parsley
⅓ cup firm tofu, pressed and crumbled
1½ to 2 tbsp. tahini
2 slices fresh ginger root, peeled
1 tsp. curry powder
3 tbsp. apple juice
1 tbsp. orange juice
salt and pepper to taste

Roast slivered almonds in 375-degree oven until light gold in color, about 6 to 8 minutes. Remove and set aside to cool. Place celery, apples, raisins, and parsley in a large bowl; set aside.

Combine tofu, tahini, ginger root, curry powder, apple juice, orange juice, and salt and pepper in a blender. Process until smooth. Remove dressing from the blender then toss with salad ingredients. Chill well. Right before serving, toss with almonds and serve over lettuce leaves.

Yield: 4 servings
Preparation Time: 15 minutes

Apricots

When the season arrives, you can spot the small fresh apricots and dried ones in most fruit stands and supermarkets. Fresh apricots are handy to have in the kitchen for breakfast with cereal or lunch snacks. Dried apricots are good with fruit curry, stewed for dessert, and for snacks.

Before you purchase fresh or dried apricots, make sure they are not sprayed with a heavy chemical sulfur dioxide, because it can be deadly for some people or can cause asthma, high blood pressure, and dizziness in others.

Benefits of Apricots

Apricots, especially dried apricots, have a highly concentrated amount of beta carotene, a form of vitamin A. Studies show that foods high in beta carotene help prevent cancer. Apricots contain other unknown protective agents and valuable vitamins and minerals, which may be responsible for the longevity of the Hunza population. Another report indicates apricots may be beneficial for anemia, asthma, bronchitis, catarrh, and toxemia. In Japan, *Umeboshi,* a pickled apricot made from the shade-dried apricot plum, is used to help in weight loss, as a blood purifier, and in many folk remedies.

APRICOT SNACK MIX

This simple recipe using dried apricots can be made ahead of time; just keep it in an airtight container. It is excellent as a snack when hiking, as a breakfast food, or sprinkled over tossed salad. If you prefer, you may substitute oats or rolled rice flakes for the rice cake. Do not freeze or cook in the microwave.

2 tbsp. oil
3 tbsp. natural sweetener
½ cup chopped dried apricot
½ cup chopped pitted dates
½ cup golden raisins
⅓ cup slivered coconut
⅓ cup slivered almonds
¼ cup sunflower seeds
¼ cup crumbled rice cake

Combine oil and natural sweetener, heat until natural sweetener becomes manageable. Combine other ingredients and place in a baking pan. Pour oil and natural sweetener mixture over combined ingredients. Mix well and place in an oven at medium heat for 10 to 15 minutes. Remove from the pan and cool. Place in an airtight container.

Yield: 2⅔ cups
Preparation Time: 20 minutes

Arrowroot Flour, Powder, or Starch

Arrowroot is a plant that grows in the Caribbean Islands. It is similar to corn or other types of starch—a common allergen—but superior in nutritional value. It provides excellent textures in finished dishes, commonly used as a thickener in sauces, soups, and desserts. Arrowroot creates a clear, tasteless sauce that can be used for more delicate cooking, such as a dessert or folk remedy.

Use arrowroot in the same proportions as you would corn starch, mixing it with cold liquids before adding to a hot sauce. For example, mix 1 tablespoon of arrowroot powder with 2 tablespoons of cold water or liquid before adding it to a hot sauce to thicken. To prevent a change in consistency, do not overcook once added to a hot sauce. To use when baking, substitute for one-fourth to one-half of total flour, and combine with other wheat alternatives.

Asafetida

An Indian spice, asafetida is used in small quantities for its flavor and digestive properties for seasoning dishes. It comes in a brown, smelly lump or in granule form. To use the lump form, break off a small piece and crush it with a hammer or cleaver to make your own powder. It is available at East Indian grocery stores.

Avocado

This plant, native to Central America, is also called an "alligator pear." In Vancouver, where I live, you can order a "California roll" in most Japanese restaurants. The main ingredient of this sushi roll is avocado rolled with other ingredients in roasted *nori* (seaweed). This must be a North American invention because I have never heard of this being served in Japan. In Japan, the avocado is called "toro of the forest" because its high fat content makes it similar to tuna belly (*toro* means the belly part of a large tuna).

Avocado is a handy fruit to have in your kitchen to expand your creativity in food preparation because it binds the oil and water well like lecithin. It can be used to prepare dips, salad dressings, sandwiches, and spreads; and it makes an excellent chilled soup, like vichyssoise. Avocados oxidize quickly, so to prevent discoloration, use vinegar or citrus juice in the ingredients.

Benefits of Avocados

It is believed that avocados are helpful for inflamed conditions of the mucus membrane, the colon, and intestines in particular; and it helps insomnia and ulcer sufferers.

ROMAINE LETTUCE, AVOCADO, AND CHILI SALAD

¼ cup olive oil
4 large dried chilies, stemmed and seeded
2 oranges
½ bunch romaine lettuce, cut into bite-size pieces
1 bunch watercress
1 large red onion, peeled and thinly sliced
1 English cucumber, peeled, seeded, and diced
½ bunch radishes, stemmed and thinly sliced

Dressing:

¼ cup white wine vinegar
¼ cup olive oil
1 tbsp. soy sauce
1 tbsp. minced garlic
Pinch cracked black pepper

Heat a small, heavy skillet, then add olive oil and cook chilies over medium heat until color of chilies starts to change, about 20 seconds. Remove chilies and place on a paper towel. Reserve oil for later use.

Peel oranges and remove segments by inserting a sharp knife between membranes. Reserve all the juice in the salad bowl. In a separate bowl, combine romaine lettuce, watercress, onions, cucumbers, and radishes. Mix dressing ingredients with reserved chili frying oil.

Before serving, drain orange segments and add with chilies and avocado to salad. Stir the dressing well and toss with salad to coat.

Yield: 6 servings
Preparation Time: 10 minutes

Bamboo Shoots (Take-no-ko)

In early spring, where a certain type of bamboo (*mo-so*) grows, shoots of bamboo start to come to the surface of the ground. The owner of the mountain or bamboo bush encourages people to dig for these shoots to remove them. This is to prevent the bamboo plant from over-growing. All the surrounding shoots of the old bamboo plant are removed to keep sufficient distance between different bamboo plants, maintaining a healthy root system, and thus avoiding serious damage to the stalks.

To find bamboo shoots, you observe the ground surface carefully to notice small shoots, about one-fourth to one-half inch tall, peeking through. You then dig a twelve-inch or larger hole around the shoot. When you reach the main root, you can break it off there, and what you have is a fresh bamboo shoot. If eaten within twenty-four hours of harvesting, it doesn't require cooking. You can then taste one of nature's most delicate foods. After twenty-four hours, you will want to cook bamboo shoots in boiling water until tender.

The Japanese call it *sashimi* of bamboo, and use a small amount of wasabi and good tamari to accompany this early spring delicacy. Bamboo shoots are available in cans or plastic vacuum-sealed bags in Chinese, Korean, and Japanese food stores. It is used to treat obesity, high blood pressure, and toxemia. In Asian countries, any plant's shoots are considered to be valuable, with bamboo shoots being no exception.

STIR-FRIED BAMBOO SHOOTS
WITH SHIITAKE

6 dried shiitake mushrooms
⅓ cup warm water
2 tbsp. sesame oil
1 tbsp. minced garlic
½ lb. sue choy, cut into 1½ x 1-inch chunks
½ cup thinly sliced boiled bamboo shoots
¼ cup dashi or vegetable stock
1 tsp. sea salt

Soak mushrooms in warm water for 2 hours, then remove stems and slice the caps into ¼-inch slices. Heat wok until hot, then add oil. Sauté garlic for a few seconds, add sue choy, and stir-fry for 1 minute. Add mushrooms, bamboo shoots, and vegetable stock. Cover and steam for 1 minute. Remove cover, reduce sauce until 4 tablespoons of liquid remain. Serve hot.

Yield: 2 to 3 servings
Preparation Time: 5 to 6 minutes

Bancha (Japanese Green Tea)

Green tea consists of the stems and leaves from tea bushes that are at least three years old. Once roasted lightly, they become *hoji-cha* or roasted tea.

Tannin, a compound found in green tea along with a high content of fluoride, was found to be effective for preventing cavities. Children who drink tea containing a high concentration of fluoride have fewer cavities. Tannin is also claimed to be a strong antimutagent in both studies of the Japanese National Institute of Genetics and British Columbia Cancer Research Center.

Drinking tea blocked the formation of nitrosamine of the cardiovascular system, which helps slow down athrosclerosis. Tea also helps break down fat in foods—when Asians eat an oily meal, they always encourage the drinking of tea instead of water.

Beets

Beets' sweet taste and bright red color add to salads and the famous Russian soup, *borscht*. The color comes from the anthocyanin pigment, coloring not only the beet, but also the cook's hands and cutting board. I was not familiar with this vegetable in Japan, apart from Japanese-style pickled large red beets, but I can find beets here almost year-round. The scarlet color becomes brighter when in acid (vinegar or lemon juice); but when in an alkaline solution (baking soda or water), it will turn slightly blue.

Scrub beets well with a brush under cold running water to remove the dirt. Cook beets whole and slice or dice, with or without the peel. Select beets which have fresh green leaves on top. Avoid beets that have soft spots or blemishes. Store beets in a cool, dry place, being sure to remove the tops. The longer you store them, the sweeter they become.

Benefits of Beets

Beets contain indigestible fiber, cellulose, and hemicellulose, vitamins C and B, and potassium. A mixture of beets and carrots makes a valuable juice by helping to build red blood corpuscles in the body. Beet juice is also used as a liver and intestinal tract cleanser, and to treat inflammation of the kidneys and bladder and hemorrhoids.

Drinking large amounts of beet juice in one serving may cause dizziness and nausea the first time. If this happens, mix more carrot juice with the beet juice until you can tolerate the cleansing effect on the liver. Beets, along with legumes and apples, are one of the best vegetables to regulate sugar balance in the body. When beets are eaten, the sugar level in the blood increases slowly.

Bok Choy

Bok choy is the one of the most popular and nutritionally important vegetables in Chinese cookery. *Bok choy* and *pai ts'ai* are the same written words in Chinese. They are names used loosely for a variety of vegetables with dark green to light yellow leaves on white stems, which look like Swiss chard. There are many species of this vegetable. Some varieties of bok choy have white stems, and others have light green stems. Some grow only in early spring, and others are able to survive the cold weather. If the winter isn't severe, a flavorful shoot from bok choy left in the ground from the previous year will come up in early spring.

Different names are given to different species, sizes, and stages of growth. They are available in most Chinese grocery stores or supermarkets. Select one that, when held sideways, does not have drooping leaves. If the leaves droop, it is dehydrated and should be avoided. Look closely at the leaves, and avoid those with brown spots or holes. When you are shopping, look for Shanghai Bok Choy, Baby Bok Choy, and Choy Sum. They look like miniature bok choys and can be prepared the same way as regular Bok Choy.

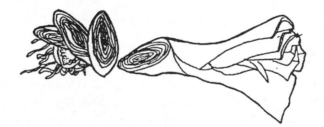

STIR-FRIED BOK CHOY

2 tbsp. olive oil
½ tsp. sesame oil
1 tsp. finely minced garlic
1 tsp. finely minced ginger root
½ lb. bok choy leaves,
    cut into ¾ x 2-inch rectangular pieces
pinch salt
2 tbsp. tamari

Heat wok or skillet until hot. Add oil, then sauté garlic and ginger until aroma rises and mixture is slightly gold in color. Add bok choy at once, stir-fry on high heat until soft but still crunchy. Add salt and tamari, toss quickly to coat the seasonings, then serve.

Note: For Stir-Fried Bok Choy with Mung Bean Sprouts, add 3 ounces of fresh bean sprouts to Stir-Fried Bok Choy at the last minute. Cook for an additional 30 seconds, no more. Toss, then serve. Sprinkle with shredded seaweed (nori).

Yield: 2 servings
Preparation Time: 3 to 4 minutes

Broccoli

Broccoli has quite a following among North Americans. Broccoli is wonderful vegetable stir-fried, deep-fried, or steamed, as a side dish, snack, or for salads.

The stems of broccoli florets are good to add to soups and stir-fry dishes—I have seen a lot of wasted stems in hotel and restaurant kitchens. When peeling broccoli stems, try to peel from the bottom up. Insert a small knife under the skin, hold the skin between thumb and forefinger, then pull. The skin will peel off easily without waste. Slice or cut the stems in various shapes for your recipes.

Benefits of Broccoli

Broccoli is sometimes called "the king of vegetables." This green member of the cruciferous family contains a high amount of protein and fiber and is a good source of calcium and vitamins C and A. Broccoli's calcium is more easily assimilated in the body than calcium contained in milk and other dairy products. According to one report, foods that are high in vitamins A and C may lower the risk of cancer of the gastrointestinal and respiratory tracts. Eating one-half cup of broccoli every day may help to prevent colon and lung cancer. Broccoli is an effective food for aiding in weight loss, toxemia, neuritis, and high blood pressure.

Purchase broccoli with tightly closed buds. Florets should look fresh, firm, and brightly colored. Avoid broccoli that has any yellowing in the buds. Avoid Chinese broccoli with yellow or wilted leaves.

BROCCOLI WITH DEEP-FRIED TOFU

This recipe, which originated as the Indonesian dish, *gado-gado,* is a simple meal you can create in no time. The combination of broccoli, tofu, sprouts, tomatoes, and nuts make an excellent dish that is nutritional as well. This salad contains high amounts of protein, calcium, and minerals. If available, use a twig of fresh mint leaves or roasted minced peanuts on top as a garnish.

> 2 tbsp. peanut butter
> 3 tbsp. warm water
> 2 tbsp. soy sauce
> 1 tbsp. rice vinegar
> 2 tbsp. sesame oil
> 2 tsp. hot chili oil
> 1 tsp. natural sweetener
> ½ tsp. salt
> ½ tsp. minced garlic
> 3 tbsp. minced scallion
> 1 tbsp. tamarind paste
> ½ tsp. finely minced ginger roots
> 2 tbsp. sake or dry sherry
> 1 cup broccoli florets, cooked
> 16 oz. deep-fried tofu, cut into bite-size pieces,
>   blanched to remove oil, and cooled
> ½ cup mung bean sprouts
> 1 ripe tomato, chopped
> 2 to 3 leaves lettuce
> 1 tbsp. sliced deep-fried shallots
> 2 tbsp. minced cilantro
> 3 tbsp. very finely minced scallion

Mix peanut butter and warm water first to make a thin paste, then add next eleven ingredients to make the peanut sauce. The thickness of the sauce may need adjusting depending on the type of peanut butter you use.

Arrange broccoli, tofu, bean sprouts, and chopped tomato in layers on lettuce leaves. Pour peanut sauce over and sprinkle with deep fried shallots and minced cilantro.

Yield: 4 to 5 servings
Preparation Time: 10 minutes

STEAMED BROCCOLI SALAD WITH MUSTARD SAUCE

This recipe may not be challenging to gourmet cooks, but to prove a point, even a small number of simple ingredients can make broccoli a unique and outstanding vegetable.

½ head broccoli tops, with 1-inch stems attached
½ tsp. sea salt
1 tbsp. dijon mustard
1 tbsp. sake
1½ tbsp. soy sauce
1 tsp. Balsamic vinegar

Blanch broccoli, drain, and dip into cold water to chill. Drain and set aside. Combine remaining ingredients and toss with broccoli. Chill for 20 minutes before serving.

Yield: 1 serving
Preparation Time: 22 minutes

Brown Rice Vinegar

Made from cooked brown rice, koji, water, and seed vinegar, brown rice vinegar is allowed to ferment for one year. The koji (rice starter) converts rice starch into sugar, and the yeast contained in the seed vinegar completes the fermentation process by converting the alcohol to acetic acid.

Good brown rice vinegar has a mild, soft, and deep mellow taste, rather than the strong sour taste you may find in cheaply produced synthetic vinegar. You may find synthetic vinegar offensive compared to brown rice vinegar.

Benefits of Vinegar

Brown rice vinegar has a significantly high amino acid content, which helps to eliminate lactic acid build-up in your body. Excess lactic acid in the blood is caused by physical exertion, which results in fatigued, stiff, sore muscles. Brown rice vinegar cleanses and helps to restore a balanced condition in the blood from acidic to normal alkali. To get the most from vinegar, avoid any product labeled distilled or grain vinegar.

Brussels Sprouts

This is one vegetable not known to win popularity contests. Do you know anybody who says, "I love brussels sprouts" or "I can't live without brussels sprouts?" Neither do I. But there must be a reason why it sits in supermarkets for Thanksgiving or Christmas time. I often wonder whether this petite and attractive vegetable began the trend toward using popular small vegetables, such as miniature squash, zucchini, and eggplant, in California cuisine.

With proper preparation and imagination, you can create amazing dishes using this vegetable. To prepare brussels sprouts, cut off the stems, then wash and soak the sprouts in cold water with a pinch of salt and a drop of vinegar for 10 minutes. Drain and cut crosswise gashes into the stem ends. Boil until barely tender, or steam, braise, or pickle.

Select brussels sprouts that are green and very firm. If the outer leaves are wilted, pull them off.

Benefits of Brussels Sprouts

Brussels sprouts belong to the cruciferous family of vegetables that protect the body from cancer—especially colon and stomach cancer. The latest research shows that eating brussels sprouts detoxifies aflatoxins (carcinogens found in contaminated peanuts, corn, and rice and linked to liver cancer). The old belief that eating too many brussels sprouts causes goiter has been disproved. The report indicates that eating cooked brussels sprouts shows no sign of affecting thyroid function.

A mixture of carrot, string bean, lettuce, and brussels sprout juice is believed to strengthen pancreatic functions of the digestive system. It is recommended to avoid carbohydrate intake while using this juice for cleansing.

BRUSSELS SPROUTS IN SESAME SAUCE

24 brussels sprouts
6 tbsp. roasted sesame seeds
2 tbsp. thin soy sauce
2 tsp. natural sweetener or other sweetener
4 tsp. dashi stock

Boil brussels sprouts until tender; remove and cool. Cut them in half. Chop sesame seeds and place in a bowl. Add brussels sprouts and remaining ingredients, toss well. Chill for half an hour, then serve.

Yield: 2 servings
Preparation Time: 35 minutes

BRUSSELS SPROUTS WITH WALNUTS

20 brussels sprouts
2 tbsp. walnuts, chopped
½ tsp. minced garlic
2 tbsp. olive oil
1½ tbsp. rice vinegar
pinch salt and pepper

Boil brussels sprouts until tender. Cool and mix with walnuts, garlic, and dressing. Chill for half an hour, then serve.

Yield: 2 servings
Preparation Time: 35 minutes

Burdock Root

This wild, hardy plant, native to Northern China and Siberia, is cultivated mainly in Japan and regarded highly by ancient practitioners of Oriental medicine. Burdock root, or *gobo* in Japanese, was thought of as a food medicine and commonly eaten as a blood purifier. In its raw state, burdock root doesn't seem to be user-friendly. Yet, when one has the knowledge of preparation and presentation, burdock root is quite a delicacy. For macrobiotic cooking, it is one of the essential ingredients.

To prepare this rather strange-looking vegetable, caution must be taken because the roots change color rapidly once peeled. To avoid discoloration, soak the roots in 2 cups of water plus 1 tablespoon vinegar or lemon juice for a half-hour or more. The famous Japanese dish, *Kimpira,* is prepared by briefly sautéing shredded burdock root and sesame seeds over high heat, then seasoning with soy sauce and mirin—simple, fast, and economical. It has been said that burdock root increases the sexual endurance of men and women.

Benefits of Burdock Root

Burdock root's cooling effect helps lower a high fever and acts as an antidote and diuretic. It's a very familiar edible vegetable in Japan, but burdock root is mainly used for medicinal purposes in China, treating catarrh, low stamina, and for sexual energy. This rather rare vegetable isn't common in North America, but is available. Fresh burdock root is solid and rigid, hairy and heavy. If you decide to be choosy, avoid wilted soft burdock roots.

GLAZED BURDOCK ROOT

This is a popular dish in Japan known as *kimpira gobo*. Kimpira is a cooking method in which shredded vegetables are stir-fried and glazed in a sweet and salty sauce.

> **2 to 3 burdock roots, peeled and cut into match sticks**
> **5 cups cold water (for soaking)**
> **1 tbsp. rice vinegar**
> **1 tbsp. sesame oil**
> **1 whole dried chili, seeds removed, cut into small rings**
> **3 tbsp. soy sauce**
> **1 tbsp. natural sweetener or other sweetener**
> **1 tbsp. sake**
> **1 tbsp. mirin**
> **½ cup water or dashi**
> **1 carrot, peeled and cut into match sticks**
> **3 tbsp. white sesame seeds, roasted**

After cutting the burdock root, soak it in cold water with added rice vinegar to prevent it from turning brown. Heat the wok until hot, add oil and sauté chili and burdock root until roots are relatively soft. Combine soy sauce, sweetener, sake, and mirin, then add with water or dashi to the wok. Bring to a boil. Turn the heat to medium low, and cook until the roots are tender. Add carrots and cook for about another 2 minutes. Turn heat to high, then reduce until 3 to 4 tablespoons of sauce remain. Remove to a serving plate and sprinkle with sesame seeds.

Note: I recommend that you remove the chili before serving. In my experience, there have been a few exciting moments when people eat their food without looking.

> **Yield: 2 servings**
> **Preparation Time: 7 minutes**

BURDOCK IN SESAME VINEGAR SAUCE

3 burdock roots (10 oz.)
1 whole dried chili
2 tbsp. natural sweetener
⅓ tsp. salt
4 tbsp. dashi
⅓ cup rice vinegar
4 tbsp. roasted sesame seeds

Scrub the skin of burdock roots with the back of a knife, then cut into a size best for your cooking pot. Boil for 2 to 4 minutes, then place in cold water. Place burdock roots on cutting board, pound lightly with a full or empty bottle to loosen the fiber. Cut into 2-inch lengths.

Mix chili, sweetener, salt, and dashi separately and bring to a boil. Add burdock root, and cook until tender, about 2 to 3 minutes. Add vinegar, and cook until liquid is almost evaporated. Chop sesame seeds and toss in. Serve at room temperature.

Yield: 2 servings
Preparation Time: 10 minutes

BURDOCK WITH NUTTY MISO PEANUT SAUCE

2 tbsp. oil
2 oz. raw peanuts
1 whole chili, seeds removed
1 small ginger root, cut into match sticks
3 oz. fresh burdock root, cut into julienne
1 tbsp. sake
1 tbsp. mirin
4 oz. red miso
4 tbsp. natural sweetener

Heat a heavy saucepan, add oil. Sauté peanuts until gold in color. Remove peanuts; set aside. In the same pan, sauté chili, ginger, and burdock root over high heat until relatively soft, about 2 minutes. Lower heat to medium, add sake, mirin, miso, and natural sweetener in that order. Stir and return peanuts to dish. Cook until burdock roots are well coated with sauce. Serve hot or at room temperature.

Note: Don't forget to remove the chili before serving.

Yield: 2 servings
Preparation Time: 6 minutes

Cabbage

Green cabbage is the most commonly consumed vegetable in Japan next to daikon, and one of the most important vegetables in Asia. The Japanese are concerned about the price of cabbage because cabbage is a big part of their food budget for everyday meals. Cabbage prices fluctuate according to demand and supply. It is locked into restaurant menus, so restaurants are obligated to purchase it at higher prices.

You can prepare cabbage in many ways, such as pickled, stir-fried, braised, steamed, or shred very fine to eat raw. Keep in mind that cooking with high heat will destroy the vitamin C contained in cabbage.

Avoid cabbage that has yellow or wilted leaves. Purchase cabbage that feels heavy for its size, and is tightly attached to the stem.

Benefits of Cabbage

Raw cabbage has a high amount of vitamin C and a moderate amount of calcium. Cabbage is the unappreciated true king of vegetables when it comes to nutrition. A large study conducted in Japan indicated that people who ate cabbage along with olive oil and yogurt on a regular basis had the lowest death rate from all causes.

Eating cabbage is associated with a lower cancer risk—especially cancer of the colon. Cabbage contains compounds that are anticancer agents, including chlorophyll, vitamin E, dithiolthiones, certain flavonoids, and phenols such as caffeic and ferulic acids. Cabbage juice is used to treat ulcers and constipation, and helps to eliminate waste putrefactive matter in the intestines. The high content of sulfur and chlorine in cabbage works as a cleansing agent in the stomach, intestinal tract, and mucous membrane.

Caution: Cabbage also contains vitamin K, which acts against anticoagulants. A person who is on anticoagulant medication and eats a large amount of cabbage and cruciferous vegetables may want to consult with a doctor.

SIMPLE SALT-PICKLED CABBAGE

½ lb. cabbage
1 tsp. salt
¼ cucumber, sliced thin
¼ carrot, sliced thin
Shiso or beefsteak leaves

Cut cabbage into ⅓ x ½-inch rectangle shapes. Sprinkle with salt and mix with sliced cucumber, carrot, and beefsteak leaves. Leave for 1 hour. Squeeze out excess water, then place vegetables on a plate. Serve with lemon slices and soy sauce on the side.

Yield: 4 servings
Preparation Time: 1 hour

Cardamom Pods (Green)

This spice looks like large dead bugs, but has a pungent exotic flavor. Cardamom originated in Ceylon and South India. It is used to flavor *chai,* a popular drink among East Indians; to season *dahl* and *sabji,* or to make *garam masala.* Refined cardamom, used to flavor Danish pastries and cakes, is more expensive than black cardamom pods. It is available at East Indian grocery stores.

Benefits of Cardamom

Slightly astringent, sweet, and a little pungent, cardamom has been thought to strengthen the heart and lungs. It is thought to relieve gas and sharpen the mind as well. In Chinese herbal remedies, cardamom is used to treat indigestion, gas in the stomach and spleen, cramps, abdominal distention (intestinal parasites), hiccups, vomiting, diarrhea, and dysentery.

Carrots

Everybody knows that carrots are good for you; we all learned that in school when we were young. I consider carrots to be the queen of the vegetables.

We usually consume the root of carrots, yet the leaves of carrots have great flavor and nutritional value as well. Carrots have that sweet unexplainable flavor and texture that is excellent for combining with other vegetables. They enhance dishes by adding color and sweetness.

In juice, soups, salads, and stews, carrots have endless menu possibilities, so keep carrots handy in the refrigerator at all times.

Choose carrots that still have their leaves attached. Carrots and their leaves should look fresh—with no brown or wilted soft spots—and have shiny and heavy roots. Avoid carrots that are limp or light in weight.

Benefits of Carrots

Carrots have the highest content of vitamin A and contain an ample supply of vitamins B, C, D, E, K, potassium, and calcium. Vitamin A in carrots is not destroyed by heat, but some of the hemicellulose is dissolved for easier digestion. Well known for protection against blindness, vitamin A is an essential nutrient for humans and is effective for lowering the risk of cancer. Carrots are ideal for people with sensitive stomachs and intestinal tracts. A carrot a day will provide enough vitamin A for a healthy adult. Additionally, carrots are an excellent means for lowering the risk of both colon cancer and high cholesterol.

As a folk remedy, carrot seeds are used to relieve kidney and urinary problems as well as constipation. Reports show that having just sixteen ounces of fresh carrot juice has more constructive body value than twenty-five pounds of calcium tablets. Carrots are used to cleanse the liver, prevent eye infections, and help respiratory organs, sinuses, and throat. Carrot juice is also recommended for pregnant women and nursing mothers.

ORANGE SNOW

This simple salad can be made one to two hours before serving. Ensure the mixture is kept in the refrigerator in an airtight container.

1 large carrot (preferably organic)
½ lemon
1 tsp. natural sweetener

Peel carrot and grate. Mix well with lemon juice, then chill for at least a half-hour in the refrigerator. Mix in natural sweetener just before serving.

Yield: 2 servings
Preparation Time: 30 minutes

CARROT SALAD

2 carrots
½ tsp. sesame oil
¼ tsp. salt
½ tsp. roasted sesame seeds

Peel carrots and cut into 1½-inch julienne strips. In a medium saucepan, heat oil with carrots and salt. Cover then cook for 5 minutes over medium heat. Remove from pan and chill. Sprinkle sesame seeds over and serve.

Yield: 2 servings
Preparation Time: 5 minutes

SPICY HERBED CHILI CARROT

7 small carrots, peeled and sliced ¼ inch thick
2 tbsp. olive oil
1 cup finely minced onion
1 tbsp. minced garlic
4 tbsp. natural sweetener
½ cup carrot cooking liquid
1 tbsp. chili pepper sauce (or hot chili bean paste)
Pinch cloves
Pinch nutmeg
Pinch cinnamon
2 bay leaves
Pinch dill weed
Pinch cardamom
1 large tomato, chopped
3 tbsp. minced green onion
4 tbsp. very coarsely chopped cilantro

Blanch carrots, saving cooking liquid. In a large heavy skillet, sauté onion and garlic in olive oil until tender. Add natural sweetener, carrot cooking liquid, chili pepper sauce, and seasonings. Bring to a boil. Add carrots, then lower heat to cook until tender. Add tomato and cook for another 2 minutes. Sprinkle with minced green onion and cilantro, toss, then serve.

Yield: 8 servings
Preparation Time: 12 minutes

Cauliflower

I had never met a person who was really crazy about cauliflower until recently. I was shopping with one of my cooking class students and she mentioned that she loved cauliflower. I stared at her in surprise. I consulted a lot of people who had problems with strong cravings for sugar, wheat, and dairy products, but not cauliflower. Cauliflower can be eaten every day, so I bought a couple of large creamy healthy cauliflower for her.

You can turn cauliflower into an exotic and marvelous dish all by itself, and it is inexpensive. Look for cauliflower with a tightly packed, creamy white head and fresh green leaves. Avoid cauliflower with small brown spots or a slimy surface on the florets.

Benefits of Cauliflower

This cabbage family vegetable has been found to be a good source of protein, vitamins A and C, potassium, phosphorus, and trace minerals. It is beneficial in cases of asthma, kidney and bladder dysfunction, high blood pressure, and gout. Additionally, cauliflower is high in carotene and chlorophyll, which are known to block lung cancers.

Three and one-half ounces of raw cauliflower will provide enough vitamin C to fulfill the recommended daily allowance for a normal adult.

CHILLED CAULIFLOWER WITH AVOCADO TARATOUR

This popular Lebanese cauliflower dish, which is easy to prepare, has excellent nutritional value. For tahini dressing, consult the index for the basic tahini recipe.

> 1 head cauliflower, separated into florets
> 1 tbsp. lemon juice
> 1 tsp. salt
> 1 tbsp. toasted sesame seeds
> 1 ripe avocado
> ¾ cup basic tahini dressing

Cover cauliflower with water, add lemon juice and salt, then boil until tender. Remove cauliflower from the pot and set aside to cool. Blend avocado and tahini dressing until a smooth sauce is formed. Pour sauce over cauliflower, sprinkle with sesame seeds, and serve.

Yield: 4 servings
Preparation Time: 10 minutes

CAULIFLOWER WITH FRESH MINT AND LIME DRESSING

1 cauliflower, separated into florets and blanched
¼ cup lime or lemon juice
⅓ tsp. cayenne pepper
1 tbsp. natural sweetener
1 tsp. minced garlic
2 tbsp. minced green onion
2 tbsp. minced fresh mint leaves
¼ tsp. fresh lemon grass, chopped
2 tbsp. vegetable oil

Mix all ingredients and toss with cauliflower. Chill for half an hour. Strain off dressing before serving, and store excess dressing in an airtight container.

Yield: 4 servings
Preparation Time: 10 minutes

Celery

This vegetable is commonly used with other vegetables to enhance their flavor. Japanese call it the "hidden actor." Otherwise, it is eaten raw as celery sticks, sometimes filled with condiments. For a true creator, this is a good chance to test your skills in the creativity department. Celery can be shredded very fine and served with unusual dressings, or it can be pickled, braised, or simply stir-fried.

Select celery that is shiny, firm, and solid. Leaves should be yellow at the ends, not brown. Before using, cut thicker bottoms off, and separate the stems to wash well.

Benefits of Celery

Celery contains an exceptionally high percentage of organic sodium, magnesium, calcium, and iron. Organic salt in the celery juice is believed to be effective in removing carbon dioxide from the system. The combination of carrot and celery juice is used to balance the mineral content in blood, which may help to cure nervous afflictions, insomnia, and anemia, and prevent gall stones.

SAUTEED CELERY KIMPIRA

This is a simple dish that you can prepare very quickly, using just celery. You can also prepare this dish with carrot, daikon skin, or other root vegetables.

4 stalks celery, cut into diagonal slices,
   leaves chopped
1½ tbsp. oil
2 tbsp. soy sauce
1 tbsp. sake
1 tbsp. mirin
½ tbsp. toasted sesame seeds

Heat a heavy saucepan until hot, then sauté celery slices in oil. Sauté until celery becomes soft. Add soy sauce and sake. Stir-fry rapidly to remove water from the celery. While still on high heat, add mirin and soy sauce, and stir quickly for another minute, or until celery becomes glossy. Serve with toasted sesame seeds.

Yield: 2 servings
Preparation Time: 5 minutes

Chard

This curly vegetable is available year-round in most markets. These leafy green vegetables, like beet greens, chicory greens, collard greens, kale, mustard greens, spinach, and turnip greens, are packed with vitamin A, carotene, vitamin C, and other important nutrients and fiber. For whose who are not familiar with cooking methods for this vegetable, try substituting chard in recipes that call for raw spinach. Add chard to soups or salad dishes to add a dark green color, or add it to stir-fry dishes for amazing results.

Benefits of Chard

Chard contains a high concentration of vitamins A, C, and B-complex, calcium, and iron. It is recommended for cases of anemia, obesity, catarrh, and loss of appetite. Chard juice, which contains organic oxalic acid, is very effective for maintaining the eliminative organs by keeping them in proper tone, stimulating peristaltic action to force waste from the body. Unfortunately, the calcium contained in chard is unavailable to the body because the high content of oxalic acid destroys the calcium once cooked.

SAUTEED SWISS CHARD WITH NEW POTATOES AND ROSEMARY

1 tbsp. olive oil
2 cloves garlic, minced
½ tsp. rosemary, minced
¾ lb. new potatoes, sliced ½ inch thick and cooked
2 cups Swiss chard

Heat a heavy skillet until hot. Add oil and cool garlic until aroma is released. Add potatoes and rosemary and cook over medium-high heat for one minute.

Add Swiss chard, then sauté until wilted, about 4 minutes. Serve with a hearty bean soup and corn bread.

Yield: 4 servings
Preparation Time: 7 minutes

Chilies

Another of nature's wonderful creations is the chili pepper. Some people love them; some people hate them; while others' stomachs are too sensitive to eat them. I have received many compliments for recipes containing chilies and an endless list of complaints because of the spiciness. Spiciness depends on the judgment of the individual. I have worked with quite a few Vietnamese and Fijian chefs who all love to eat spicy, burning-hot jalapeño, or seleno chilies as condiments. I cannot figure out why some people can enjoy many spicy foods and others cannot.

A small amount of chili does give a punch or lift to various meals. The Japanese use chilies called hawk's claw for antibacterial purposes, but otherwise make minimum use of chilies. Indian, Southeast Asian, Mexican, South American, and chefs in other tropical countries use this aggressive spice extensively. There are quite a few different kinds of fresh chilies available in North America in dried, whole, or flaked form.

Look for dried chilies that are large in size, shiny, evenly colored, and still pliable in a clear plastic bag. It is a good investment because less than two dollars will buy enough chilies to last about six months—depending on how many chilies you use. For fresh chilies, choose those that look fresh, shiny, and heavy. Avoid those with wrinkles, spots, or blemishes.

Benefits of Chilies

Chilies are a good source of vitamins C and A and calcium. Small amounts of chili pepper increase your appetite. The compound capsaicin, found in almost all types of chilies, provides not only the hot taste in the seasoning department, but also does wonderful things for your body—especially your respiratory system. After eating chilies (the hotter, the better) your body produces liquid to flush out and eliminate the invading substance, according to one study. Thus, chilies aid the body's natural protective mechanism, removing mucus from the lungs—good for smokers and those with breathing problems. Capsaicin is also an effective painkiller for rheumatoid arthritis—the only side effect being a slightly burning mouth.

Chilies are also used in India as a folk remedy to treat ulcers, which may sound funny, but is true, and to treat hemorrhages. Chilies contain other chemical compounds that prevent air pockets in the intestinal tract and relieve constipation. They are also used in the kitchen to prevent insects and bacteria from contaminating flour, rice, and various pickles.

SICHUAN CHILI BEAN PASTE

To use this bean paste, I suggest that you sauté it with oil until the full aroma starts to fill your kitchen before adding the rest of your ingredients.

20 large dried chili peppers
½ cup water
1 lb. fresh red pepper, minced
6 tbsp. oil
2 tbsp. minced garlic
¼ cup brown bean paste

Soak dried chilies in water until soft. Drain, reserving soaking liquid. Cut red pepper in half, remove seeds, and chop into small pieces. Heat wok, add oil, and sauté chili peppers and garlic. Stir-fry for 2 to 3 minutes, until the aroma is released. Add red pepper, brown bean paste, and the chili soaking liquid. Bring to a boil, reduce heat to low, and cook until liquid has evaporated, stirring occasionally. Store in an airtight container.

Yield: 1¼ cups
Preparation Time: 12 minutes

HOT AND SOUR DRESSING

4 tbsp. tamari
¼ tsp. salt
3 tbsp. lime juice
2 cloves garlic, minced
½ tsp. cayenne pepper or hot chili oil
2 tbsp. lemon grass, minced
2 stalk green onion, diced
1 tbsp. cilantro, minced
½ red onion, thinly sliced

Mix all the ingredients except red onion. Store in an airtight jar for at least 2 days. Add thinly cut red onion after salad is tossed with the dressing.

Yield: about ½ cup
Preparation Time: 5 minutes

CHILI BEAN PASTE

½ cup oil
2 tbsp. minced garlic
3 tbsp. fermented black bean, chopped
10 dried chilies, seeds removed and chopped
10 Sichuan peppercorn, crushed
1 dried tangerine peel
2 tbsp. Chinese brown bean paste

Combine all the ingredients together in a pot. Cook over medium heat until the aromas are transferred to the oil, about 30 to 40 minutes. Remove from heat and cool.

Yield: ⅔ cup
Preparation Time: 40 minutes

JALAPEÑO PEPPER DIP

1 cup pinto beans
4 cups water
¼ cup chopped onion
1 tbsp. chopped fresh garlic
⅛ cup olive oil
¼ tsp. cumin, ground
¼ tsp. oregano, ground
1 tsp. chili powder
¼ cup reserved juice
¼ cup crushed tomato
½ tsp. sea salt
1 tsp. green onion, chopped
1 tsp. pickled jalapeño pepper, chopped
½ tsp. fresh jalapeño pepper, chopped

Pressure cook pinto beans in water for 1 hour. Drain juice, reserving for later use. Sauté onion, garlic, and olive oil for 2 to 3 minutes until transparent. Add cumin, oregano, and chili powder. Cook for 2 to 3 more minutes, then remove and cool. In a food processor or blender, process cooked beans until smooth, adjusting the thickness by adding reserved juice. Combine remaining ingredients and mix. Taste and season as necessary.

Yield: 2¾ cups
Preparation Time: 1 hour 10 minutes

HOT CHILI OIL

½ cup oil
2 tbsp. ground chili pepper

Heat oil in a wok or pot until hot. Turn off heat, wait for 2 to 3 minutes, then add ground chili powder. Stir well and let sit until the solids settle to the bottom. Strain oil through a strainer lined with a paper towel. Transfer to a glass bottle for storage.

Yield: ½ cup
Preparation Time: 3 minutes

Chinese Cabbage

This cabbage has pale yellow leaves and a white stem. Called *haku-sai* in Japan, or sold under the name of *nappa,* this cabbage is available at most supermarkets in North America. This is an inexpensive vegetable that will last a long time in the refrigerator when properly wrapped. After daikon and green cabbage, the Japanese use this vegetable more than any other vegetable. They are pickled, sautéed, boiled, and used for braised dishes and hot pots. In Korea, they are used to make a very popular spicy pickled *kimchee.*

Choose Chinese cabbage that feels heavy when lifted. Avoid those that have small brown spots; these indicate age. Look at leaf tips, and avoid brown ones.

Benefits of Chinese Cabbage

This vegetable contains a high amount of vitamins C and A as well as various trace minerals.

Chiang (Brown Bean Paste or Chinese Miso)

Chiang is the equivalent of Japanese miso. It is a Chinese product that has a wheat base instead of a rice base. It is made from a mixture of various cooked beans and wheat as a starter, then fermented for almost the same length of time as miso. Chiang and miso are versatile seasonings used to flavor soups, stews, dips, dressings, marinades, or a dairy product substitute with other ingredients. Because it is a salt seasoning, it lasts a long time in the refrigerator. Normally, one teaspoon of miso or chiang is adequate to flavor one serving of soup, while less is required for other purposes. Once blended with other ingredients, it changes its taste and name.

There are several kinds of chiang available in North America, including chunky, garlic, chili, sweet, Hoisin, yellow bean, and brown bean chiang. Basic chiang is called brown bean paste or soybean paste, and is sold in bottles or tins. The following is a list of a variety of chiang sauces available in Chinese or Oriental food stores.

CHIANG VARIETIES

Hoisin Chiang (sweet bean paste)
Dou-Ban-Chiang (chili bean paste)
Garlic Chiang (with minced garlic)
Black bean Chiang (with ginger, garlic, and salted black beans)
Yellow bean Chiang (yellow bean paste)
Koch'ujang (Korean chili bean paste)
Toenjang (Korean bean paste)

Chrysanthemum Greens

After all these years, I'm still not crazy about this green that my mother used to put into miso soup and hot pots. I do know people, however, who just love this green vegetable. This cultivated green, also known as crown daisy, *shun-giku, or tung hao ts'ai,* grows like a weed and should be eaten before it begins to bloom. The seedlings are eaten first. Then, as it grows, the vegetable is harvested by picking off the top several inches of the stem where the leaves and stems are still tender. It is sold by the bunch or by weight. Because it grows so easily, it can be grown at home in almost any type of soil. You may find this green at selected Chinese grocery stores when in season.

Choosing this green is little tricky because not many people buy this type of green. If you happen to see unwilted, fresh-looking greens with no brown spots or blemishes, buy them and experiment. It may be a brand new experience for you.

CHRYSANTHEMUM GREEN SALAD

½ lb. chrysanthemum greens, leaves only
4 to 5 large mushrooms, sliced thin
1 tbsp. olive oil
1 tbsp. soy sauce
1 tsp. sesame seeds
1½ tsp. rice vinegar
1½ tbsp. roasted sesame seeds

Wash greens well and pick only the leaves. Mix with mushrooms and place in a salad bowl. Mix together olive oil, soy sauce, sesame seeds, and rice vinegar, then pour over greens just before serving. Top with roasted sesame seeds.

Yield: 1 serving
Preparation Time: 5 minutes

Cilantro (Coriander Leaves, Chinese Parsley)

This pungent herb adds an exotic flavor to salsas, tacos, salad dressings, and many other preparations from many different countries. It is an essential herb to spice up Chinese, Spanish, Mexican, Thai, Indian, and Southeast Asian dishes.

When choosing your cilantro, look for bright, fresh green leaves with small, strong stems. Store in a glass container, covered, in the refrigerator.

Benefits of Cilantro

Cilantro is very high in calcium, iron, and vitamins A, B1, B2, and C. It is a powerful remedy that stops vomiting and diarrhea almost instantly. It is best used as a fresh ingredient, because fresh leaves are fragile and nutrients are destroyed once cooked. Make it a habit to sprinkle freshly minced cilantro on your salads or favorite meals.

TOMATO SALSA

5 large ripe tomatoes, peeled and diced
1 green pepper, seeded and finely chopped
1 fresh jalapeño pepper, seeded and diced
3 tbsp. minced garlic
¼ tsp. dry oregano
1 to 2 tbsp. chopped cilantro

Combine all ingredients and refrigerate until needed.

Yield: 2½ to 3 cups
Preparation Time: 5 minutes

THAI-STYLE FIVE-FLAVORED SPINACH

This sauce is seasoned with sweet, sour, salt, hot, and bitter spices. This combination of seasonings can be used for almost all vegetables and dishes. It is a very unique blend that can be used over almost all vegetables.

3 tbsp. oil
1 tbsp. minced garlic
½ tsp. minced ginger
3 tbsp. natural sweetener
1 tbsp. soy sauce
½ tsp. Thai chili sauce or 3 whole dried chilies,
   seeds removed
Juice of 1 lemon or 2 limes
1 bunch spinach, whole and cooked
1 tbsp. minced cilantro
2 tbsp. minced green onion (white part only), shredded
2 tbsp. lemon grass, chopped

Heat wok until hot, then add oil and sauté garlic and ginger until aroma is released. If using dried chilies, add them with the garlic and ginger to sauté. Reduce heat to medium. Add natural sweetener, soy sauce, chili sauce, and lemon juice. Bring the sauce to a boil. Add spinach. Cook for 1 minute. Sprinkle with cilantro, minced green onion, and lemon grass. Serve hot.

Yield: 2 to 3 servings
Preparation Time: 7 minutes

Cinnamon

This aromatic and popular spice is used in everything from tea to curry powder.

Benefits of Cinnamon

According to Ayurveda, cinnamon strengthens and energizes tissues, promotes digestion, and has a cleansing action. A mixture of cinnamon, cardamom, ginger, and cloves are used in very small quantities as a tea to relieve cough and congestion and to promote digestion. According to Chinese herbal medicine, cinnamon warms the kidneys and supplements the body fire, dispels colds, and alleviates pain.

Cloves

Produced mainly in India and Indonesia as well as Madagascar, Zambia, and Tanzania, cloves derived their name from the French word, *clou*, meaning "nail." Cloves are used widely to give flavor to meat, such as ham and pork, and to season sauces, gravies, and vegetables. Ground cloves are an important spice for seasoning desserts and baked goods as well. In India, cloves are a common spice used in curry powder. Cloves have also been used for cosmetic purposes, for fragrance in incense, as a mouth freshener, and as an insect repellent.

Benefits of Cloves

Cloves are a natural pain reliever. Oil of clove is used to relieve toothaches. The steam from boiling water with a few drops of clove oil is inhaled as a decongestant. In Chinese herbal medicine, cloves are used in treating certain types of colds, vomiting, hiccups, pains in the heart and abdomen, and hernia.

Coconut Milk

Coconut milk is a good substitute for dairy milk, but use it with caution. Coconut milk is high in saturated fat just like dairy milk and cheese. If you decide to use coconut milk, make sure you burn off all the saturated fat you consume.

Benefits of Coconut Milk

Coconut contains all the essential amino acids, vitamins A and B-complex, and various minerals. It is used for treating urinary diseases, constipation, vomiting, fatigue, and weakness. Coconut meat is recommended for preventing thyroid gland problems because of the high content of the organic iodine.

COCONUT AND BASMATI PILAF

2 tbsp. flaked coconut
3¾ cups basmati rice
3½ cups water
2 340-ml cans coconut milk
Pinch saffron
½ cup golden raisins
2 tbsp. oil
2 tbsp. cumin seeds
2 tbsp. sesame seeds
½ cup cashew nuts
1 tbsp. chopped cilantro

Place coconut in a flat skillet and cook over medium heat until lightly toasted. Remove and set aside to cool. Wash basmati well, place in a large pot, and combine with water, coconut milk, and saffron. Bring to a boil, stirring constantly. Add raisins, then lower heat to simmer and cover with a lid. Cook for 10 minutes, or until all the liquid is absorbed. Turn off the heat and leave for 10 minutes.

Heat oil in a large frying pan, then add cumin and cook for 10 seconds. Lower the heat to medium and add cashews and sesame seeds. Cook until golden in color. Remove from heat and stir into fluffed rice. Mix and place on a serving platter. Sprinkle with toasted coconut and cilantro.

Yield: 8 cups
Preparation Time: 35 minutes

Coriander

Coriander originated in southern Europe and along the Mediterranean coast, but is widely produced in Russia, Eastern Europe, South America, and India as well. Coriander plants can grow as high as ninety centimeters tall, and they have either white or pink flowers. When the seeds are ripe, they are picked and dried. Once dried, seeds have a mellow, sweet flavor. In Southeast Asia, China, and South America, fresh coriander leaves are also used in cooking. Coriander is an essential spice in making curry, spice soups, stews, sauces, and salad dressings.

Benefits of Coriander

In Ayurveda medicine, coriander is believed to be a stimulating substance that aids in digestion and acts as a natural diuretic. It is useful for eliminating gas, indigestion, nausea, and vomiting. In Chinese herbal medicine, coriander is used to treat measles, stomach aches, nausea, and painful hernia.

Corn

Fresh young corn is naturally sweet, but after a few hours off the stalk, changes take place causing a depreciation of flavor and vitamin C, A, and B1, in that order.

After purchasing fresh corn, peel off the husk and pick a few kernels to taste for sweetness. Keep the husks on and place in the refrigerator until ready to use.

Benefits of Corn

Corn oil has been connected to lower blood cholesterol levels than other polyunsaturated vegetable oils. It is also known as a diuretic and mild stimulant in American folk remedies.

CORN AND TOMATO CHOWDER

Chowder doesn't have to be made with clams. With only vegetables, you can create anything you can imagine. Start by picking one vegetable as the main actor. For example, if you want the potato to play the leading role in your soup, consider onion and garlic as supporting actors. Then surround them with the cast: seasonings, herbs, and spices. With you as director and your choice of audience, it's a bound to be a hit.

10 tbsp. olive oil
1 tbsp. garlic, minced
1 cup onion, minced
1 stalk celery, diced
1 carrot, diced
2 potatoes, peeled, diced
3 tomatoes, seeded, diced
1 cup fresh or frozen corn
1 tsp. salt
pinch pepper
½ tsp. dry basil
4 cup vegetable stock
2 tbsp. chopped parsley
1 cup soy milk or nut milk
1 tbsp. tahini

Heat a medium-size saucepan, add oil and sauté garlic, onion, and celery until soft and transparent, stirring occasionally. Add remaining ingredients, except milk and tahini. Bring to a boil, then reduce heat to low. Simmer until potatoes are almost tender. Stir tahini and milk into the soup, and stir well. Bring to a boil, continuing to stir. Cook for another 5 minutes. Season and serve.

Yield: 4 to 5 servings
Preparation Time: 25 minutes

Cucumber (English and Japanese)

Japanese cucumber is slightly smaller than English cucumber and has fewer seeds and a thinner skin. Rubbing salt into the cut cucumbers is done to remove some of the unpleasant bitter tartness. The salt will, however, remove the liquid from the cucumber at the same time, so for salads, remove the bitterness instead by soaking cut cucumbers in cold water with a small amount of salt.

Choose cucumbers that are rigid, all green, and have a lustrous skin. Remove the ends, peel when waxy, and remove the seeds if desired. Japanese cucumbers tend to have a better flavor than English cucumbers. They are available in Japanese or Korean food stores in season only.

Benefits of Cucumbers

Cucumber is a well-known diuretic, helping the kidney secrete and promoting the flow of urine. The high content of potassium in cucumbers makes it useful for both high and low blood pressure. Cucumbers are used as a tonic for conditioning the skin, preventing nails from splitting, and promoting healthy hair. They are high in barium and vitamins B and C, along with the protein digestive enzyme, erepsin. Cucumber juice has a high potassium, organic salt, calcium, phosphorus, and chlorine content. Combined with carrot juice, cucumber has been documented to be effective in removing uric acid crystal from the circulatory and muscular system.

PICKLED CUCUMBER WITH EGGPLANT

In the preparation of this basic recipe, you will remove water from the vegetables. If you like the end result, which is crunchy textured vegetables, you can experiment with this less common method of preparing them.

2 Japanese eggplants
1 Japanese cucumber
3 slices fresh ginger root, cut into julienne strips
1 tsp. salt

Cut cucumber and eggplant into thin slices. Sprinkle with salt and rub gently. Leave at room temperature for 30 minutes to 1 hour. Squeeze out excess water. Place on a serving plate with lemon slices and soy sauce on the side.

Yield: 4 servings
Preparation Time: 1 hour

Cumin Seeds (Regular or Black)

This spice is mostly produced in western Asia, India, and Indonesia. It originated in the Nile Canyon in Egypt. Its leaves are dark green and its flowers are white or light blue. The seeds are yellow-brown and about six millimeters in size. Once seeds are dried, they become sharp and pungent. Cumin seeds are a very popular spice among European, North African, Indian, and Mexican diners. They are used to flavor bread, cheese, and cakes in Germany and Switzerland, and are also used often in Mexican, Arabian, and Spanish cooking.

Cumin seeds were cultivated long ago in India, and are therefore an essential seasoning in garam-masala, curry powder, and chutney. Once dry-roasted to increase aroma and pungency, they should be kept in an airtight container.

Benefits of Cumin

Cumin is known to aid in digestion and the secretion of digestive juices. In Ayurveda medicine, roasted cumin powder is used to treat intesinal disorders such as diarrhea and dysentery.

Curry Powder

Curry is a popular blend of herbs and spices used in many countries. India, Southeast Asia, Japan, and Hong Kong consume a large amount of curry. There are different blends available; curry powder is commonly the manufacturer's secret recipe of various spices and herbs. Curry may contain a combination of allspice, cumin, cardamom, cinnamon, cloves, coriander, fennel, mustard seeds, turmeric, or other spices. In India, the mixture of spices is blended and adjusted for the family health needs.

Use curry spices to flavor various bean and vegetable dishes. It may be difficult to find a curry powder that you like; regular supermarkets may carry a rather expensive curry powder whose quality is not that great. You can make your own curry powder or try those in an East Indian store.

CURRY POWDER

This recipe will make a large amount of curry powder at once.

¼ cup coriander
5 tbsp. ground turmeric
4 tbsp. cumin
4 tsp. allspice
4 tsp. cinnamon
3 tsp. cardamom
1 tsp. cloves
3 tsp. fennel
4 tsp. fenugreek
4 tsp. ginger
2 tsp. mace
4 tsp. ground chili
4 tsp. white pepper

Mix all spices, which should be ground or powdered. Store in an airtight container.

Yield: 1⅓ cups

YELLOW CURRY PASTE

6 dried red chilies
1 tsp. coriander seed
½ tsp. ground cinnamon
½ tsp. cloves, ground
2 tbsp. minced red onion
1 tbsp. minced garlic
1 tbsp. minced fresh lemon grass
1 tsp. sea salt
1 tbsp. curry powder
1 tsp. dry mustard powder

Seed chilies, soften in warm water, then mince. In a dry skillet, heat coriander seeds over low heat until brown and aromatic. Grind in a blender to make a powder. Add the remaining ingredients to the powder to make a paste. Adjust the texture by adding small amounts of water or oil. This paste can be stored in a glass container for quite a long time; but for better flavor, use soon. Add the paste to recipes or thin with stock to make an instant curry sauce.

Yield: ¼ cup

CURRY POWDER II

¼ cup coriander seed
2 tbsp. poppy seed
1 tbsp. cardamom seed
1 tbsp. fenugreek seed
2 tsp. black mustard seeds
2 tsp. white mustard seeds
1 tbsp. black peppercorns
2 tsp. crushed dried chilies
2 tbsp. turmeric powder
2 tbsp. cumin, ground
2 tbsp. ginger, ground
1 tsp. cloves, ground
1 tsp. cinnamon, ground
1 tsp. mace, ground

In a dry skillet, toast coriander, poppy seeds, cardamom, fenugreek, and black and white mustard seeds, stirring over medium heat until seeds start to darken slightly and an aroma is released, about 5 minutes. Let cool, then transfer to a blender. Add peppercorn and chilies, blend until finely ground. In small bowl, combine mixture with turmeric, cumin, ginger, cloves, cinnamon, and mace. Store in a clean dry jar with a tight-fitting lid.

Yield: 1 cup

GARAM MASALA

1 tbsp. cardamom seeds
1 tsp. whole cloves
1-inch stick cinnamon
1 tsp. black cumin seeds
1 tsp. black peppercorn
1 whole dried chili, seeds removed
2 tsp. anardana (dried pomegranate seeds, optional)

Grind all ingredients in an electric blender or coffee grinder. Store in an airtight container.

Yield: ¼ cup

Daikon

Daikon, also known as *lo-bok* or Japanese white radish, is Japan's most prized, most familiar, and most widely used vegetable. Pickled, raw, dried, or cooked, folk healers and scientists have noted its outstanding nutritional and medicinal qualities. In Japanese, *daikon* translates to "large root" or "big root." The word *daikon* is used in many different expressions, such as *daikon ashi* for a woman with large legs, or *daikon yakusha* for actor with no talent.

Raw daikon, abundant in digestive enzymes, complements the oily or raw foods eaten in Japan by aiding in their digestion. From stew in the cold wintertime to a summertime condiment with cold noodles, daikon is used year-round. It looks like a little girl's leg, white to beige in color, with green leaves on top. It is relatively inexpensive for its weight, and it is widely available in North America.

The Japanese always serve grated daikon or ginger with broiled fish, tempura, deep-fried tofu, cold soba, and udon. The fact that daikon always appeared with high protein dishes made me curious. After making a few inquiries and going through several books, I discovered the wisdom of the old culture—prior to scientific proof, people combined foods for nutritional benefit.

Choose daikon that feels heavy for its size. If it feels light, avoid it. Chances are that a light daikon has worm holes inside or may have been forced to grow too rapidly.

Benefits of Daikon

Enzymes similar to diastase, amylase, and esterase are found in raw daikon juice, and help in the digestion of fats, proteins, and carbohydrates. The raw juice is proven to inhibit nitrosamine (carcinogen) formation in the stomach. Daikon has high amounts of vitamins E (twice as much in the skin), A, B1, and B2. Daikon is used as a diuretic, decongestant, cleanser for the liver, and balancing agent for female hormones including estrogen.

DAIKON STICKS SAUTEED WITH GINGER

2 tbsp. oil
1 oz. ginger, peeled, cut into very fine julienne
1 whole dried chili
1 lb. daikon, cut into match sticks
3 tbsp. white sesame seeds, roasted
3 tbsp. tamari or soy sauce
½ tsp. salt

Heat a flat skillet until hot, then add oil. Stir-fry ginger first, then chili and daikon over high heat, stirring constantly for 2 to 3 minutes. Lower the heat to medium high. Add sesame seeds, stir, and cook for another minute until daikon becomes slightly transparent. Add tamari and salt. Stir-fry for 30 more seconds. Remove from heat. Serve hot or at room temperature.

Yield: 3 servings
Preparation Time: 5 minutes

STEWED DAIKON WITH MISO SAUCE

3 tbsp. white miso
1 tbsp. natural sweetener
1 tbsp. minced scallion
1 tbsp. minced ginger
1 tbsp. sake
1 tbsp. mirin
1 tbsp. tamari
1 tbsp. dry mustard powder
1 lb. daikon, peeled and cut into ½-inch-thick half-moon shape
1 6 x 6-inch piece kombu (dashi kombu)
½ tsp. salt
3 cups water

Combine miso, sweetener, scallion, ginger, sake, mirin, tamari, and dry mustard; set aside. Place daikon, kombu, water, and salt in a pot. Bring to a boil, then lower heat to medium. Cook until daikon is tender. Serve sauce on the side. Keep leftover miso sauce refrigerated in an airtight container.

Yield: 4 servings
Preparation Time: 25 to 30 minutes

DAIKON AND CARROT
IN SWEET DIJON VINEGAR SAUCE

1 cup daikon, peeled and cut into 2-inch cubes
2 cups carrot, peeled and cut into 1-inch cubes
½ cup finely minced onion
3 tbsp. olive oil
⅓ cup cider vinegar
½ cup natural sweetener
1 tbsp. dijon mustard
½ tsp. salt
1 tbsp. dill weed
2 bay leaves
Minced parsley
½ cup green peas, fresh or frozen

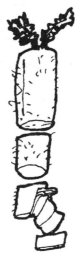

Blanch carrots and daikon; remove and set aside. In a large skillet, sauté onion until tender. Add vinegar, natural sweetener, and mustard; then bring liquid to a boil. Add carrot and daikon and cook for 2 to 3 minutes, stirring constantly. Cover and simmer over the low heat until carrots are tender and well seasoned. Season with salt, if needed, and herbs. Remove from heat and sprinkle with minced parsley. Add green peas, stir for 30 seconds, and serve.

Yield: 4 servings
Preparation Time: 15 minutes

DAIKON WITH MINCED SHIITAKE SAUCE

Even though a small amount of shiitake is used for this dish to simulate minced chicken, the main actor of this meal is daikon, not shiitake mushrooms.

2 to 3 slices ginger root, cut into very fine julienne
3 tbsp. thin soy sauce
2 tbsp. natural sweetener
1 tbsp. sake
1 tbsp. mirin
1 cup dashi
1 lb. small daikon, peeled
   and cut into ½-inch-thick half-moon shapes
1 oz. shiitake, soaked then minced
1 tbsp. arrowroot powder
1 tbsp. water

In a 7-inch saucepan, place ginger, soy sauce, sweetener, sake, mirin, and dashi; bring to a boil. Add shiitake, stirring slowly. Add daikon and water, cover with drop lid, then cook for 7 to 8 minutes over medium heat, or until daikon is tender.

Combine arrowroot and water, then slowly stir arrowroot mixture into sauce to thicken. Serve hot.

Yield: 2 servings
Preparation Time: 15 minutes

SAUTEED GLAZED DAIKON PEEL

1 lb. dry daikon peel, cut into julienne
1 whole dried red chili, seeds removed
2 tbsp. sesame oil
2 tbsp. sake
½ tsp. sea salt
½ tbsp. soy sauce

Dry daikon peel in the sun or place on a plate and leave in the refrigerator overnight, uncovered. Cut chili into very thin slices. Heat a flat skillet, then quickly sauté daikon peel and chili in sesame oil over high heat. Add sake, salt, and soy sauce; then toss quickly and remove onto a flat platter to cool. Serve as a condiment with a meal or with high-protein food such as tofu, tempeh, or seitan.

Yield: 2 servings
Preparation Time: 5 minutes (plus drying overnight)

Dates

Dates are an excellent sweetener used in many ways. From my point of view, they are a must as a vegetarian snack fruit and for vegetarian cooking.

To select quality dates is to select the best bulk health food store in your area. Avoid any type of packaged dates even though the price may be lower than fresh dates. There are several kinds of dates available—imported and local—try them.

Benefits of Dates

Dates are high in calcium, potassium, iron, and traces of various vitamins. They are low in fat, making them an ideal snack food. As a remedy, dates are used as a laxative and to treat anemia, low blood pressure, stomach ulcers, colitis, and tuberculosis. In India, they are used to promote recovery from fever. They are also recommended for nursing mothers.

SESAME DATE SHAKE

2 tbsp. tahini
½ cup apple juice
½ banana, peeled and cut into chunks
2 whole pitted dates
5 to 6 ice cubes
Sprinkle nutmeg

Blend all ingredients in an electric blender until flossy, then pour into a chilled glass and sprinkle with nutmeg.

Yield: 1 serving
Preparation Time: 5 minutes

Eggplant (Japanese)

In Japan, summer and autumn eggplant is considered so special that according to an old saying, "It's not to be wasted or given to a daughter-in-law." Eggplants are excellent grilled, simmered, or deep-fried. Eggplant oxidizes very quickly, and the bitterness should be removed before cooking. To remove bitterness, soak the cut eggplant in salted water immediately after cutting. Leave in water for 30 minutes to 1 hour, drain, pat dry, and use. If western eggplant is used, salt it first, wait 30 minutes, press, then rinse.

Eggplant and oil go together well. In many countries, eggplant is always cooked with plenty of oil or fats, yet studies show that eggplant somehow reduces the build-up of fatty acids in arteries. Less fat, however, is better when cooking eggplant because the pulp absorbs oil when deep-fried or sautéed and intensifies when the temperature of the oil is too low.

Japanese eggplant, which is small compared to the western eggplant, is available year-round in North America. Japanese eggplant is available in supermarkets and Oriental markets. Look for gleaming purple eggplants. Any signs of brown, yellow, or other color spots indicate the eggplant may be old and should be avoided.

Benefits of Japanese Eggplant

Eggplant has a little of every nutrient, but not much of any particular nutrient known to westerners. In Asia, dried or burnt eggplant is used to treat several diseases such as alcoholism, lumbago, stomach ulcers, and stomach cancer. In Japan, a mixture of sea salt and burnt eggplant skin is used as toothpaste.

When one is taking an antidepressant medication that inhibits an enzyme known as monoamine oxidase (MAO), eating food rich in tyramine, such as eggplant, is not advised, as it may cause hypertensive crisis. In a recent study in Japan, it was shown that protease (trypsin) inhibitors contained in eggplant counteract cancer-causing agents. Eggplant is considered excellent for both energy and sexual stamina.

EGGPLANT AND CHICKPEA DIP

3 to 4 lb. Japanese eggplant
4 tbsp. olive oil
1 tbsp. minced garlic
3 tbsp. chili bean paste
½ cup finely chopped onion
½ cup diced green pepper
1 cup cooked chickpeas (reserve cooking liquid)
4 large dried chilies, seeds removed
2 tsp. sea salt
4 tbsp. chopped cilantro
1 tbsp. natural sweetener
2 cups diced ripe tomatoes
¼ tsp. ground cumin seed

Cut eggplant into ¼-inch cubes, sprinkle with salt, and spread on a paper towel. Let sit for 30 minutes. Heat oil in a large flat skillet. Sauté garlic, bean paste, onion, and pepper until soft and gold in color. Add eggplant and stir-fry until eggplant becomes soft. Remove to mixing bowl.

Process chickpeas in food processor for 10 seconds with ½ cup of chickpea cooking liquid. Combine all the ingredients together, chill for 1 hour. Serve with thin taco chips or tortilla chips.

Yield: 4½ cups
Preparation Time: 1 hour 35 minutes (including chilling time)

BRAISED EGGPLANT WITH GINGER

1½ lb. Japanese eggplant
1 cup plus 1 tsp. oil
2 tbsp. minced ginger root
3 tbsp. tamari or soy sauce
1 tbsp. natural sweetener
¼ cup water

Remove and discard eggplant stems, but leave the skin. Cut into 3 x 1 x 1-inch slices and set aside. Heat 1 cup oil until hot. To test oil temperature, drop one slice into oil; if it surfaces immediately, then the temperature is right. When the oil is the right temperature, add eggplant slices and fry until gold in color. Drain, then dry on paper towels and set aside.

Heat wok, then add 1 teaspoon oil and sauté ginger for 30 seconds. Add remaining ingredients and sauté very quickly. Return eggplant to the mixture in the wok. Braise over medium low heat for 2 to 3 minutes, stirring occasionally. Remove when sauce is absorbed by the eggplant. Serve hot.

Yield: 3 to 4 servings
Preparation Time: 9 minutes

LEBANESE-STYLE EGGPLANT SALAD (BABA GHANNOUJ)

1 large eggplant
3 tbsp. tahini
3 tbsp. water
¼ cup lemon juice
1 tbsp. minced garlic
½ tsp. salt
1 tbsp. olive oil

Roast eggplant over an open flame, turning it over the direct heat until all the skin is dark brown (or broil in the oven). Remove from heat and cool for 1 minute. Peel off skin and place eggplant in a strainer to drain the liquid. Chop eggplant, then mix with next five ingredients. Cover with oil at the last minute to prevent oxidation and darkening of the eggplant. Serve with toasted pita bread.

Yield: 1½ cups
Preparation Time: 5 minutes

BRAISED EGGPLANT IN MISO

This is a classic Japanese dish that has three marvelous foods combined together in one dish. Miso, eggplant, and oil complement each other well.

1 lb. Japanese eggplant
½ cup dashi
2 tbsp. white miso
2 tbsp. natural sweetener
1 tbsp. mirin
3 tbsp. sesame oil

Wash eggplant and cut into ½-inch round pieces. Soak for 15 to 30 minutes in cold water with a pinch of salt. Drain, then set aside. Combine dashi, miso, natural sweetener, and mirin; set aside. Heat a thick skillet, then sauté eggplant in sesame oil until light gold in color. Add sauce mixture, lower heat, and cook until sauce is almost gone and the surface of the eggplant is well coated. Serve hot or at room temperature.

Yield: 2 servings
Preparation Time: 5 minutes

DEEP-FRIED EGGPLANT
WITH GRATED DAIKON SAUCE

3 small Japanese eggplants
2 cups oil (for deep-frying)
1 cup dashi
¼ cup mirin
¼ cup thin soy sauce
2 tbsp. daikon, very finely grated

Cut eggplants in half lengthwise. With a sharp knife, cut a fine criss-cross pattern on a skin side, then release into cold water with a pinch of salt for 10 minutes. Drain and pat dry. Deep-fry in 380-degree oil, skin side down. Remove eggplant when light gold in color. Combine dashi, mirin and soy sauce in a small pot and keep warm. Serve eggplant on a platter with grated daikon and dipping sauce on the side.

Yield: 4 servings
Preparation Time: 20 minutes

JAPANESE-STYLE BROILED EGGPLANT

¼ cup dashi
¼ cup soy sauce
¼ cup brown rice vinegar
1 tbsp. mirin
1 tbsp. sake
1 4 x 4-inch piece kombu
3 small Japanese eggplants
1 tbsp. roasted sesame seeds
1 thumb-sized piece of ginger root, grated

Combine first six ingredients and boil for 5 seconds. Strain, and set aside. Broil eggplant until soft, soak in very cold water to cool, then peel quickly and remove the stems. Tear into 5 or 6 pieces, then cut into 1½-inch slices. Serve eggplant in individual dishes. Pour dressing over eggplant, sprinkle with sesame seeds, and serve with grated ginger on the side.

Yield: 2 to 3 servings
Preparation Time: 8 minutes

Fennel

Fennel originated on southern Europe and is cultivated widely in Europe, North Africa, India, and Japan. It is a perennial herb; in the fall, yellow flowers appear. After a cluster is ripe, it is harvested and dried. Two seeds are taken from each cluster. The seeds have a pleasant, aromatic fragrance, and they are sharp and sweet tasting.

Benefits of Fennel

Fennel is used to treat indigestion and to refresh the mouth after a meal to prevent bad breath. It resolves phlegm and stimulates milk production. In Chinese herbal medicine, fennel is used to treat gastroenteritis, hernia, indigestion, and abdominal pain.

Flax Seeds and Flax Seed Oil

Benefits of Flax Seeds

Flax seeds contain 12 percent complete protein, 10 percent fiber, 4 percent mucilage, and 45 percent quality oil. They are used in the treatment of many digestive diseases, including gastritis, ileitis, and diverticulitis. A substance found in flax resembles prostaglandins, which may be responsible for part of its therapeutic value. The function of prostaglandins includes regulation of blood pressure, heart function, calcium, and energy metabolism. Flax seeds increase the bulk of stools and prevent toxin build-up in the colon. They also contain a complete array of trace minerals—potassium, phosphorus, magnesium, calcium, sulfur, sodium, chlorine, iron, zinc, manganese, silicon, copper, fluorine, aluminum, nickel, cobalt, iodine, chromium, selenium, and vanadium.

In recent years, flax seed oil has been gaining popularity. More and more medical practitioners are using flax seed oil in various therapeutic treatments for fatty degeneration, cardiovascular disease, cancer, high cholesterol, and hardening of the arteries.

Flax seed oil contains 25 percent LA and 55 percent LNA—both essential fatty acids necessary for a healthy body, with oleic and saturated fatty acids. It also contains lecithin and vitamins A, E, C, B1, and B2.

Gai-Lan (Chinese Broccoli)

Another kind of broccoli, *gai-lan*, or Chinese broccoli, is popular among the Chinese and is available at Chinese markets or produce stores. Chinese broccoli does not have any resemblance to western broccoli. It has a hint of a delicate bitter taste, so when seasoning, don't overpower the flavor of gai-lan with a strong sauce. When cooked properly, has a delicious crunchy texture.

Prepare Chinese broccoli by steaming or blanching first then adding to your stir-fry dish with garlic and ginger; or serve with an oil and stock-based sauce with added soy sauce. Before steaming, the bottom tough part of the gai-lan should be removed, just as you do with asparagus.

STEAMED GAI-LAN

2 lb. gai-lan
2 tbsp. oil
2 tbsp. soy sauce
Pinch white pepper
1 tbsp. natural sweetener
1 tbsp. minced ginger

Combine oil, soy sauce, pepper, and ginger in a small bowl; set aside. Cut gai-lan such that one stem is attached to one branch. Wash gai-lan, and remove the tough bottom portion. Steam until tender-crisp. Remove from the steamer and set aside. In a large bowl, toss hot steamed gai-lan with soy sauce mixture. Arrange on a serving plate and serve hot.

Yield: 4 servings
Preparation Time: 4 to 5 minutes

Garlic

Garlic is a wonderful creation of nature—the world wouldn't be the same without it. Garlic is available everywhere in North America, and a large portion of the population loves it. I keep one or two whole fresh garlic cloves beside my cutting board at all times. I use at least half a garlic bud every day, and my family doesn't complain.

My father prepared pickled garlic every year when garlic harvesting season arrived. He purchased large quantities from the market, and all the kids peeled the cloves, trying to be careful not to break them. The garlic was then marinated in a good soy sauce for six months to a year in a glass jar, completely sealed and stored in a cool dark place, usually under the floor. When it was done marinating, he transferred the garlic to a small ceramic container with the soy sauce and ate at least two or three cloves a day. The remaining soy sauce was used to season vegetables, fish, and marinades. All the nutrients are preserved either in the soy sauce or in the garlic. Pickled garlic is not as pungent as raw garlic.

If you don't mind the strong taste, I recommend you eat two to three raw garlic cloves a day. If you begin to receive stares of suspicion from strangers, you can always take odorless garlic pills.

Look for firm, solid cloves with tightly clinging skin. Lift to judge the weight—if it feels heavy for its size, it's a good one. Avoid garlic buds with empty sections or those with a new shoot; this is an indication of old garlic.

Benefits of Garlic

The trick is to eat enough garlic to get a measurable amount of nutrients. Garlic has a large amount of vitamins C, thiamin, and B1, and traces of potassium and iron. Garlic contains alliin and allicin, both of which have antibiotic activity. Garlic is effective for gastrointestinal disorders, septic poisoning, typhus, cholera, infections, cancer, and for lowering blood pressure and blood cholesterol (LDL). Studies indicate some anti-clotting effects of ajoene, a natural derivative of allicin.

Ginger Root

Fresh ginger root has a distinctive, sweetly clean, sharp, pungent flavor. It is an essential condiment in all Oriental cooking and cooking in other tropical parts of the world, but it is widely available in North America. Most ginger root comes from China or Hawaii.

The potato-like skin of ginger should be peeled or scrubbed off using the back of a small knife, then the ginger should be grated or chopped. You can find a fine-tooth economical grater from your local Japanese or Korean food store called *Oroshi-gane,* which will give you a nice, fine grate. It looks like a small (3 x 4-inch) metal washing board.

Old ginger has thicker skin and a stronger aroma and taste than young ginger. Ginger should not be kept in a plastic bag. Keep it in a cool, dry place for storage. Don't substitute fresh ginger for powdered ginger; it is not the same.

Select ginger with a solid weight for its size. Break off a small part, and smell it. It should have a strong, sweet, tangy smell. Ginger that feels light when lifted, is soft to touch, is wrinkled, or has dark spots should be avoided, as those are signs of bad ginger.

Benefits of Ginger

In Chinese medicine, ginger is used for about sixty or seventy different kinds of remedies, in addition to being widely used in cooking in most of Asia. Ginger juice is well known as an effective antioxidant, digestive stimulant, antidote for food poisoning, and as a treatment for bronchial cough, flu, and fever. Ginger's warming effect is used when it is applied as a pack to relieve pain from rheumatism, arthritis, and back aches. When the ginger root is finely grated, its pungency is increased, and the paste becomes more effective to use as a pack.

GINGER MISO SAUCE

2 tbsp. finely grated ginger
1 tbsp. oil
½ cup vegetable stock
4 tbsp. red miso
1 tbsp. natural sweetener
1½ tbsp. arrowroot powder
2 tbsp. water

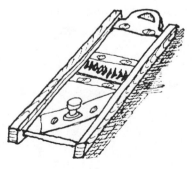

Heat a small saucepan. Sauté ginger root in oil for 20 seconds. Add half of the stock, along with the miso and natural sweetener. Sauté for 1 minute over medium heat, then add remaining stock and bring to a boil. Dissolve arrowroot powder in water, then slowly stir it into the sauce. Cook until thick. Serve over cooked vegetables or tofu.

Yield: 1 cup
Preparation Time: 5 minutes

Gingko Nuts

Fresh gingko nuts are available in the fall and the beginning of winter. Once purchased, they should be cracked open with a hammer or nutcracker. Blanch them quickly, to turn the nuts light green in color. They can be deep-fried, steamed with egg, skewered and broiled, or added to tempura dishes. You can buy them canned, but the taste and flavor is not as great as that of fresh ones. Store gingko nuts in the refrigerator, and they will last a long time.

Gingko first appeared 250 million years ago. It is sacred to Buddhists and a favorite of urban landscapers.

Benefits of Gingko

In Chinese herbal medicine, the seeds and fruit have been used for nearly four thousand years for asthma, bronchitis, gonorrhea, and tuberculosis. In recent years, Europeans have prescribed the drugs from gingko leaves for circulatory disorders such as stroke and blocked arteries.

Gomashio

This is a mixture of roasted unhulled sesame seeds and sea salt. It is excellent when sprinkled on top of rice, noodles, vegetables, or other grains. The essential amino acids in sesame seeds perfectly complement those in brown rice; and these two foods eaten together provide plenty of high-quality protein.

ROASTED GOMASHIO

1 tbsp. sea salt
1½ cups unhulled sesame seeds, roasted and chopped
2 tbsp. tangerine peels, chopped very fine
3 tbsp. kelp powder

Place salt in a cast iron pan, then roast for 2 minutes over medium heat. Remove from heat and add tangerine peels and kelp powder. Mix and cool. Place in an airtight container to store. Serve over rice.

Yield: 1½ cups
Preparation Time: 5 minutes

Gourd (Kampyo)

This Japanese vegetable is usually only used in Japanese cooking, but it is versatile enough to use in vegetarian cuisine. Gourd is the stem of a plant from which the skin is stripped and then dehydrated. It is excellent for sushi stuffings, grain salads, and to tie things with. Use it to tie an asparagus bunch for braising or to wrap tofu with seaweed for marinating. In Japan, this ingredient is used to tie kombu, which is then braised for a celebration box dinner or for lunch snacks. It comes in clear cellophane packages, found mainly in Japanese food stores.

BRAISED SWEET GOURD

1½ oz. dried gourd
5 cups water
1 tsp. sea salt
4 tbsp. soy sauce
2 tbsp. sake
2½ cups water
2 tbsp. natural sweetener
2 tbsp. mirin
1 tbsp. white sesame seeds

Wash and scrub gourd under cold water, then place in a pot. Add water and salt, then boil for 2 to 3 minutes, drain, and set aside. Combine next six ingredients, place in a pot with gourd, and bring to a boil. Cook for 20 minutes over medium low heat, until only a small amount of cooking liquid is left in the pot. Remove from heat and cool gourd in sauce. Cut into bite-size pieces and arrange on dish. Sprinkle with sesame seeds before serving.

Yield: ½ cup
Preparation Time: 25 minutes

Grapes and Raisins

I met a lady in California in 1985, who was healthy and attractive. What she truly believed in was eating just fruit—nothing else. Most of the time, she ate grapes, raisins, and currants with grape juice—no bread, no grains, no vegetables—nothing else. She exercised every day and was in terrific shape. She wore a black belt in karate with pride. I don't think I could follow what she does for even a week. She mentioned *The Grape Cure* by Johanna Brandt from South Africa, and she was one of the fanatical grape cure believers.

Benefits of Grapes

Grapes are a good source of vitamin C, manganese, and potassium, and they have a high concentration of polyphenols and tannins. Tannin, also found in green tea, is antibacterial, antiviral, and prevents tooth decay. Grapes are known to be a good blood purifier, a detoxifier in chronic diseases, and are an excellent laxative. There is no reason to say no to grapes when someone offers them.

Green Beans, String Beans

When I was working in a large hotel kitchen, I saw green beans every day. They were either shredded or French-cut and came in two-pound frozen packages. We were serving beans with almost every dish to fill the space on the plate beside the meat or fish. As a result, they all came back at the end of the meal and went into the garbage. What a shame!

Green beans bring back another memory I will never forget. On a Sunday afternoon, I took one of my cooking classes, with mostly women students, to Chinatown. It was a really busy afternoon. One of the students asked me about a couple of Chinese ladies who were busily occupied in front of a batch of green beans. My answer was that they were selecting good green beans. For some people, it is hard to understand the culture behind food choices and the time spent choosing. Asians are serious about their vegetables and the food they eat. They know what is best for the money, and they spend time to select the best.

I honestly didn't discover the true goodness of beans until 1984 when I found one dish I really admired and enjoyed. I said to myself, "I love string beans," and that was that. Ever since then, I have created many recipes using just string beans. Green beans are good to sauté, deep-fry, steam, or blanch for use in cold salads, casseroles, and mixed with grains and pasta.

Benefits of Green Beans

Green beans are a good source of vitamins A and C, and have a moderate amount of iron and potassium. The vitamin C value will be reduced by the cooking process. To minimize this effect, use a small amount of water or steam when cooking string beans. Cooking for too long not only destroys vitamin C, but will also change the color of the beans because of the acidic reaction between the water and the vegetables.

GREEN BEANS IN FIVE-FLAVORED SAUCE

2 tbsp. oil
2 whole dried chilies (or ½ tsp. chili bean paste)
1 tbsp. minced garlic
1 tbsp. minced ginger
1 lb. green beans, cooked and cut into 1½-inch lengths
3 tbsp. natural sweetener
3 tbsp. soy sauce
4 tbsp. roasted white sesame seeds
3 tbsp. minced green onion (or scallion)

Heat a wok or flat skillet until hot, add oil and chilies, then add garlic and ginger and sauté until aroma is released. Add green beans, and stir-fry over high heat for about a minute. Add natural sweetener, soy sauce, and sesame seeds. Reduce heat to medium. Cook until sauce coats green beans, about 2 to 3 more minutes. Serve hot or at room temperature with minced scallions on top.

Yield: 2 to 3 servings
Preparation Time: 5 minutes

GREEN BEANS IN ZESTY SWEET MUSTARD SAUCE

2 tbsp. dijon mustard
1 tsp. mustard seed
2 tbsp. natural sweetener
3 tbsp. oil
½ tsp. salt
2 to 3 tbsp. lemon juice
1½ lb. green beans, cooked
    and cut into 2-inch lengths

In a cooking pot, heat mustard, mustard seeds, natural sweetener, oil, salt, and lemon juice over medium heat, stirring constantly. Add beans, and heat thoroughly for about 3 minutes. Serve hot.

Yield: 3 to 4 servings
Preparation Time: 4 minutes

GREEN BEANS IN HERB SAUCE

3 tbsp. oil
½ cup minced onion
1 tbsp. minced garlic
3 tbsp. white roasted sesame seeds
1½ lb. whole green beans, trimmed
¼ cup minced celery
¼ tsp. whole rosemary
¼ tsp. basil
⅓ cup water
½ tsp. sea salt

Heat skillet until hot, then sauté onion, celery, garlic, and sesame seeds until light brown in color. Add beans and remaining ingredients to the pot. Cover and simmer for 6 to 7 minutes. Season to taste and serve.

Yield: 3 to 4 servings
Preparation Time: 10 minutes

GREEN BEANS AND PLANTAIN SAUTE

This exotic dish is not only beautiful to look at but its combination of tastes is very unique. Try it one day just for fun. If you like it, elaborate by adding other ingredients.

2 plantains or large green bananas
4 tbsp. oil
1 lb. green beans, cut into 1½-inch strips
½ tsp. garlic powder
¼ tsp. ground cardamom
1 cup mixed sunflower seeds, almonds, and walnuts
4 tbsp. currants
Pinch salt
Chopped parsley

Peel and cut plantains diagonally into 1½-inch pieces. Heat a large, flat skillet, then cook plantains in oil until brown. Add green beans and sauté together. Sprinkle with garlic and cardamom. Continue to cook for 5 to 6 minutes. Toss nut mixture and currants into the skillet, and cook over medium heat until the beans are tender. Season with salt. Toss in parsley at the last minute.

Yield: 4 servings
Preparation Time: 12 minutes

BLACK GREEN BEANS

2 tbsp. fermented black beans, whole
1 lb. green beans, cooked
3 tbsp. oil
1 tbsp. minced garlic
1 tbsp. minced ginger
3 tbsp. minced green onion (white part only)
2 tbsp. soy sauce or tamari
4 tbsp. water
2 to 3 tbsp. natural sweetener

Soak black beans in warm water for 30 minutes. Drain, then mince fine. Set aside. Heat wok until hot. Add oil, and sauté garlic and ginger until aroma is released. Add black beans and green onion. Sauté for another 10 seconds. Add soy sauce, water, natural sweetener, and green beans. Cook, uncovered, until green beans are tender. Serve hot.

Yield: 2 to 3 servings
Preparation Time: 35 minutes

STIR-FRIED GREEN BEANS WITH FERMENTED BEAN CURD

Fermented bean curd is a Chinese product made from tofu and salt which goes through a fermentation process before it is marinated in an alcohol-based brine.

1½ lb. whole green beans, trimmed
3 tbsp. oil
1½ tbsp. fermented bean curd,
   mashed with a little liquid from the jar
1 tsp. natural sweetener
¼ cup water
½ tsp. salt

Heat wok until hot. Add oil and stir-fry fresh green beans over high heat for 2 minutes. Add fermented bean curd and cook for another minute. Add natural sweetener, water, and salt. Cook until tender. Sauce should just coat the green beans. Serve hot.

Yield: 3 to 4 servings
Preparation Time: 4 minutes

Green Onions (Scallions)

Green onion is one vegetable that has a bitter taste. You will find scallions everywhere in Japan. The Japanese stock them in their kitchens at all times because they are an absolutely essential Japanese vegetable. Green onions are used to make nuta-miso, scallion salad, one-pot dishes in winter, miso soup, sho-jin tempura, and many other dishes. Green onions are used extensively to increase the aroma of Chinese cooking. Different cooking techniques produce different tastes and textures.

Select the smallest green onions possible. Before using, wash well to remove grit and mud from the inside. Cut into desired shapes and lengths. Scallions are important garnishing ingredients in Japanese cookery for their color, aroma, and versatility. Scallions are shredded extra fine then soaked in cold water to remove the sliminess.

Benefits of Green Onions

In Japanese folk remedies, they mix two to three tablespoons of finely shredded scallions with one tablespoon of miso, then pour hot water over the mixture, stir, and drink the liquid while still burning hot to treat cold symptoms and fever. It really works if taken at the beginning of a cold. Mixing half of a freshly grated ginger root with a scallion and hot water works for the same symptoms.

In Chinese folk remedies, the white part of the scallion is used as a diuretic to relieve swelling and water retention. Generally, bitter foods are good to clear the throat, sharpen the intellect, and improve the skin. Green onions have a cooling and calming effect on both the nervous and digestive systems. Similar to garlic, scallion is used for strengthening the stomach and appetite and for curing general cold symptoms.

Kalonji

Kalonji, black seeds, or *siyah-daneh* is a spice used for pickling, baking bread, and adding to vegetables and legumes, mainly in Middle Eastern and Indian cooking. Also called onion seeds, kalonji is used to flavor the bean dish, dahl. It is available at Middle Eastern or Indian food stores.

STEAMED CAULIFLOWER WITH AROMATIC HERBS

3 lb. cauliflower
4 tbsp. oil
1 tsp. cumin seeds
1 tsp coriander seeds
1 tsp. kalonji
2 whole chilies, seeds removed
1 tbsp. ginger root
1 cup minced onion
2 tbsp. minced garlic
2½ tbsp. garam masala
1 tsp. ground turmeric
1 tsp. salt
¼ cup water

Break cauliflower into 1-inch long florets. Heat a flat skillet over medium heat, then add oil. Add cumin, coriander, and kalonji and cook for 2 seconds. Add whole chilies and brown both sides. Lower heat and add onion, ginger, and garlic. Cook until onion is slightly browned, about 4 to 5 minutes. Add cauliflower, garam masala, turmeric, and salt. Stir to mix. Add water and bring to a boil. Cover and cook over low heat for 10 to 12 minutes, or until tender. Stir ever 3 to 4 minutes, replacing the lid each time. Remove lid to evaporate the water when the cauliflower is cooked.

Yield: 4 servings
Preparation Time: 20 minutes

Koji

Koji is a fermented rice starter used to make miso, sake, soy sauce, mirin, rice vinegar, and pickles. It is available in the frozen food section of Japanese grocery stores.

Kudzu

This white powder is a starch made from the root of the wild plant, kudzu or *kuzu* in Japanese. Once harvested, it is washed then grated and goes through three days of natural refining processes. Normally, it takes fifty to fifty-three days after harvest to complete the natural drying process. There are imitation kudzus available that are sold under the name of kudzu, but are made from yam potatoes. To determine the quality of kudzu, look at the price of the product. If the price is lower than twelve dollars per pound, then it is almost certain that it's imitation.

Kudzu is unsurpassed as a thickening agent in cooking, but it is rather expensive. Normally, it comes in a coarse small block or a flaky unprocessed shape. Kudzu gives a superior texture and flavor when used as a thickener in sauces, gravies, soups, and noodle broths. It is also used in place of wheat flour to coat food before cooking. Kudzu is ideal in thickened desserts such as toppings, puddings, and pie fillings.

Benefits of Kudzu

Kudzu quickly remedies various intestinal and digestive problems, especially diarrhea, upset stomach, and disorders related to excess acidity. For the early stages of the flu, a kudzu and ginger juice mixture with hot water is recommended.

Laos

Laos, also known as Siamese ginger or galangal, is part of the ginger family commonly grown in Southeast Asia and Iran. Laos was regarded as an aphrodisiac in Europe in the Middle Ages. It is available in dried, powder, or whole forms in most Southeast Asian food stores.

Lecithin

Lecithin is a useful ingredient for making your own butter or mayonnaise substitute without using eggs. Granulated lecithin can be found in most natural food stores.

Benefits of Lecithin

Lecithin is one of the important lipids that functions with the help of enzymes in the transport and utilization of fatty acids. Soybeans and egg yolks are rich in lecithin, which is effective for treating high blood pressure, heart problems, and poor circulation. It stimulates hair growth, improves memory, and is used to treat various mental disorders. Lecithin is widely publicized as a cholesterol sweeper.

Lemons

Benefits of Lemons

Lemons are an excellent source of vitamin C, calcium, potassium, and magnesium. They are used as a blood purifier, for treating liver disorders, sore throat, colds, or fever. Sour lemon juice works well when combined with nutty foods, to cut the oily taste of nuts or seeds. Vitamin C assists with calcium absorption from nuts or seeds.

TART LEMON AND FIG CHUTNEY

1 cup dried fig, chopped
1 apple, cored and chopped
1 lemon, seeds removed and chopped (including peels)
½ cup black strap molasses
¼ cup apple cider vinegar
1 tsp. allspice
½ tsp. cinnamon powder

Place all the ingredients in a heavy pot and bring to a boil. Lower heat, skim, and continue to cook for 25 to 30 minutes. Remove to cool and store in a glass airtight container.

Yield: 1½ cups
Preparation Time: 30 minutes

Lemon Grass

One of the common herbs used in Thai and East Asian cuisine is lemon grass. This plant has long spearlike leaves. The juicy base is chopped to season curry, soup, and other dishes for a lemony flavor. It is grown commercially in India, Australia, South America, and in the state of Florida. It is available dried, as dried flakes, and fresh.

Lotus Root

Lotus root has been a delicacy in Asian cooking for centuries. Harvested in fall or winter, it is an exotic plant that grows in muddy ponds or paddies in mild tropical climates. Fresh lotus root is becoming more common in North American markets. It is used in stir-fried, deep-fried, or braised dishes. It can be filled with rice, used in salads, or prepared in many other ways. It is an important ingredient for Chinese and Japanese macrobiotic cooking.

Lotus root is a great vegetable because of its texture, taste, and unusual shape. During preparation, lotus root oxidizes or darkens. To avoid discoloration, peel or slice lotus roots and completely submerge in vinegar and water (1 teaspoon of vinegar to five cups of water). Lotus roots are excellent deep-fried, sautéed, and simmered. Canned and packaged lotus root is available to substitute fresh lotus root, but the precooked lotus root lacks flavor and texture.

Select firm, cream-colored or grayish-white lotus roots with no bruises, soft spots, or blemishes. Pick them up and choose those that feel heavy for their size. Store in a cool, dark place.

Lotus Root Flour

Lotus root flour is available in powder or flake form from Chinese food stores or herbal shops. It is an excellent thickener for sauces, soups, and desserts.

Benefits of Lotus Root

Lotus roots, seeds, and stems are all used for food or for medicinal properties. Lotus root juice and fresh ginger are used for diarrhea, food poisoning, stomach inflammation, and for lung-related ailments such as tuberculosis, asthma, and coughs. Lotus root increases energy and vitality. In Asia, lotus roots—along with burdock root—are considered to be one of the best blood purifiers. The dried end section of the lotus root, where the portions join, is believed to have the greatest effect as a diuretic, and is effective for hemorrhoids and kidney problems.

LOTUS ROOT IN SWEET VINEGAR SAUCE

16 oz. fresh lotus root, peeled and sliced ½-inch-thick
5 cups water with 1 tbsp. vinegar (for soaking)
4 tbsp. rice vinegar
1 red dried chili
½ tsp. salt
2 tbsp. natural sweetener
5 cups water
sesame seeds, roasted

Place lotus root in 5 cups water mixed with 1 tablespoon vinegar for 30 minutes to 1 hour; remove and drain. Combine rice vinegar, chili, salt, sweetener, and remaining 5 cups water in a pot and bring to a boil. Add the lotus root.

Cook over high heat for 4 to 5 minutes until lotus root becomes transparent. Continue to cook until 2 to 3 tablespoons of liquid remain. Serve at room temperature, sprinkled with roasted sesame seeds.

Yield: 2 to 3 servings
Preparation Time: 40 minutes

LOTUS ROOT IN SALTY SWEET SAUCE

2 sections small, fresh lotus root
1 dried chili
1 cup dashi
1 tbsp. natural sweetener
1 tbsp. mirin
1 tbsp. sake
4 tbsp. soy sauce

Peel and cut lotus root into ¼-inch-thick slices; place in water. Boil remaining ingredients in a pot. Add lotus root, return to boiling, then lower heat to medium. Braise for 4 to 5 minutes, stirring constantly until sauce is reduced to have just enough to coat the lotus root. Serve hot or at room temperature.

Yield: 2 to 3 servings
Preparation Time: 7 minutes

Mandarin Oranges

When Mandarin oranges show up in grocery stores, I realize the Christmas season is near and my Christmas spirit awakens with memories of gift wrapping, last-minute shopping in crowded shopping malls, screaming kids, and shouting parents. It's hard to believe that it is all in the name of good spirit. I would rather recall my memory of mandarin oranges and New Year's Day in Japan. Every family member, except my mother, did absolutely nothing—not a thing. We just sat around *kotatsu,* a type of small table with a little heater attached underneath and covered with a blanket. This was an arrangement I used to call Japanese-style central heating. We would grab Mandarin oranges and eat until our fingers turned yellow.

Benefits of Mandarin Oranges

Mandarin oranges are helpful for asthma, high blood pressure, and ailments of the heart and liver. They are high in vitamins C and A, phosphorus, potassium, calcium, sodium, and magnesium. Dried Mandarin orange peels, or *chen pi*, are used for digestive ailments, bloating, lack of appetite, abdominal pain, and nausea in Chinese herbal medicine. It is kept in traditional Chinese families—sometimes for many generations. They are convinced that with age, *chen pi* increases its healing properties. Chen pi is burnt at night to ward off mosquitoes in southern China, Taiwan, and Vietnam.

Mangoes

When the price of mangoes goes down, I recognize that the season is changing; spring is over and summer is near. Mangoes are an excellent sweetener for curry, and they taste great eaten as plain fruit. Purée them, cut them into various shapes, or add mangoes to your fruit salads to provide an exotic flavor. Imported mangoes from Mexico, Haiti, Hawaii, and India are all available in North America. You can purchase mangoes at any supermarket when in season, but I found that they are better and cheaper to buy at ethnic food stores.

Benefits of Mangoes

Mangoes are used for liver and menstrual disorders. They are excellent for improving eyesight, constipation, indigestion, and sexual weakness.

Mirin

Mirin is an essential seasoning in Japanese cooking, used mainly to sweeten foods and to give a distinctive taste. This sweetener is made from cooked white rice, koji, and water. The mixture is fermented for one month, then undergoes a distillation process. The clear distillate, *shochu,* is a famous strong drink, similar to vodka, produced on Southern Kyushu Island. It is then mixed with more sweet rice and koji. After three more months of natural fermentation, the shochu mixture is pressed and kept in ceramic containers for three months to two years. When the fermentation is completed, you have an extremely sweet and syrupy liquid with a sweet fragrance. Bottled mirin is available in Japanese grocery stores or health food stores.

Miso

Miso is a thick Japanese soybean paste made from a mixture of soybeans, rice, and rice koji starter placed in a container to ferment. The combination of salt, enzymes in the koji, and microorganisms in the environment breaks down the soybeans into easily digestible amino acids, fatty acids, and sugar. Miso is available in paste form or red miso, white miso, or miso categorized by  ingredients and length of fermentation. The most popular miso for North Americans is white miso, also called sweet mellow miso.

Because miso comes in paste form, it needs to be dissolved in water before it is added to soups or sautéed dishes. Miso can keep in a glass or porcelain container with a lid in the refrigerator for a long time. To select a good miso, find a health food company that doesn't use any preservatives, caramel, or artificial flavoring in their miso.

Red Miso

Red miso (also called aka miso, barley miso, gen-mai miso, Inaka miso, or Haccho miso) is usually stronger than white miso and primarily used as a salt seasoning. The various types indicate the ingredients used and fermentation length. It is generally a strong dark paste made from soybeans, koji, and rice. Red miso contains more salt than other types of miso, and is used mainly to make red miso soup, marinades, and sauces. Fermentation of aka miso takes longer than white miso, usually as long as one to two years. It has a higher salt content than white miso and contains less koji (rice starter). Length of fermentation and salt content determines the flavor, color, and aroma. The amount of koji used in the miso affects the sweetness. Aka miso is usually sold in a clear plastic package or container in either Oriental or health food stores.

Shiro Miso, White Miso

Shiro miso is often described as white miso or mellow miso. The fermentation process for making shiro miso takes only two to eight weeks. It is high in koji, which means that more rice and less salt are used and it is sweeter and milder than red miso.

Shiro miso is used most often for salad dressings, marinades for tofu dishes, stir-fried dishes, and dinner soups. It is better combined with sake, mirin, or vinegar to enhance the flavor. Along with other types of miso, you can find shiro miso in Japanese and natural food stores.

Benefits of Miso

The nutritional benefit of shiro miso includes a high amount of niacin and lactic acid bacteria that aids in digestion. The regular use of miso by the Japanese has been practiced for many centuries. Miso is thought to not only neutralize the effects of pollution, but is also believed to be a cholesterol discharger and a reliever of hangovers. Miso contains all the essential amino acids, approximately .17 microgram of vitamin B12 (depending on the type of miso and the way it was aged), various minerals, and an average of 5 percent fat. One tablespoon of miso used in a soup or dish will supply as much as 12 grams of complete protein.

MISO GLAZING SAUCE

You can make this simple sauce using red miso ahead of time, and storing it in the refrigerator. It will keep for almost a month. With this sauce, you can make dips, salad dressings, and various other sauces by adjusting the thickness with either vinegar or water, or by adding one of the three remaining seasonings: sour, bitter, or hot.

6 tbsp. red miso
3 tbsp. sake or white vermouth
2 tbsp. mirin
1 tsp. sesame oil
1 tsp. grated ginger juice
1 tbsp. minced garlic
1 tbsp. natural sweetener
½ tsp. English mustard powder

Combine all ingredients and stir well, until smooth. Store in an airtight container.

Note: To make Miso Lemon Sauce, just add one teaspoon of grated lemon rind to miso glazing sauce. To make Shiitake Miso Sauce, sauté ½ cup presoaked shiitake or regular mushrooms in one tablespoon of oil, then add them to the miso glazing sauce.

Yield: ¾ cup
Preparation Time: 2 minutes

Mochi

This sweet rice cake is made from steamed and pounded sweet rice. Mochi is sold in vacuum-sealed containers in Japanese or health food stores. It is easy to digest and an excellent ingredient for soups or snacks—or even baked in the oven or a low-temperature barbecue broiler until crisp and puffy, then dipped in soy sauce or ground roasted soy flour (*kinako*). Some people prefer to wrap it with *nori* (Japanese seaweed sheet).

Mochi symbolizes longevity and wealth, and is normally eaten at the new year to celebrate the traditional holiday season. In the old days in Japan, around December 27 and 28, all the neighbors got together to celebrate the happy holiday season with all-day mochi-making. One group, usually the women, steamed the rice, while the men pounded the steaming-hot rice on a wooden pallet with a large curved wooden hammer until the rice was completely crushed and formed a sticky homogenous mass. The mochi was formed into two-inch balls, then flattened. Some were stuffed with cooked sweet azuki beans, some were coated with corn starch, and some were left for an immediate snack for the rice pounders to eat with soy sauce and grated daikon.

Benefits of Mochi

Mochi is an excellent source of protein, and is recommended for such health problems as anemia, blood sugar imbalances, and weak intestines. It is also an excellent food for pregnant women and nursing mothers.

QUICK-MADE MOCHI

Sweet rice works as a strong cohesive agent, providing a chewy and dense texture when it is needed. This microwave method of sweet rice cooking will cut the mochi-making to a short fifteen minutes. Authentic mochi-making takes at least 3 to 4 hours of cooking and pounding. Eat mochi coated with roasted sesame seeds or roasted soybean flour, in a sweet azuki bean soup, dry, baked, or fresh with grated daikon and a good quality tamari sauce. Potential stuffing ideas for mochi include: tahini, peanut butter, sweet red bean paste, and peach spread.

1 cup glutinous rice
2 cups cold water
4 tbsp. corn starch
1 to 2 tbsp. sesame seed oil

Wash rice in a sieve under cold running water until water runs relatively clear. Leave the rice in the sieve for 2 hours. In a blender, process water and rice until a thick liquid forms, about 3 to 4 minutes. Place the liquid in a bowl and cover with plastic. Place in a microwave oven and cook for 8 to 9 minutes on high heat. Remove, let cool for 2 to 3 minutes, and remove plastic. Stir well, wet your hands with cold water, and roll the dough into golfball-size portions. Flatten, stuff if desired, then roll into desired flour or into sesame oil to prevent from drying out. Cover tightly with plastic.

Mochi freezes well if sealed in plastics. It can be coated with roasted soybean powder (*kinako*), chopped sesame seeds, or other seeds or nuts to keep it from sticking. The Japanese roast mochi over direct heat until it puffs up, then they coat it with kinako or wrap it in toasted seaweed, and dip it in soy sauce before eating.

Yield: about 16 patties
Preparation Time: 2 hours 15 minutes

Mushrooms

There are many different kinds of mushrooms available in North America. One secret of making elaborate dishes is to know where to purchase mushrooms, what to look for, and how to prepare and cook them. You'll find local and imported dried or fresh, canned or bottled mushrooms in North America.

Mushrooms are in a different category than other foods. I encourage you to eat these fungi. They come in various shapes and colors and have a variety of textures and flavors. I don't know how many kinds of edible mushrooms grow in the world, but they certainly add variety to vegetarian cooking.

There are a few things to remember to help you with your selection when purchasing quality dried black mushrooms. Most dried mushrooms (shiitake, don-gou, and flower) come in plastic bags. To inspect them, shake the bag a couple of times and check the bottom of the bag. If you can spot powdered mushroom dust settling at the bottom of the bag, chances are the mushrooms in the bag contain insects, so avoid this package of mushrooms.

Thick mushroom caps are more expensive than thin mushroom caps because they are usually of higher quality. Take your time to compare prices of mushrooms and cap thicknesses. The flavor of the mushrooms also determines their quality. Depending on the season, area, or type of mushroom, the aroma will vary. When the mushrooms come in bulk, take a whiff. If they have a strong pleasant aroma and the caps are thick with no dust, they are the ones you want.

Soaking dried mushrooms overnight and preparing them in small quantities really doesn't make sense. If you want the convenience of having mushrooms ready to go at all times, here's the way to go: First, soak all the mushrooms you have in a large enough bowl to cover them with water. Leave them covered overnight in the refrigerator. The next day, remove the stems, saving them for making stews or soup stocks. Drain the liquid and reserve it for soup. Sprinkle a small amount of sugar over the mushrooms, rub them well, and place them in a large bowl that will fit into your steamer. Cover with water, add two fresh ginger slices and two stalks of green onion cut into two-inch lengths, then seal with a lid and steam over high heat for two hours, checking the water level constantly. After two hours, your mushrooms should be tender, and the aromatic smell should fill your kitchen. Remove the bowl from the steamer and cool completely. Drain the liquid and reserve it for stock, then separate the mushrooms into batches for your household needs. Put them into freezer bags, tightly sealed. Freeze until you are ready to use them. Frozen mushrooms are convenient, and they defrost quickly. They should last at least three months in the freezer.

Most mushrooms are hard to recognize once dried, packaged, and labeled with non-English words. Black mushrooms (don-gou, shiitake, far-gou) usually have Chinese labels when sold in bulk. Don't pay attention to what the Chinese character is, just compare the price and description of the mushrooms to those in this book. The label may not always be correct.

VARIETIES OF MUSHROOMS

Chanterelle Mushrooms

There are quite a few varieties of chanterelle mushrooms (*Cantharellus cibarius*) harvested in North American forests, from the popular common yellow chanterelle, to the white, funnel-shaped woolly, to the clustered blue chanterelle. They are normally found in late summer to late fall, often under Douglas fir, hemlock, or spruce trees in old forests.

These slippery mushrooms have a delicate mild flavor. You should wash these mushrooms quickly to remove any twigs or leaves, then drain and use them as soon as you can. They are available fresh and dried; both are rather expensive to purchase but go well in stir-fried dishes with lemon, a touch of tamari, and mild flavorings. Never overpower or kill the flavor of mushrooms with strong seasonings.

Cloud Ear Fungi

Cloud ear fungi, also known as *won-yheer* or *won-yhe* in Chinese or *kikurage* in Japanese, are a variety of wooden ear fungi that is imported from China. Unfortunately, it is rather difficult to find this mushroom in North America, but I have seen this type of mushroom in herbal stores in Vancouver's Chinatown. It's a relatively inexpensive way to compensate for a lack of various proteins, minerals, and vitamins. In China, won-yhe is widely believed to give strength to the body, moisten beautiful skin, and stop hemorrhoidal bleedings.

Enoki Mushrooms

This tiny 2 to 3-inch-long, white-stemmed Japanese mushroom (*Flammulina velutipes*) resembles the stems of mung bean sprouts. They can be found in Japanese grocery stores in the refrigerated section, in a vacuum-sealed plastic package. The texture and peculiar look adds a unique touch to your salads, soups, stews, and fillings. Before using, remove the bottom of the stem, where the color is different.

Flower Mushrooms

Most of the flower mushrooms, which are called *far-gou* in Chinese, are produced in mainland China and in Japan. It is hard for the first-timer to differentiate between this mushroom and other types of black mushrooms. *Fa-gou,* or *far-gou,* translates to "flower mushroom"—a name that probably comes from the pattern on top of its caps that resembles a flower. Its cap shape generally looks like shiitake mushrooms, with the top part of the cap having a pattern of cracked lines.

To determine the quality of this mushroom, check the under side of it. If the color is white, then it's considered to be better. Some people consider far-gou to be the best mushroom in the world to eat; for others, it is don-gou. It is up to you to decide. Far-gou are available in large Chinese grocery stores or Chinese herbal shops.

Golden Mushrooms

Don't confuse the golden ear fungi with golden mushrooms. This mushroom is produced mainly in Taiwan, and it comes in a can. It has an almost unnoticeable flavor, but the texture is something else. It looks almost like the enoki mushroom, and it is slightly gold in color. Golden mushrooms are available from Chinese grocery stores.

Matsutake Mushrooms

Harvested in early to late fall, the pungently sweet and aromatic odor is the distinguishing feature of matsutake mushrooms (*Tricholoma ponderosum*)—and it is not easily forgotten once experienced. When these delicate Japanese mushrooms begin to appear on the menus of Japanese restaurants in North America, I know that autumn is here.

As far as I know, these expensive mushrooms are rare, and nobody—including Japan, China, Australia, and the United States—has successfully cultivated them yet. It grows around two to three-year-old dead pine trees and in thickets of black huckleberry and rhododendron bushes. They grow from the northwest coast of the United States to the mountain tops in Mexico. In autumn, these mushrooms are available only from special Japanese or Korean grocery stores.

All the picked mushrooms are sorted into four to five grades, then they are cleaned, boxed, and shipped to Japan or expensive Japanese restaurants in large North American cities. The ones the Japanese avoid are mainly sold in North American markets or are dehydrated and processed, then shipped to various other countries. If you have a friend who knows and enjoys the outdoors and knows about mushrooms, try to find this delicacy of nature.

Black and Edible Morel Mushrooms

These expensive mushrooms have spongy elongated caps and come fresh or dried. Edible morel and black morel mushrooms (*Morchella elata* and *Morchella esculenta*) are both available in specialty stores. Dried morel should be soaked in water overnight, then rinsed well. They are considered to be one of the most elegant and exotic mushrooms in French and European cuisine. Locally, you may find them growing in forests, orchards, yards, gardens, and areas where a forest fire occurred in April, May, and sometimes June.

Oyster Mushrooms

Oyster mushrooms (*Pleurotus ostreatus*), known as *shimeji* in Japanese, are harvested in spring to summer, normally on stumps or logs of alder, willow, maple, or cotton wood. Oyster gray to white in color with white flesh, these are superb when young. This meaty mushroom has become increasingly available in many supermarkets. It is a handy mushroom and easy to use in many dishes—just like white mushrooms.

Shiitake (Don-Gou, Japanese or Chinese Black Mushrooms)

These Japanese forest mushrooms are delicious and versatile and have a long history of use as a folk medicine. They are used for making broth, in sautéed or stir-fried dishes, soups, stews, sauces, and for many other purposes. Japanese and Chinese black mushrooms are an important ingredient in both Chinese and Japanese cookery. Called *don-gou* or "winter mushrooms" in Chinese, they are considered a prized food for medicinal use and flavorful cooking.

The best way to use these rather expensive mushrooms is to first wash, then soak them in warm water with a pinch of sugar for 1 to 2 hours to reconstitute them. Save the soaking liquid because it has plenty of flavor and is highly nutritious. Squeeze the excess water out of the mushrooms, remove the stems, and use according to your recipe. Dried mushrooms will expand to three to four times their size after soaking in warm water for several hours.

Fresh shiitake mushrooms are available in most Oriental food stores and supermarkets. For flavor as well as medicinal and nutritional value, dried ones are superior to fresh ones. Examine the dried shiitake package; the best mushrooms are thick, medium size, and dark brown. Good quality mushrooms have thick caps once reconstituted. Thick shiitake mushrooms are superior in taste, flavor, and texture. Avoid those in which the cap is already opened and appears light beige in color. The price varies depending on quality. Store dried shiitake mushrooms in an airtight glass or ceramic container in a cool, dry place.

Benefits of Shiitake Mushrooms

The ability of shiitake to lower cholesterol and cause the body to reject foreign substances has been studied and documented. Eritadenine, the isolated active agent in these mushrooms, helps to lower blood cholesterol. As summarized by Dr. Mori Kisaku, mushrooms are health food. Shiitake mushrooms are effective for treating high blood pressure, diabetes, cancer, anemia, and for strengthening the immune system. Shiitake mushrooms contain vitamins D, B1, B2, and calcium.

A study conducted at the University of Michigan by Dr. Kenneth Cochran indicated a compound lentinan, a long chain of polysaccharides found in shiitake mushrooms, contains a powerful antiviral material that boosts immune system functions.

As a folk remedy, they are used to stop vomiting, asthma, and diarrhea. Shiitake mushrooms are high in many enzymes that do not usually occur in plants.

Straw Mushrooms

Someone once said that this is the most sensuous mushroom, and I agree. Straw mushrooms, or *sou-gou* in Chinese, have thin envelopes inside. When stewed or added to soups whole, the sauce will burst out when you bite into this mushroom. There are certain tricks you can apply to avoid this type of incident when you want, but I think that it is rather sensuous not to.

Snow Ear Fungi

Also called "silver ear" or *sue't-yhee* in Chinese, this mushroom is named for its white-silver color. They come from the Fukken and Sichuan province in mainland China and from Taiwan. They grow naturally on oak trees and look like delicate balls of seaweed, with their light ivory color. They are neatly packaged in expensive gift boxes, but avoid buying this mushroom when pure white in color; chances are they have been chemically bleached.

In China, snow ear fungi is widely believed to help balance *yin* and *yang* energy in the body, and is especially helpful for aliments of the lungs and sexual organs. They are also believed to help maintain smooth, moist skin, and are effective in stopping hemorrhoidal bleeding and constipation. They are a common ingredient in soups, various desserts, and herbal medicines.

Yellow Ear Fungi

Dried yellow ear fungi, known to the Chinese as *wong yhee* or *wong yheer,* are produced mostly in the Hunan province in China. They are another rare kind of small fungus, sometimes available in Chinese herbal stores. Also called "golden mushrooms" in North America, this fungi is found on hardwood trees year-round with the right weather and location. A similar spice, called orange jelly or witch's butter, can be found in the Pacific Northwest in late fall to early winter.

Winter Mushrooms

Winter mushrooms are produced in China, Japan, and Taiwan. *Don-gou,* produced in Japan, is considered to be of better quality. The cap of don-gou is dark brown to black. To select better quality winter mushrooms, check the thickness of the mushrooms; the thicker the better and the more expensive.

Wooden Ear Fungus

This curious mushroom (*Aurucularia auricula*) has the consistency of rubbery gelatin when fresh. They can be found on conifer or fir logs. This jelly fungi appears after the heavy rain in summer, fall, and winter. Also called wooden mushroom, *mok yhee, or ki-kurage,* these black, thin dried mushrooms give excellent contrast to any dish, and are not to be confused with black shiitake mushrooms or Chinese winter mushrooms (*don-gou*).

With their chewy crunchy texture and soft, almost slippery consistency, these thin mushrooms are not only interesting to eat, but are more than they appear to be in the medicinal department. Wooden ear fungus is used in many countries, including Japan, China, and Korea. They are added to soups, salads, fillings, cold dishes, noodles, and medicinal remedies.

When cooked fresh, they usually melt, leaving only thin membranes. Once dried, they gain a crunchy texture. To prepare wooden ear fungus, soak in warm water for 10 to 15 minutes with a pinch of sugar (I don't know why you add sugar; that's how I learned and it works well). After soaking, discard soaking water. Wash well under cold running water to remove any particles and grit. Squeeze out excess water. If there are hard black stems or pieces of wood attached, remove them before using. Once hydrated, wrap them, and they will last at least four to five days in the refrigerator.

The wooden ear fungi, or "sea jelly fish" in Japanese, come in clear cellophane packages or in bulk in most Chinese herbal and Japanese food stores.

Benefits of Wooden Ear Fungus

Eating small amounts of wooden ear fungus will prevent blood from clotting. It acts as a blood thinner or anticoagulant according to a new discovery by Dr. Hammerschmidt, a hematologist at the University of Minnesota Medical School. He and his colleagues reported that eating a small amount of black fungus stopped blood from clotting, just as aspirin does, but without serious side effects. The team succeeded in isolating a powerful anticoagulant chemical from black mushroom called adenosine, and reported it in the New England Journal of Medicine in 1980.

When I asked a Chinese herbal doctor about black fungus, his reply was, "Good for women; live longer, and thins blood." They knew all along.

MARINATED MUSHROOM SALAD

2 lb. small white mushrooms
½ cup olive oil
¼ cup lemon juice
1 tbsp. brown rice vinegar
1 stalk celery, minced
½ onion, minced
1 tsp. sea salt
½ tsp. ground coriander
Salt and pepper
1 cup water

In a stainless steel saucepan, combine all ingredients and bring to a boil. Cook for 10 minutes. Remove from heat and transfer to a bowl. Chill well before serving.

Yield: 4 to 5 servings
Preparation Time: 20 minutes

MUSHROOM AND BARLEY PILAF

10 medium white mushrooms, sliced
1 small onion, chopped
½ tsp. minced garlic
3 tbsp. oil
1 cup barley
3 cups boiling water
½ cup cranberries
1 tbsp. soy sauce
1 tbsp. onion powder
4 tbsp. wheat germ
¼ tsp. dill weed
½ tsp. sea salt
⅛ tsp. fresh ground pepper

Sauté white mushrooms, onion, and garlic in oil in a heavy skillet until onion becomes soft. Add barley and boiling water. When water resumes boiling, transfer mixture to a baking dish. Add remaining ingredients. Bake in an oven preheated to 325 degrees for 30 minutes, or until barley has absorbed all the liquid. Adjust by adding more boiling water if barley is not tender and requires more cooking. Serve hot immediately.

Yield: 4 to 5 servings
Preparation Time: 35 to 40 minutes

SHIITAKE BRAISED
IN TERIYAKI SAUCE

12 medium dried shiitake
4 tbsp. soy sauce
2 tbsp. natural sweetener
1 tbsp. sake
1 tbsp. mirin

Soak dried shiitake mushrooms in water for 3 to 4 hours until tender. Save the soaking liquid. Squeeze out excess water, remove the stems, and discard. Combine 1 cup of soaking liquid with soy sauce, natural sweetener, sake, mirin, and shiitake; braise over low heat for 30 to 40 minutes. Increase heat to high and reduce the sauce until 3 tablespoons of sauce remain. Remove and serve hot.

Yield: 4 servings
Preparation Time: 4 hours (including soaking time)

WARM SPINACH SALAD
WITH FOUR KINDS OF MUSHROOMS

You can substitute brown rice vinegar for lemon juice.

3 tbsp. olive oil
1 tsp. minced garlic
4 to 5 whole white mushrooms, sliced
4 to 5 whole fresh shiitake mushrooms, sliced
½ pkg. enoki mushrooms, ¼-inch bottom part removed and separated
4 to 5 fresh oyster mushrooms, sliced
Pinch salt and freshly ground black pepper
1 to 2 tbsp. fresh lemon juice
1 bunch fresh spinach, cleaned and trimmed
1 small tomato, cored and diced

Heat a small frying pan, then add olive oil and garlic. Cook over high heat until the garlic becomes a slightly golden color. Add all the mushrooms and cook until soft, about 1 minute. Season with salt and pepper, toss, and remove from the heat. Add lemon juice, then toss with spinach and tomato. Toss well and serve when salad is still warm.

Yield: 4 servings
Preparation Time: 10 minutes

PUNGENT BLACK FUNGUS SALAD

To make this salad more elaborate, add blanched seasonal vegetables with nuts and seeds.

1 cup soaked black fungus, washed and cleaned
2 tbsp. soy sauce
2 tbsp. brown rice vinegar
1 tbsp. sesame seed oil
2 tbsp. minced ginger root
3 tbsp. minced green onion

Toss all the ingredients together, chill for 2 hours, and serve.

Yield: 1 cup
Preparation Time: 2 hours (including chilling time)

Mustard Greens

Mustard greens, known to the Chinese as *gai-choy,* belongs to the cabbage family, which has many varieties. Chinese mustard greens all have about the same taste, stronger than *gai-lan* (Chinese broccoli) or *choy-sum* (miniature bok-choy), but with a touch of bitterness. All of them have dark stems and leaves, are available year-round, and are easily found in Chinese markets. Another pickled product called *takana-zuke,* is one of the famous pickles that come from Kyushu Island, southwest of the main island of Japan. These sour and slightly bitter pickles are excellent sautéed with oil, ginger, and sesame seeds. They are sold at Japanese grocery stores.

When you see this curly light brown vegetable in the market, like other greens, the leaves should look fresh and crispy. Wilted leaves or spots are signs that the vegetable is not fresh.

Benefits of Mustard Greens

Mustard greens are high in vitamins A and C and are well supplied in the calcium department.

Mustard Seeds

Mustard seeds originated in southern Europe and along the Mediterranean Coast. They are mainly produced in Canada, Denmark, Holland, China, and India. Mustard seeds are pungent, hot, sharp, and also oily. They are used in making pickles, mayonaisse, salad dressings, white vinegar, and curry powder. In India, these tiny dark brown seeds are used to season almost everything from beans to drinks. They can be found in East Indian grocery stores.

Mustard seeds are toasted or popped in hot oil. Foods are cooked or seasoned with oil, and mustard seeds are poured over the cooked food.

Benefits of Mustard Seeds

In Ayurveda medicine, mustard seeds are used to neutralize toxins in the blood, as an analgesic, and to relieve indigestion and distention of the abdomen.

Nuts and Seeds

A variety of nuts and seeds make excellent flour and milk substitutes for both drinking and cooking purposes. They are easy to make and can take the place of dairy milk in almost any recipe. The recipes below are for three types of milk: one for drinking, one to be used as a milk substitute when cooking, and one to be used as a cream substitute when cooking.

Nut and Seed Flour

I use nut or seed flour when I don't have wheat germ in the kitchen. Ground nuts and seeds make an excellent wheat flour substitute in many recipes. Use nut and seed flour for one-fourth of the wheat flour requested in recipes or to taste. Because seeds and nuts become rancid quickly, you should only grind the amount you need.

Benefits of Nuts and Seeds

All nuts and seeds (e.g., peanuts, almonds, Brazil nuts, cashews, sunflower seeds, sesame seeds) contain protease inhibitor. This compound found in beans, nuts, and seeds is known to block cancer. Nuts and seeds are nutritious and contain high levels of trace minerals and vitamin E. Vitamin E is an antioxidant, which protects the body from damaging free radical chain reactions, prevents skin from aging and wrinkling, and may also prevent cancer.

MILK SUBSTITUTE FOR DRINKING

½ cups cashew pieces
½ cup blanched almonds
2 cups water
1 tbsp. molasses

In a blender, grind cashew pieces and blanched almonds until fine. Add water and molasses. Blend well and transfer from blender to a glass container. Leave at room temperature for 1 hour. Strain through a fine sieve into a jar. Chill well.

Yield: 2 cups

MILK SUBSTITUTE FOR COOKING

1 cup cashew pieces
2 cups water

In a blender, blend cashew pieces with water. Blend well and transfer to a glass container. Leave for 1 hour, then strain through a fine sieve into a jar.

Yield: 2 cups

CREAM SUBSTITUTE FOR COOKING

1 cup almond pieces
1¼ cups water

In a blender, blend almond pieces with water. Blend well, then strain. Leftover pulp can be added to granola, muffins, breads, and porridges before cooking or baking, or dried for preservation.

Yield: 1⅓ cups

NUT OR SEED FLOUR

1 cup blanched almonds, sunflower seeds,
**   or other peeled nuts**

Add ¼ cup of seeds or nuts at a time to a blender, blend until fine, then strain through a fine sieve. Return any lumpy nuts or seeds to the blender, add more seeds or nuts, and repeat the process.

Yield: varies, depending on type of nuts

Nutritional Yeast

This yellow flaky yeast is grown on molasses and has a mild, chicken-soup sort of taste and smell. It is a wonderful seasoning that is used commercially by many spice companies in their seasonings, but the average consumer knows little about it. Stored in a jar, it keeps a long time. In dairy-free cooking, it is used to make "cheese" with a flavor and color like cheddar. It is used as a flavoring for food, but it also has good nutritional value. It is available for purchase in most natural food stores.

Benefits of Nutritional Yeast

Nutritional yeast contains variable amounts of vitamin B12, high-quality protein, and trace minerals. One teaspoon of yeast sprinkled over salad, pasta, or rice dishes every day will provide enough vitamin B12 for an average adult.

Onions

Onions are a common vegetables in almost all cultures. We use them every day, but not often as star vegetables such as asparagus in spring or snow peas in summer. Just because they are cheap and readily available in stores, does not mean we should underestimate the value of onions. They are one of the basic food ingredients and one of the top food medicines.

Benefits of Onions

There are many exotic vegetables in the world, but the common onion's medicinal power is one of the most misunderstood and undervalued. For centuries, the onion has been used in folk remedies for treating earaches, colds, fever, dizziness, laryngitis, diarrhea, insomnia, and vomiting. Onions stimulate blood production, help to cleanse the liver, aid in digestion, and eliminate mucus. Half a cup of onions a day, cooked or otherwise, will keep your blood and heart in good condition. A research group in the United States reported that eating onions boosts HDL cholesterol (the good type) an average of 30 percent while at the same time lowering LDL cholesterol (the bad type). Try adding this simple food to your meals every day. Onions prevent blood clots by thinning the blood and lowering blood pressure.

Another study shows that the compounds isolated from onions—one called diphenylamine and the other an antidiabetic compound similar to tolbutamide—have both been found to be effective in lowering blood sugar levels. Another test shows that eating onions prevents cancer in animals.

Parsley

This is a vegetable that I call a decoration vegetable. It seems that people are just not too keen on eating parsley or orange slices when they are used as garnishes on the side of the plate. But for vegetarians, I recommend you use a lot of minced parsley in your meals. You can drink fresh juiced parsley or chop it and add it to dishes just before serving. It contains a high amount of minerals and vitamins you don't want to destroy by oxidation.

Benefits of Parsley

Parsley juice is used in treating kidney problems, cleansing the kidneys, and regulating and maintaining calcium balance in the body.

Parsnips

To bring out the best flavor of this vegetable, store it for several weeks at room temperature. Parsnips discolor easily. To avoid discoloration, cook them unpeeled. If cooking peeled parsnips, cook with 3 cups of water, one tablespoon of flour, two tablespoons of lemon juice, and ½ teaspoon salt.

Persimmons

When the autumn season arrives, suddenly all sorts of fruits and nuts begin to appear on the dining table at home and on restaurant menus. Chestnuts, gingko nuts, walnuts, and many kinds of late autumn fruits appear. One of the most intriguing of the fruits is persimmons. In late autumn, when all the leaves begin to fall, the only things left on the persimmon tree branches are these bright red-orange colored fruit, which hang like red dots against the gray sky. Persimmons have a strong bitter taste when not ripe. Once ripened, they are distinguished by a sweet tart taste that is hard to describe. Asians eat a great quantity of persimmons, preserving them for winter by hanging them with rice straw. There are semidried persimmons and fresh persimmons available in late summer in North American markets.

Benefits of Persimmons

Dried persimmon strengthens the stomach and intestinal tract and is effective for catarrh and coughing. The young leaves of persimmons are used as a tea and juice treatment.

Potatoes and Yams

A long time ago in Japan, I remember a street vendor who pulled his two-wheeled wagon containing hot roasted sweet potatoes among rocks inside a huge cast-iron container. People, especially young females, rushed to the vendor to purchase piping hot, roasted potatoes wrapped in newspaper.

Now that people are talking about nutrition and healthy ways of eating, I often hear, "I grew up in a meat-and-potatoes family." There is nothing wrong with potatoes. They are an excellent vegetable that is easy to prepare in so many ways.

In Japan, there is one kind of potato known in the northern part of the country as *danshaku,* which translates in English to "baron." The Japanese believe sweet potatoes increase sexual stamina. Insofar as variety is concerned, I think the North Americans know more about the potato than the Japanese. They are a very economical vegetable and are always handy to have in the kitchen.

There are usually three kinds of sweet potatoes in regular markets. To avoid confusion, I will clarify the definition of sweet potato here. Normally, when we refer to sweet potatoes, we mean a potato that is pale inside and out. Yams are darker outside and orange inside. However, at the market, you may see them marked as sweet potatoes, jewelled yams (the plumper and lighter of the two) and garnet yams (the longer and darker). They are all sweet potatoes, but the jewelled yam or garnet yam are sweeter and moister.

Avoid potatoes of any kind with peeling or blemished skin. Look for firm, unscarred potatoes. Moldy or sprouting potatoes are especially hazardous, as they contain solanine, a poisonous substance. It is safer to peel regular potatoes, although this does not apply to yams or sweet potatoes. Store them in a cool, dry, dark place.

Potato Starch and Flour

Potato starch is just like cornstarch but made from potatoes, so the corn allergen is not present. It is best used in recipes as a thickener or in pancake batters in place of eggs to hold the ingredients together when cooked. Potato flour and potato starch are not the same thing. Potato starch is made from raw potatoes and is suitable for cakes but not for breads. To make bread with potato starch requires eggs, baking powder, or other leavenings. It is also suitable for breading.

Potato flour is made from cooked potatoes. It is a good substitute for wheat flour or when making cookie dough with brown rice flour. Use ½ to ⅝ cup potato flour for each cup of wheat flour. It is not suitable as a thickening agent or as a breading flour.

Benefits of Potatoes

Both potatoes and sweet potatoes contain cellulose, hemicellulose, pectin, gums, and lignin—the fiber found in plant stems, leaves, and peels. Potatoes contain vitamins C and B6, and yams contain vitamin A. Both kinds of potatoes are good sources of potassium. Potatoes contain protein, but lack some amino acids. To provide complete essential amino acids, combine potatoes with grains or legumes. Potato juice and potato water is used to relieve pain from rheumatism and gout. Reports indicate the skin of the potato not only contains chlorogenic acids and polyphenol, but also contains an antioxidant that helps to fight free radical chain reactions and prevent cancer. Potatoes are known to help such conditions as asthma and diarrhea, and cleanse the body by neutralizing acid waste.

OLD-FASHIONED RED POTATO SALAD

2 lb. red potatoes
⅓ cup minced green onion
¼ cup minced celery
2 tbsp. capers, rinsed
1 tsp. minced garlic
3 tbsp. olive oil
1 tbsp. dijon mustard
2 tbsp. chopped parsley
Salt and pepper to taste

Cut red potatoes in ½-inch cubes. Cook until tender, then cool. Combine remaining ingredients in a bowl. Toss well and chill for 1 to 2 hours. Toss again, and serve.

Yield: 4 servings
Preparation Time: 2 hours

SAMOSA PASTRIES

Wrapping Pastry

3 cups unbleached pastry flour
½ tsp. salt
12 tbsp. very cold water
8 tbsp. oil

Samosa Filling

4 tbsp. black or yellow mustard seeds
3 tbsp. oil
2 cups finely minced onion
2 tsp. grated ginger
2 to 10 oz. large potatoes, peeled, cooked,
    and cut into 1-inch cubes
1⅓ cups peas
2 to 3 tbsp. water
½ tsp. ground coriander
½ tsp. whole cumin
½ tsp. turmeric
1 tsp. salt

Process all the wrapping pastry ingredients in a food processor to form a coarse meal. Wrap in a plastic bag and keep in the refrigerator, preferably overnight or a minimum of 4 to 5 hours.

In a flat skillet, fry mustard seeds until they begin to pop. Add oil, and sauté onion and ginger. Cook until onions are soft and transparent. Add cooked and cubed potato, peas, and water and mix in. Add seasonings. Cover pan and cook for 3 to 5 minutes, or until potatoes are tender. Stir and set aside to cool.

Roll dough into balls the size of golf balls, then roll to make 10-inch diameter crêpes and cut in half. Hold the half crêpe in your left hand, straight side up, then bring one end to the other end to make a triangular shape. Place a small amount of water between the cut edge of the seam, and press. Place 2 to 3 tablespoons of stuffing inside the triangle pocket, and fold the edge of the pastry to close, moistening with a touch of water under the seam. Repeat using the remaining stuffing.

Heat 3 cups of oil to 360 degrees. Deep-fry samosas until light gold in color.

Yield: about 25 samosa pastries
Preparation Time: overnight for pastry; 10 minutes for filling

SWEET POTATO AND CARROT ROSTI

Sweet potatoes, yams, potatoes, lotus roots, and carrots make great pancakes. Pancakes are great before a main course, as an appetizer, or for breakfast. For more variety, add different vegetables and your favorite nuts or seeds for more flavor.

2 cups grated uncooked yams
½ cup grated carrot
2 tbsp. minced parsley
⅛ tsp. basil
⅛ tsp. oregano
Pinch salt
Pinch pepper
3 tbsp. rice cake crumbs (or 2 tbsp. flour)
4 to 5 tbsp. olive oil

In a bowl, combine all ingredients, reserving the oil for frying. Form pancake-shaped patties ¼ inch thick with a 3-inch diameter. Heat a flat skillet and sauté pancakes in medium high heat until golden and crisp on the outside then flip to cook the other side. Cook until tender inside, about 4 to 5 minutes.

Note: To prevent oxidation, use 1 to 2 tablespoons of vinegar or lemon juice with root vegetables. You can make homemade rice cake crumbs by processing rice cakes in a food processor until fine crumbs are formed.

Yield: 10 to 12 pancakes
Preparation Time: 10 minutes

GREEK-STYLE LEMONY SWEET POTATO WEDGES

3 medium sweet potatoes, not peeled
2 tbsp. olive oil
2 tbsp. minced garlic
3 tbsp. lemon juice
1 tbsp. dried rosemary
1 tsp. dried oregano
⅓ cup minced red onion
Pinch salt and pepper

Cut each potato into wedges lengthwise, then place all ingredients in a large bowl and toss well. Place in a roasting pan and bake in a preheated 450-degree oven for 13 minutes. Turn and bake other side until golden. Adjust seasoning as needed.

Yield: 4 servings
Preparation Time: 30 minutes

WARM NORTH AFRICAN SWEET POTATO SALAD

2 lb. sweet potatoes
4 tbsp. oilive oil
1 cup minced onion
½ tsp. salt
1 tsp. minced ginger root
1½ cup water
½ tsp. ground cumin
Juice of 1 lemon
4 tbsp. minced cilantro
¼ tsp. ground chili
Spinach leaves (for garnish)

Peel sweet potatoes and cut into ¾-inch dice. Place diced potatoes in a heavy saucepan with water, ginger, and salt. Bring to a boil, then lower heat to medium. Cover and cook until potatoes are almost tender, about 7 minutes. Remove lid, add cumin and paprika, and simmer uncovered until all the water is evaporated.

In a separate skillet, sauté onion until transparent over medium-low heat, about 4 to 5 minutes. Remove from heat and add onion to the potato mixture. Add lemon juice and chili with half of the cilantro. Toss and place on a large platter with spinach leaves. Serve warm.

Yield: 4 servings
Preparation Time: 17 minutes

Rice Syrup

Brown rice syrup is a natural sweetener, lightly processed from grains. The grain is sprouted or malted, then allowed to ferment to a natural sugar. The result is a sweet liquid cooked down into a syrup. Brown rice syrup sweetener is significantly more nutritious than table sugar, but is still a highly concentrated sugar.

Sake-Kasu

Sake-kasu or *sake-lees* is the fermented residue left after making sake. It is used to make pickles and special types of soups, which are a popular dish in the cold winter season in Japan. It is also used in Chinese cooking as a flavoring agent for sauces and dips.

Seitan (Wheat Gluten)

Seitan is made from whole wheat flour, high gluten flour, or a mixture of both. If you mix flour and water then knead, you'll create a sticky dough, which is gluten (wheat protein). It is used in many dishes such as stews, soups, or deep-fried and sautéed dishes. In Chinese and Japanese vegetarian cuisine, seitan is used to make mock chicken, mock duck, and other meat-simulated products. In Japan, dried gluten is called *fu,* which is added to miso and clear soups. This is an excellent source of protein.

HOMEMADE SEITAN

3 cups gluten flour
1 tsp. salt
1 tsp. dried yeast
1¼ cups cup warm water

Place gluten flour in a large stainless steel mixing bowl. In another bowl, dissolve salt and yeast in warm water. Pour liquid mixture onto gluten flour while stirring slowly to make it into a firm dough. Knead the dough until smooth, about 30 minutes. Cover the bowl with a damp cloth and leave at room temperature for at least 4 hours.

Remove the dough from the bowl and puncture. Knead into a ball. Return the dough to the bowl, cover, and keep in the refrigerator for 3 hours. Remove the dough, place under cold running water and wash until the water becomes clear, squeezing constantly to remove the starch. (If it separates, add 1 teaspoon of salt and knead again.) Gluten seitan is then ready to roll into balls, steam, boil, deep-fry, or dry.

Yield: 2 dozen balls
Preparation Time: 40 minutes (plus 7 hours rising time)

Sesame Oil

The delightful nutty aroma of dark sesame oil is made from whole toasted unhulled sesame seeds, which gives a distinctive character to Oriental cooking. Used in small amounts for sautéing and stir-frying, it is preferably mixed with other oils to prevent from overpowering the delicate taste of vegetables. Use it in sauces and dressings, and to enhance the flavor of other foods by adding few drops of oil at the last minute along with a nutty enhancer like vinegar.

Dark roasted sesame oil is available in Oriental or health food stores. Look for the label that reads "pure roasted sesame oil" and nothing else. Avoid dark sesame oil products that are blended with other types of oil. Good dark roasted sesame oil has an appetizing fragrance and is rich in flavor. Low-grade dark sesame oil does not have the aroma that you get from pure roasted oil. Once opened, store in cool, dark place.

Benefits of Sesame Oil

Sesame oil is high in vitamin E, nature's protector against aging skin and wrinkles. It also contains lecithin, a cholesterol sweeper.

Sesame Seeds

Both black and white sesame seeds, *kuro-goma* (black) and *shiro-goma* (white) in Japanese, are usually roasted to bring out their flavor and aroma, then ground or chopped finely before they are used. To roast your own sesame seeds, heat a thick cast-iron pan until warm, add unhulled sesame seeds to the pan, and stir continuously over medium heat until a few seeds begin to pop. Remove all seeds from the pan immediately and cool. Good quality sesame seeds should have a trace of aromatic oil when rubbed between your fingers after roasting.

Select only unhulled large plump seeds at bulk food stores.

Benefits of Sesame Seeds

Sesame seeds are nutritious; they are high in protein, lecithin, calcium, potassium, and magnesium and contain traces of iron, vitamin A, vitamin B1, vitamin B2, vitamin B6, and niacin. They can be used to rejuvenate mental and physical capacity and endurance, and to increase the secretions of the pituitary, pineal, and sex glands. Sesame oil helps to balance calcium and magnesium in the body. The high quantity of vitamin E in the oil from sesame seeds protects the skin from aging and wrinkling.

GREEN BEANS GOMA-AE

The term *ae* is often used in Japanese cookery (*shiro-ae, miso-ae, konome-ae*) and means "mixed" or "coated." Foods are usually mixed with a thick sauce and served chilled or at room temperature. *Goma-ae* is one of the most popular ways to prepare foods. For example, carrots, spinach, eggplant, and pressed tofu are all foods suitable for *ae*.

- ½ lb. green beans, ends removed
- 3 tbsp. roasted sesame seeds
- 1½ tbsp. dashi
- 2 tsp. soy sauce
- ½ tsp. natural sweetener or maple syrup

Boil green beans for 3 to 5 minutes. Drain and cool. Cut into 2-inch lengths. Dry-sauté sesame seeds in a frying pan on low heat until seeds start to pop. Pound and grind sesame seeds in a spice mortar or Japanese mortar. Mix all seasonings with ground sesame and toss green beans in. Marinate for 1 hour, then serve.

Shichimi Togarashi

As a mixture of spices, use shichimi togarashi, or Japanese seven chili pepper, to sprinkle over noodles, broiled foods, cooked vegetables, and other dishes. It is a mixture of crushed chili flakes, sansho, white and black sesame seeds, poppy and hemp seeds, tangerine peel, roasted nori, and other ingredients. It is sold in premixed bottles in Japanese and Korean food stores.

Shiso (Perilla Leaves)

These exotic-tasting leaves, whose taste resembles a mixture of basil and mint, are used in many Japanese preparations. There are two kinds of shiso leaves available in North America: blue and red. They are found in most Japanese grocery stores; and they are normally packaged in plastic containers in the refrigerated section.

Red shiso is used mainly for umeboshi pickles (see index) to give them a pink color and added nutritional value. If you are a curious and adventurous person and happen to see these leaves in the store, pick up a package and try them. Chop them up and add them to salads; mince and sprinkle on pastas; sprinkle over rice dishes; or use as a wrapper for sushi preparation. I'm sure you will not forget this pleasant aromatic herb once you've tried it.

Soy Sauce

This wonderful and popular creation comes from Asia. Soy sauce is made from roasted wheat, soybeans, salt, rice koji, and water. These ingredients are naturally fermented for over a year to establish a mellow tart-tasting dark sauce.

It is very confusing for the first-timer to select a good soy sauce for any particular purpose because there are a great number of soy sauces to choose from. Each culture has its own types of soy sauce and brands that add to the confusion. There are also soy sauce-based premade sauces designed especially for North Americans.

VARIETIES OF SOY SAUCE

Before selecting a soy sauce, take a little time and effort to study how soy sauces are made, what kinds of soy sauce are available to you, and how to use them properly. Read the labels. Quality soy sauces, with the exception of tamari, contain only wheat, sea salt, soybeans, rice koji as a starter, and water. Avoid soy sauce if it contains caramel, dehydrated vegetable protein, or artificial ingredients. Experiment by tasting the soy sauce. If you like the taste of the soy sauce, use that brand until you discover a better one.

I recommend having three or four kinds of quality soy sauce in your kitchen—one for cooking, another for non-cooked purposes such as salad dressings and dipping sauces, and a third type for seasoning when you don't want too much color in the food. For example, light soy sauce, tamari soy sauce, mushroom soy sauce, and all-purpose soy sauce are a good combination of soy sauces to have in your kitchen for everyday cooking purposes.

When using soy sauce in cooking, remember that soy sauce is a mixture of water (one of the basic elements) with a high salt content. For those with sodium-restricted diets, use soy sauce with caution. When soy sauce reduces from heat, the water evaporates, leaving the salt. You can add water to help adjust the taste.

Soy sauces are divided into the following categories. Each category of soy sauce is intended for a different purpose.

All-Purpose Soy Sauce

As indicated by its name, all-purpose soy sauce can be use for almost all types of cooking, from braising vegetables to noncooked seasonings to dipping sauces.

Light Soy Sauce

Light in color but high in salt, light soy sauce is used to season food when you don't want to make dark colors. Use it in soups, when braising light-colored foods, such as white turnip, daikon, or sue choy, to add more seasoning than ordinary salt.

Dark Soy Sauce

This sauce is much darker than other types of soy sauce, so use it when you want color added to your foods.

Mushroom Soy Sauce

This is a dark sweet soy sauce you can use when you want a bright dark color in the food and an added touch of sweetness.

Low-Sodium Soy Sauce (Lite Soy Sauce)

Use low-sodium or lite soy sauce when you don't want to add salt but want some seasoning.

Tamari Soy Sauce

Pure tamari soy sauce is made from soybeans, rice koji starter, and water. It contains no wheat. Subtle, mellow, and tart, tamari soy sauce is superior to any other soy sauce for all aspects of cooking. Unfortunately, because this sauce is made only from soybeans, this product is rather expensive compared to others.

Spinach

Spinach is a popular vegetable all over the world. That delicate, sweet flavor comes from both the gleaming stems and dark green leaves. It is one of my favorite vegetables, and is good steamed, stir-fried, and cold in salads with sesame seed sauce. Spinach grows in muddy soils; wash it well to remove all the sand and grit before cooking. One grain of sand can ruin your reputation as a good cook.

Choose spinach with fresh dark green leaves, avoiding those with wilted yellow leaves.

Benefits of Spinach

This vegetable has a good reputation in research reports conducted in various countries. Spinach is an excellent source of vitamins A, C, and B1, potassium, calcium, and iron. It is used therapeutically for anemia and heart disturbances. Spinach also contains extremely high concentrations of carotinoids—including beta carotene—and high amounts of chlorophyll, both of which are known as anticancer agents.

The oxalic acid found in spinach binds some of the iron and calcium, making both minerals unusable to the body. The old wisdom in many countries' food combinations solved this problem by mixing other foods to allow for nutritional balance. Japan, for instance, created a unique dish called *goma-ae,* using spinach and sesame seeds along with a dashi-based sauce. Calcium and other nutrients in sesame seeds compensate for the ones that aren't available because of the oxalic acid.

Caution: A person on anticoagulant medication or MAO inhibitor should avoid eating large amounts of spinach.

SPINACH SAUTEED WITH GARLIC AND TAHINI

2 tbsp. olive oil
3 cloves garlic, minced
1 bunch cooked spinach, cut to your favorite size
1 tbsp. tahini
Pinch sea salt
Fresh ground pepper
½ tsp. rice vinegar

Heat a flat skillet or wok until hot, add oil, and sauté garlic until browned. Add spinach and sauté quickly. Add tahini and toss well. Season with salt and pepper if desired. Add vinegar before serving.

Yield: 4 servings
Preparation Time: 5 minutes

SLOW SIMMERED SPINACH AND TOFU IN BROTH

In this recipe, the tofu and kombu will compensate for calcium loss. Tofu and spinach combine well for taste and color. Customarily, this dish is served in the pot with dipping sauce and condiments on the side. Each person adds condiments to the sauce then dips tofu in sauce.

¼ cup dashi
⅓ cup tamari
3 tbsp. mirin
2 cups water
Pinch sea salt
1 4 x 4-inch piece dashi kombu
2 16-oz. blocks soft or medium tofu
1 bunch spinach, blanched
2 tbsp. minced scallion
2 tsp. grated ginger

To make a dipping sauce, boil dashi, tamari, and mirin for 10 seconds. Remove and cool. Place water, salt, and kombu in a ceramic pot. Bring to a simmer, uncovered, over medium heat. Cut each block of tofu into ten pieces and place it and the spinach into the pot. Cook until tofu begins to rise to the surface and is warm inside, but never bring the liquid to a raging boil. Remove the pot from heat, and use a slotted spoon to remove tofu from ceramic pot. Serve with individual condiments and dipping sauce. Add condiments to the dipping sauce to season, and dip tofu into sauce before eating.

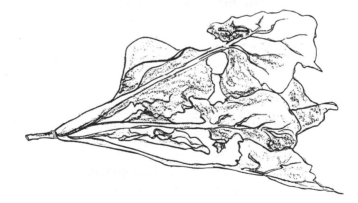

SPICY SICHUAN TOFU WITH SPINACH

3 tbsp. oil
1 bunch spinach, cooked and cut into 2-inch lengths
1 tbsp. minced garlic
1 tsp. minced ginger
2 whole dried chilies, seeds removed
1 tbsp. red miso or dou ban chiang
3 tbsp. soy sauce or tamari
1 tbsp. natural sweetener or other sweetener
5 to 6 tbsp. water
1 16-oz. block medium soft tofu
2 tbsp. arrowroot powder
1 tbsp. water
1 tbsp. vinegar
½ tsp. sesame oil
Pinch ground Sichuan peppercorn

Heat wok until hot. Add 1 tablespoon oil, then stir-fry spinach until hot. Place spinach on top of platter and keep warm. Reheat wok and add remaining 2 tablespoons of oil. Sauté garlic, ginger, chilies, and miso until aroma is released. Add soy sauce, sweetener, and water. Bring to a boil, then reduce heat to medium. Cut tofu into ½ x ½-inch cubes, add to sauce, and simmer for 2 minutes. Mix together arrowroot powder and water, and carefully add to thicken. Add vinegar and sesame oil. Serve over warm spinach. Sprinkle with roasted Sichuan ground pepper and serve.

Yield: 3 or 4 servings
Preparation Time: 10 minutes

SPINACH STIR-FRIED WITH TOFU POUCH

2 tbsp. oil
1 bunch spinach, cooked
2 tbsp. all-purpose soy sauce
2 tbsp. mirin
1 3 x 6-inch usu-age tofu pouch, prepared and shredded
2 tbsp. white roasted sesame seeds

Heat wok or frying pan until hot. Add oil and sauté over high heat. Add soy sauce and mirin at once. Reduce heat to medium, add tofu skin, and cook for 4 to 5 more minutes. Sprinkle with sesame seeds before serving.

Yield: 2 or 3 servings
Preparation Time: 6 minutes

SPINACH PESTO

2 tbsp. garlic, minced
2 tbsp. scallion, minced
2 cups washed fresh spinach, firmly packed
3 cups fresh basil, firmly packed
1 tbsp. lemon juice
2 to 3 tbsp. olive oil
Pinch sea salt
½ cup pine nuts or chopped nuts

Place garlic and scallion in a food processor and process for 30 seconds. Add spinach, process for another 30 seconds. Add basil, lemon juice, oil, and salt. Purée until it forms a paste. Blend in a tablespoon or two of water for a smoother consistency. Add nuts if desired. Process for 30 more seconds for a creamier sauce.

Yield: 1½ cups
Preparation Time: 5 minutes

Squash

Squash are common, with many kinds available in North America. At least sixty varieties of winter and summer squash are recognized by horticulturists. Winter squash is packed with more vitamins, minerals, and protein than summer squash.

When choosing winter squash, choose those with hard skins and avoid those with watery spots. Unless baked whole, remove the seeds and stringy portions, or peel and cut into small pieces.

Benefits of Squash

Deep orange vegetables such as carrots and squash have been proven to prevent cancers—stomach, esophageal, bladder, and lung cancers in particular.

BRAISED WINTER SQUASH

This recipe's ingredient list is simple, but I think it is one of the best ways to cook pumpkin without loosing the flavor of this nutritious vegetable.

1½ lb. winter squash or Japanese pumpkin
1½ cups water or dashi stock
1 tbsp. soy sauce
4 tbsp. natural sweetener or other sweetener

Remove seeds from squash, and cut it into ½-inch cubes. Place in cold water for 5 minutes. Drain and set aside. Place remaining ingredients into the pot with the squash, and bring to a boil over high heat. Reduce heat to medium high. Cook until squash is tender. Serve hot or at room temperature.

Yield: 4 servings
Preparation Time: 10 minutes

Sunflower Seeds

This is one of nature's foods I recommend to eat every day. Add to the salads, muffins, pancakes, vegetables, or eat as a snack. As a rule, they should be eaten raw. The nutritional information for sunflower seeds is included in the Benefits of Nuts and Seeds (see index).

SUNFLOWER SEED DRESSING

This wonderful dressing is made from sunflower seeds and cider vinegar. If you prefer to use another type of vinegar, give it a try. Adjust the dressing's thickness by adding water. This dressing has a tendency to get thick once left at room temperature.

½ cup natural sweetener
¼ tsp. asafetida (hing)
2 tsp. dry mustard
1 cup sunflower seeds
¾ cup cider vinegar
3 tbsp. minced onion
1 tsp. lemon rind, grated
¼ tsp. dill
2 tsp. salt

Blend all ingredients together.

Yield: 2½ cups
Preparation Time: 2 minutes

Tahini

Tahini is a paste, which some call a butter, made from ground sesame seeds. Tahini is a versatile food, and its usage is almost endless. It is an essential ingredient in Mediterranean cuisine. It has a light flavor, especially when made from raw instead of roasted sesame seeds. Tahini is a wonderful substitute for cream in making cream soups, for egg in custards, and for milk in salad dressings. It is available in Greek, Arab, Iranian, and Mediterranean food stores and most health food stores. It can be stored for up to two months at room temperature once opened.

Benefits of Tahini

Tahini has nutritional values almost identical to sesame seeds or *gi-ma-chiang* (Chinese sesame paste). Tahini is high in protein, calcium, vitamin A, vitamin B-complex, minerals, and other nutrients. See Benefits of Nuts and Seeds for additional nutritional information.

BASIC TAHINI DRESSING

For herb seasonings, use parsley, coriander, mint, or dill.

1 tbsp. minced garlic
½ tsp. salt
1 cup lemon juice
1 cup tahini
2 to 3 tbsp. olive oil

Combine ingredients, then adjust thickness by adding water if desired.

Yield: 2¼ cups
Preparation Time: 2 minutes

TAHINI GINGER DRESSING

½ cup tahini
½ cup water
2 tbsp. soy sauce
4 tbsp. finely minced ginger
1 tbsp. finely minced garlic
3 tbsp. minced onion
1 stalk green onion, chopped
1 tbsp. tomato paste
4 tbsp. lemon juice

Blend all the ingredients in a blender until smooth. Keep in an airtight glass container and refrigerate.

Yield: over 2 cups
Preparation Time: 2 minutes

TAHINI DRESSING

2 tbsp. tahini
1 tsp. natural sweetener
⅓ tsp. sea salt
1 tbsp. soy sauce
1½ tbsp. rice vinegar
1½ tbsp. dashi

Mix all ingredients together well.

Yield: less than ½ cup
Preparation Time: 2 minutes

Takuwan

These wonderfully chewy sweet pickles, *takuwan,* were created by a famous Buddhist monk. They are an excellent condiment for rice dishes, and they make a delicious snack. Good natural takuwan is made with fermented rice bran and dried daikon, and is light beige in color. It is sold in natural food stores, Japanese stores, and stores specializing in macrobiotic foods.

Avoid takuwan that are bright yellow in color, as they probably contain yellow food coloring. Naturally pickled takuwan have a dull light beige color and are superior in taste to chemically pickled takuwan.

Benefits of Takuwan

Takuwan (daikon pickled in rice bran) is a good source of vitamin B12, which is lacking in other vegetarian foods.

Tamari

As a by-product of the miso-making process, this dark liquid pools on top of *aka miso*. Miso makers remove this aromatic liquid using a special wooden toll in the miso mixture. After collecting this rare, expensive liquid, the miso maker bottles it and usually divides it among the workers or gives it to special customers.

Real tamari has a rich, sweet, deep taste and a thick texture in comparison to soy sauce. Be cautious, real tamari does not contain wheat; it is made only with soybeans and koji. In supermarkets or health food stores, you'll find tamari brand names containing wheat, but they are not real tamari.

Tamarind

Tamarind's name comes from the Arabic *tamar-i-hind*. It is also called the Indian date from the pods of the feathery tamarind tree. The pulp of the ripe tamarind fruit is separated from the fiber and squeezed repeatedly through water. The concentrated pulp, without fibers and seeds, can be found in packages or jars. Before using, the pulp must be soaked in water. It is used as a souring agent for curries. For convenience, try tamarind concentrate, a syrupy liquid available in a plastic bottles that you can add directly to sauces or with other ingredients. Both are available in Indian or Chinese food stores.

Taro

In Chinese or Japanese markets, you will find a hairy vegetable, slightly larger than a golf ball, called taro, taro root, or sato-imo. It's also called yucca or tapioca. There are about twenty different kinds of taro roots available throughout Japan. In North America, you can find large (cassava), medium, and small (most expensive) ones. Taro is an essential vegetable for one-pot cookery, soups, and a famous braised dish, *Ni-coro-gashi,* which translates to "roll while braising." Taro root is an important staple food

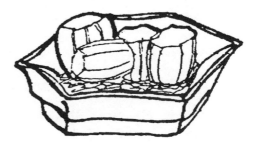

for tropical natives. Grated and steamed cassava is a staple in the Philippines. The taste of taro root is similar to potatoes. Once cooked, it turns slightly glutinous.

To prepare taro root, scrub the skin well using the back of a knife, then place in water containing vinegar (1 cup water to 1 teaspoon vinegar) to stop oxidation.

When buying taro, grab a root and press gently. If it is solid and feels heavy, has no soft spots or blemishes, and has strong-looking hair, then it is a good one to buy.

Benefits of Taro

Taro contains vitamins C, B6, and potassium. It also contains a moderate amount of protein, but taro root protein is deficient in essential amino acids. Combine taro root with grains and legumes to provide complete protein. Taro miso soup is effective in removing catarrh and relieving asthma.

TARO ROOT NIKOROGASHI

1½ lb. small taro roots
1 tbsp. salt
1 4 x 4-inch piece kombu
3½ cups water
3½ tbsp. soy sauce
2 tbsp. natural sweetener
1 tbsp. sake
1 tbsp. mirin

Scrub the skin of the taro root with a knife. Sprinkle salt over taro root, then rub lightly. Wash under cold running water to remove any slimy substance. Drain and set aside.

In a cooking pot, place kombu, water, and taro root. Bring to a boil, cooking over high heat for 3 minutes. Lower heat to medium, and add remaining seasonings. Cook for 15 to 18 minutes covered. When the taro roots can be pierced with a skewer, remove kombu and cook without a lid until taro roots are well glazed, moving the pot to roll the roots. Serve hot or at room temperature over grains.

Yield: 4 servings
Preparation Time: 21 minutes

SWEET BRAISED TARO ROOT

2 lb. small taro root, washed and peeled
1½ cups dashi or vegetable stock
2 tbsp. raw natural sweetener
2 tbsp. soy sauce

Place peeled taro root in cold water for 10 minutes before cooking; drain. Place taro root and dashi together in a large saucepan and bring to a boil. Cook for 2 to 3 minutes. Add natural sweetener to the pan and cook for 3 to 4 minutes more. Add soy sauce and bring to a boil. Cover with a waxed paper lid over the pan, then cook for 9 to 10 minutes over medium low heat. Serve when the taro roots can be pierced with a skewer easily.

Yield: 4 servings
Preparation Time: 17 minutes

Tekka

Tekka is a condiment made by sautéing burdock root, carrots, and lotus roots in sesame oil for 5 to 6 hours over low heat. Minced ginger is added at the last minute. It is delicious sprinkled on rice, noodles, and other vegetables.

Tomato

Almost everyone is familiar with what a tomato looks like, what it tastes like, and how to select it. Tomatoes are popular and a very handy vegetable to have in your kitchen. Some recipes call for peeling tomatoes, but unless you are entertaining fussy friends, you really don't have to peel and seed tomatoes. All the good nutrients are concentrated between the skin and meat of the tomatoes. For fussy friends, skin tomatoes by slitting the bottom end and submerging in boiling hot water for 10 to 15 seconds. Remove and place in cold water. The peel should come off easily.

For immediate use, choose tomatoes that are deep red in color with no bruised or soft spots.

Benefits of Tomatoes

Mostly carbohydrates, tomatoes have a slight trace of fat, only 23 calories, and are rich in beta carotene, vitamin C, and potassium. Scientists have found that foods containing beta carotene may lower the risk of cancer of the larynx, esophagus, lungs, and bladder. Potassium helps to release the energy from carbohydrates, proteins, and fats, and maintains the fluid and electrolyte balance in the body.

MILLET AND FRUIT-FILLED TOMATOES WITH ORANGE MARMALADE GLAZE

4 large tomatoes, tops removed and pulp scooped out
2 tbsp. olive oil
½ cup minced onion
2 cups cooked millet
½ cup currants
½ cup blanched almonds, chopped
½ cup dried apricots, presoaked and chopped
2 tbsp. orange marmalade
2 tbsp. lemon juice
1 tbsp. fresh mint, chopped
1 tbsp. natural sweetener
½ tsp. allspice
½ tsp. cinnamon
¼ tsp. salt

Glaze

½ cup marmalade
2 tbsp. natural sweetener
1 tsp. dijon mustard

Place tomatoes upside down to drain liquid, reserve pulp for stuffing. Heat skillet until hot, sauté onion in oil until soft and transparent. Mix with remaining stuffing ingredients including pulp. Stuff tomatoes with mixture. Combine glaze ingredients and drizzle over stuffed tomatoes. Bake in a 350-degree oven for 20 minutes. Serve cold.

Yield: 4 servings
Preparation Time: 20 to 22 minutes

BARBECUE SAUCE

1 medium onion, minced
2 tbsp. minced garlic
4 tbsp. olive oil
1 cup sorghum
2½ cups canned whole tomatoes with juice,
processed in a blender
3 tbsp. tomato paste
1 tsp. powdered English mustard
1 tbsp. salt
1 tbsp. allspice
1 tbsp. ground chili
¾ cup lemon juice
2 tbsp. soy sauce

Heat a large, heavy pot. Add oil and cook onion and garlic until transparent and light gold in color. Add remaining ingredients, and cook for 1 hour, skimming occasionally. Add lemon juice and soy sauce, and cook for 10 more minutes. Remove to cool, and store in a refrigerator for up to 10 days.

Yield: 4¼ cups
Preparation Time: 1 hour 15 minutes

TOMATO MISO SAUCE

This is an unusual combination of tomato and miso sauce in which the miso seems to mellow the tartness of the tomato, blending well with the other ingredients. Use Tomato Miso Sauce to braise tofu or a mixture of vegetables, in casserole dishes, or when baking potatoes.

2 tbsp. olive oil
1 tbsp. minced garlic
1 onion, chopped fine
1 small carrot, chopped
1 celery stick, chopped
1 green pepper, chopped
6 medium tomatoes, diced
½ cup sliced mushrooms
2 cups vegetable stock
1 bay leaf
Pinch salt
Pinch pepper
¼ cup fresh basil, minced
  (or pinch dried basil)
4 tbsp. red miso

Heat a heavy sauce pot. Add oil and sauté garlic and onion until soft. Add carrot, celery, green pepper, tomatoes, and mushrooms. Sauté until vegetables become soft, then add remaining ingredients. Simmer for one hour.

Yield: 3½ cups
Preparation Time: 1 hour

TOMATO CHOCOLATE SAUCE

This sauce can be prepared ahead of time and stored in an airtight container in the refrigerator. It will last for up to two weeks. It can be served with any kind of steamed vegetables, pasta, or grains. For a more elaborate dish, try braising deep-fried tempeh with this sauce. It is quite unique.

½ cup minced onion
4 tbsp. oil
1 tbsp. minced garlic
½ cup chopped green pepper
1 16-oz. can whole tomatoes, chopped
1 oz. bitter chocolate
4 tsp. black strap molasses
¼ tsp. ground cloves
¼ tsp. ground nutmeg
1 tbsp. chili powder
½ tsp. whole cumin
½ tsp. oregano powder
1 tsp. salt
½ tsp. black pepper

In a skillet, sauté onion in oil until soft, then add garlic and green pepper, and sauté for another 2 minutes. Add chopped tomatoes, cook for 30 minutes. Melt chocolate and add to tomato mixture. Add dark molasses and other spices. Cook for 10 minutes; season with salt and pepper.

Yield: 2¼ cups
Preparation Time: 45 to 50 minutes

TOMATO VINAIGRETTE

1 cup tomato juice
1 tsp. minced garlic
3 tbsp. lemon juice
1 tbsp. dried chives
¼ tsp. dry English mustard
¼ tsp. prepared horseradish
2 tsp. natural sweetener
4 tbsp. olive oil
2 tbsp. chopped parsley

Place all ingredients in an airtight glass container. Shake well. Refrigerate until ready to use.

Yield: 1¾ cups
Preparation Time: 2 minutes

Turmeric

This close relative of the ginger and arrowroot family is bright orange-yellow inside. Turmeric is used in many dishes in India and neighboring countries as a flavoring agent. It originated in Southeast Asia, and is cultivated and produced in India, Haiti, Jamaica, and Peru. In commercial use, it is used to color curry powder, mustard powder, chili powder, and French dressings. It is also used to dye clothing material and paper. In Thailand, turmeric is used to color the robes of Buddhist monks.

In North America, we can only purchase it in powder form instead of fresh or dried, at any ethnic bulk food store.

Benefits of Tumeric

Turmeric is excellent for improving the complexion of the skin, for strengthening mucus membranes, and for treating problems associated with joints. In Ayurveda medicine, turmeric is used to relieve congestion, soothe respiratory ailments such as coughs or asthma, and to relieve inflammation of the tonsils and throat. A current study shows that a compound found in turmeric is effective in treating diabetes and certain types of cancer.

Turnips

There are several kinds of turnips available in North America. In most supermarkets, you can find yellow and white turnips. Yellow turnips are good to use in soups, stews, purées, and other dishes, where the sweet taste of yellow turnip blends well with the other ingredients. White turnips go well with sour flavorings, especially where the sweet bitter taste of the turnips will not be overpowered by other flavorings and ingredients. They therefore taste best prepared simply.

When selecting turnips, especially white ones, those that feel heavy, solid, hard, and plump are the ones that you want. Avoid hollow, light turnips with any spots or blemishes.

BRAISED TURNIP
AND DEEP-FRIED TOFU

2½ cups water
1 8 x 4-inch piece kombu, wiped with damp cloth
1½ lb. white turnip, peeled and cut into bite-size pieces
1 lb. deep-fried tofu (atsu-age), cut into bite-size pieces
2 tbsp. mirin
2 tbsp. sake
3 tbsp. thin soy sauce
⅓ tsp. sea salt

In a pot, combine water and kombu, then place turnip and tofu in the pot. Place over high heat. When water begins to boil, reduce heat to medium, cover with a lid, and cook for 20 minutes or more until tender. Remove kombu, reserving for later use. Add remaining seasonings, and cook for 10 to 12 minutes more. Remove from heat and serve hot or at room temperature.

Yield: 4 to 5 servings
Preparation Time: 36 minutes

JAPANESE-STYLE INSTANT
PICKLED TURNIPS

Normally, Japanese pickles are served with other condiments, grains, and soup at the same time. Serve a small amount of these pickles with your favorite grain or serve with a noodle or pasta dish as a condiment.

4 very small white turnips, sliced very thin
2 tsp. salt
½ lemon, sliced

In a large bowl, combine sliced turnips and salt, rub together thoroughly, and leave at room temperature for 1 to 2 hours. Squeeze the turnip slices by hand to remove as much excess water as possible. Place on a serving plate, garnish with lemon slices, and serve with soy sauce on the side for dipping.

Yield: 1 cup
Preparation Time: 2 hours

Umeboshi

Umeboshi is a product made by sun-drying and pickling Japanese plums in sea salt brine and red shiso (perilla) leaves. Properly made, good umeboshi has a taste that is not too salty and naturally sweet with a subtle tangy taste. It comes in a jar with brine, available in health food and Japanese food stores. Umeboshi is eaten as food and as a remedy for many purposes.

Benefits of Umeboshi

Umeboshi is very effective for all sorts of stomach disorders and indigestion—especially morning sickness in pregnant women—and provides an almost instant cure for a hangover. In Japan, umeboshi is known to cure almost all minor sicknesses and is kept in every household as a food medicine.

As a folk remedy, umeboshi is used to cure headaches and stomach aches by peeling off the skin of the plums and placing the skin on the temples or on top of the belly button for half an hour.

Umeboshi counteracts fatigue and stimulates the liver and kidney functions of removing toxins, thus balancing and purifying the blood at the same time. Umeboshi paste is made from the flesh of umeboshi and is handy to have as a powerful medicine or excellent flavoring agent. When you have extra time and patience, prepare some for emergency use.

UMEBOSHI PASTE

Add this to accent your salad dressings and dips or dilute it with hot water to make tea.

5 (1½ oz.) umeboshi plums
2 tsp. natural sweetener
½ tbsp. sake
1 tsp. mirin
1 tsp. soy sauce (optional)

Remove pits from umeboshi. Strain umeboshi flesh through a fine sieve, then mix with remaining ingredients. Keep in an airtight container.

Yield: 4 tablespoons
Preparation Time: 5 minutes

Ume-Su (Pickled Plum Vinegar)

This brine drawn from kegs of mature umeboshi is both pleasantly tart and salty. *Ume-su* is used on cooked vegetables, in spreads, and to liven up salad dressings. It is available in most natural food and Japanese food stores.

Wasabi

Wasabi, or Japanese horseradish, has a fresh, stimulating flavor that adds zest not only to your foods but to your sinuses as well. Its abundance of protein-digesting enzymes makes it a perfect condiment to eat along with food that has a high protein content.

In North America, only powdered wasabi is available in tins or pouches at Oriental stores or supermarkets. To prepare wasabi, add several drops of lukewarm water to one tablespoon of wasabi powder in a small cup. Mix vigorously to make a paste. Flip the cup and let it sit for 10 minutes to allow the pungency to heighten; this trick was taught to me by my mother. To test the pungency, lift the container and bring it to your friend's nostrils. If they don't react, then the wasabi needs a little more time. If the strong pungency hits your sinus when you taste it, the wasabi is ready to use.

Wasabi is used mostly for sushi, as a dipping sauce for cold soba noodles, rice porridge, and for making various salad dressings. Once mixed, be sure to use all the wasabi as soon as possible.

Watercress

I first saw watercress in 1965, when I was in hotel training. The elder cook asked me to clean this strange vegetable, but I did not know how. He showed me how to clean the whiskers off the stems and how to pinch younger leaves for salad preparation. Back then, watercress was mostly used as a garnish with grilled steaks or other meat dishes. Sometimes it was deep-fried until crisp and served with fish dishes. I never had a chance to taste it when I was in Japan. Now, watercress is used in salads, soups, sautéed dishes, and salad dressings.

Benefits of Watercress

Watercress is high in minerals such as sulfur, chlorine, and calcium, and is good for reducing water retention and high blood pressure.

WATERCRESS AND MINTED PARSLEY SALAD

½ cup bulgur wheat
1 cup chopped parsley
1 cup chopped parsley
1 cup chopped watercress, leaves only
10 cherry tomatoes
½ English cucumber, sliced in half-moon shapes
1 stalk celery, finely chopped
⅓ cup minced fresh mint leaves
⅓ cup lemon juice
2 tbsp. olive oil
Salt and pepper to taste

Place bulgur in a bowl and cover with boiling water for 15 minutes. Strain through a fine sieve, then wash under cold running water. Leave in sieve for 1 hour to dry.

Mix the remaining ingredients with bulgur and toss well. Season with salt and pepper to taste. Chill for 1 hour before serving.

Yield: 4 servings
Preparation Time: 2 hours 15 minutes
(including drying and chilling time)

TOFU WITH HOT CHILI AND WATERCRESS SAUCE

1 large bunch (about 5 oz.) watercress
1 fresh hot chili (sereno or jalapeño)
½ small red pepper, cored and chopped
½ tsp. salt
16 oz. tofu
2¼ cups stock
2 tbsp. oil
2 tbsp. minced garlic
1 tbsp. minced ginger
2 tbsp. soy sauce
1 tsp. sesame oil
½ tsp. natural sweetener
1 tsp. arrowroot starch mixed with 2 tsp. water
1 tsp. sesame seeds, roasted

Mince watercress, stalks and leaves. Remove seeds from chilies and mince. Place watercress, chilies, and chopped red pepper in a bowl and sprinkle with salt. Mix well and leave for 25 minutes.

Place 2 cups of stock and tofu in a pot, and simmer over low heat for 7 to 9 minutes. Do not boil.

In a wok, sauté ginger and garlic in oil until almost dark. Add watercress mixture, and sauté until watercress is wilted. Lower heat and add remaining ¼ cup stock, soy sauce, sesame oil, and sweetener. Add arrowroot starch mixture and stir for 30 seconds while it thickens.

Remove tofu from stock and cut into 8 pieces. Place tofu on a serving platter and pour sauce over it. Sprinkle with sesame seeds and serve.

Yield: 4 servings
Preparation Time: 35 minutes

Yard Long Beans

Also called the asparagus bean or *dau godka,* this bean is best consumed when 1 ½ to 2 feet long. It is excellent sautéed with a small amount of oil or braised with seasonings. When you are shopping for any type of green bean, select those that are shiny, not too dry, firm, solid, and bright in color with no bruises or sweat spots. Look also for crispy beans with no brown spots, streaks, or blemishes. Avoid those that are dry or wrinkled.

YARD LONG BEANS WITH ASPARAGUS STIR-FRY

This dish is best cooked close to serving time to taste the crunchy beans and asparagus. Do not overcook either vegetable.

1 lb. yard long beans, washed and cut into 2-inch lengths
1 lb. asparagus, bottoms removed
3 tbsp. oil
2 tbsp. minced garlic
¼ cup water
¼ tsp. salt
2 tbsp. soy sauce
2 tbsp. lemon juice
4 tbsp. pine nuts
3 tbsp. minced chives

Heat a wok until hot, then add oil and sauté beans for 1 minute, tossing constantly to cook all sides. Remove beans from wok to a plate, then add asparagus to the wok and sauté for 1 minute, stirring constantly. Add asparagus to beans on plate. Add minced garlic to wok, and sauté until golden and aromatic. Return asparagus and beans to the wok. Toss quickly, then add ¼ cup water. Cover and steam until tender, about 3 or 4 minutes. Remove lid and season with salt and soy sauce. Toss and cook until all sauce is gone. Add lemon juice, toss, and remove from heat. Add pine nuts and serve with chives sprinkled on top.

Yield: 4 servings
Preparation Time: 4 minutes

Za-Choy, Za-Sai

This spicy Sichuan pickled preserved vegetable, called *za-sai* in Japanese, is used in many vegetarian and non-vegetarian dishes. Normally it is sold in a tin or a vacuum-sealed package in the refrigerated section of Oriental food stores. *Za-choy* is a rather salty vegetable and needs desalting by soaking in cold water with a pinch of salt. This simple trick of a pinch of salt is always successful in wicking salt out of salty foods.

Zucchini, Summer Squash

Zucchini is a popular vegetable in North America. It is readily available all year at reasonable prices. I love to use zucchini because of its color, flavor, sweet taste, and texture. The sweetness of the zucchini can compensate for refined sugar in cooking. Zucchini is good in soups, stewed dishes, braised by itself, deep-fried, stir-fried with various seasonings, salt pickled Japanese-style, or stuffed to make an elaborate main course meal.

When choosing zucchini, avoid any that are limp, bruised, cut, or have soft spots. Choose dark green slender zucchini that have shiny skins.

Benefits of Zucchini

Zucchini contains sufficient amounts of vitamins A and C, potassium, and a fair amount of vitamins B1, B2, and niacin.

QUICK ZUCCHINI SAUTE

2 tbsp. olive oil
1 tbsp. minced garlic
1 lb. zucchini, cut into large matchsticks
2 tbsp. minced parsley
Salt and pepper to taste

Heat skillet until hot, then add oil and sauté garlic for 5 seconds or until the aroma of the garlic is released. Add zucchini at once. Stir-fry over high heat until limp, but still crunchy and tender inside, about 30 seconds or more. Season and toss. Sprinkle with parsley, season to taste with salt and pepper, and serve.

Yield: 2 to 3 servings
Preparation Time: 2 minutes

SAUTEED BRAISED ZUCCHINI WITH NUTTY PINE NUT MISO

2 tbsp. cooking oil
1 tbsp. minced garlic
1 tsp. chopped ginger
1 onion, cut into small dice
2 lb. zucchini, cut into 1-inch half-moon shapes
3 tbsp. white miso
2 tbsp. water
4 tbsp. natural sweetener
½ tbsp. sesame oil
⅓ cup roasted pine nuts

Heat wok until hot. Add 1 tablespoon of oil, then fry garlic, ginger, and onion together. Sauté until transparent. Remove from wok and set aside to cool. Return wok to the heat, add remaining tablespoon of oil, and sauté zucchini lightly over high heat until soft, about 1 minute. Return garlic and onion mixture to wok and toss quickly. Combine miso, water, sweetener, and sesame oil until dissolved, then pour over the zucchini mixture. Over medium heat, cook zucchini until miso seasoning is absorbed, about 2 to 3 minutes. Add pine nuts and toss. Serve hot or at room temperature.

Yield: 4 to 5 servings
Preparation Time: 7 minutes

Soups

Soup is a wonderful thing to eat any time of the day—in the morning, for lunch, for dinner, or for late night snacks. From hearty warming soups in the winter to cool refreshing soups in the lazy, hot summer, they reflect the seasonal changes and provide comfort and satisfaction year-round. You will find that soup making is an easy process, and basic soup stocks are simple and nutritious. All you need is water, seasonings, and one or a combination of vegetables, legumes, and grains. Select the best and freshest vegetables you find in the market, and create your own recipes. The following chapter contains quite a few excellent soup recipes. I hope you enjoy making them as well as tasting them.

Basic Soup Stocks

Soup stocks can be prepared ahead of time and stored in the refrigerator for convenience. Some of the nutrients will be destroyed by the long cooking process, but don't worry, plenty of nutrients and digestive aids remain, including the protease inhibitors contained in grains and legumes, minerals, and some vitamins.

DASHI (JAPANESE BASIC SOUP STOCK)

This simple stock is made from kelp (*kombu*), and can be prepared in a very short amount of time. It is tasty and nutritious, as well as versatile. Add this to your basic recipe list and have the ingredients handy for your convenience. The Japanese say that eating kelp will give you beautiful skin, hair, and nails.

2 cups cold water
1 4 x 4-inch piece kombu

Wipe kombu lightly with a damp cloth. Combine kelp with water in a pot, then place over high heat. Bring water to a boil, cook for one minute or more, then remove kombu from the stock. Cool the stock for later use, saving kombu for another purpose. Store for up to four days in the refrigerator.

Yield: 2 cups
Preparation Time: 2 minutes

PRESEASONED DASHI

This simply wonderful tasty soup stock is made from kombu and sometimes shiitake mushrooms. Shiitake mushrooms give a distinctive aroma and taste. This stock is the foundation of various sauces, soups, stocks, and dressings. It is very handy to have a basic nonfat, convenient stock base. Practice this until you master the method. This stock will keep for up to four days in the refrigerator.

5 cups water
4 to 5 dried shiitake
1 5 x 5-inch piece kombu
2½ tbsp. all-purpose soy sauce
3½ tbsp. mirin

Soak dry shiitake in warm water for 3 hours. Remove shiitake from soaking liquid. Combine shiitake liquid and all other ingredients in a pot. Bring to a boil, then remove kombu, setting aside for later use. Remove pot from heat and cool stock. Stock is then ready to use. Kombu and shiitake can be used for other dishes.

Yield: 5⅓ cups
Preparation Time: 3 hours (including soaking time)

PRESEASONED BASIC STOCK

This is a another type of basic stock that is much richer than dashi or preseasoned dashi, but is also easy to prepare. As you can see by the ingredient list, this stock has many more ingredients than other basic stocks. This stock has salty, bitter, nutty, sweet, and pungent tastes all in one. It also lasts for up to four or five days in the refrigerator.

> **3 slices fresh ginger root**
> **5 medium dried shiitake**
> **6 scallions, cut into 2-inch lengths**
> **2 carrots, coarsely cut**
> **½ tsp. salt**
> **1 4 x 4-inch piece kombu**
> **2 tsp. soy sauce**
> **¼ tsp. natural sweetener or rice syrup**
> **1 tsp. mirin**
> **½ tsp. sesame oil**
> **5 cups water**

In a pot, boil all the ingredients together first, then simmer for 30 to 45 minutes over low heat, skimming continuously. Strain stock, reserving vegetables for later use. Stock is then ready to use or store in the refrigerator.

> **Yield: 4 cups**
> **Preparation Time: 45 minutes**

VEGETARIAN BASIC STOCK

This is one of the most wonderful, full-flavored soup stocks that is used by Chinese vegetarian restaurants. I obtained this secret recipe from a Chinese chef. Making this soup stock in a large quantity gives superior results to making small amounts. For a darker color soup stock, use mushroom soy sauce instead of soy sauce and reduce the amount of salt.

¼ cup dried don-gou or shiitake stems
5 to 6 whole shiitake mushrooms
½ cup fresh mushroom stems
¼ cup raw peanuts
½ cup soybeans
1 cup mixture of carrots, turnips, cabbage, cauliflower
   or celery, coarsely chopped
7 cups water
Pinch salt
Pinch pepper
2 tbsp. soy sauce
2 tbsp. nutritional yeast

Combine all the vegetables in a pot and add water. Bring to a boil, then lower the heat to simmer. Cook for 2 hours over very low heat, skimming continuously. Strain broth, keeping vegetables for other recipes. Season broth with salt, pepper, and soy sauce, if needed. Add nutritional yeast for a richer flavor.

Yield: 6 cups
Preparation Time: 2 hours

Miso Soup

When I was young, I used to wake to the wonderful smell of miso in the morning. The smell of certain foods and the memories of youth are hard to separate, even after three decades. I'm sure many of us have memories of wonderful aromas associated with experiences—the smell of oven-baked bread in the morning, freshly brewed coffee, or steaming-hot homemade soup. They fill the body with warmth and pleasant emotions. For me, most of the nostalgic memories come from the smell of miso, the burnt sweet scent of soy sauce, and the sour aromas of rice bran pickles—an odd combination.

Most Japanese love miso soup—the sweet mellow-tasting one is for breakfast, the aka-dashi miso soup is for lunch, and the strong red miso soup is for dinner. The old Japanese saying, "A good wife is determined by the miso soup and pickles she prepares," signifies the importance of this soup. Japanese take miso soup, rice bran pickles, and cooked rice seriously. Unfortunately, in recent years, advanced food technologies have introduced instant foods—from instant miso soup to noodles—so people can have more private time to enjoy. But this results in a loss of quality food value. Dehydrated food does not contain as much nutritional value as fresh food made from fresh ingredients.

Miso has been used in many preparations and folk remedies over the past few hundred years in Japan. It is an excellent substitute for dairy products. For example, instead of cream in mashed potatoes, cream soups, spreads, dips, or salad dressings, use a combination of shiro miso, tofu, and lemon juice or brown rice vinegar. Shiro miso combines well with baked or broiled dishes, stir-fried vegetables, soups, and many other foods. The light color, sweet taste, and creamy texture of sweet shiro miso is recommended for those who prefer mild flavorings. Aka miso is used mainly for miso soup and various marinades, pickling bases, and sauces.

The secret to miso cookery is not to overpower dishes with the strong taste and flavor of miso, but to integrate the color and flavor, balancing it with other ingredients. Most importantly, do not overcook miso in soups, especially miso soups. Once miso soup is boiled, the miso will lose its flavor and aroma. Add miso only when the stock begins to boil, then remove it from the heat before the soup boils again, and serve it piping hot.

In this book, miso is used in many areas because miso is easy to use, not fattening, economical, nutritious, and an excellent seasoning. You can have fun preparing simple, tasty, yet nutritious foods, so be creative. Why not use miso once a day? It will make your day, I'm sure.

Making Good Miso Soup

Start with good dashi or vegetable stock and quality miso. Select only good fresh vegetables for *mi*. Do not boil the soup once miso is added, and stop the cooking process before the soup begins to boil again after adding miso. Serve immediately.

Mi

The Japanese put various vegetables in their miso soup, called *mi,* which translates to "fruit, condiment, or content." You can add anything you like to your soup, but make sure it is cut into very small pieces so that it will cook quickly—remember you are making miso soup, not a vegetable stew. An average serving contains about 1 to 1½ ounces or less of added vegetables. *Mi* is merely a condiment to signify the seasonal changes in a small bowl, so use only a small amount of one of the following:

Usu-age	eggplant
tofu	green beans
cabbage	bamboo shoots
carrot	taro root
daikon	potato
squash	shiitake mushrooms
shimeji mushrooms	sweet potato
wakame seaweed	mochi
hijiki seaweed	burdock root
white turnip	Chinese cabbage
chrysanthemum leaves	

WHITE MISO SOUP

2 cups dashi stock
4 to 5 tbsp. white miso
Pinch sea salt

In a small pot, bring dashi to a boil. Cook over medium heat for 30 seconds. Using a ladle, remove ½ cup of hot soup and add miso to the soup in the ladle. Stir to dissolve, return to the pot, and stir. Taste your soup and add more miso or salt if needed. Wait until just before soup starts to boil, then remove from heat and serve immediately in individual soup bowls.

Yield: 2 servings
Preparation Time: 2 minutes

RED MISO SOUP

2 cups dashi stock
2½ to 3 tbsp. red miso

In a small pot, add dashi and bring to a boil. Cook over medium heat for 30 seconds. Using a ladle, remove ½ cup of hot soup and add miso in the ladle. Stir to dissolve, return to the pot, and stir. Taste your soup and add more miso if needed. Wait until just before the soup starts to boil, then remove from heat and serve immediately in individual soup bowls.

Yield: 2 servings
Preparation Time: 2 minutes

TOFU AND WAKAME MISO SOUP

This simple yet wonderful miso soup recipe is popular among Japanese people. Practice making this soup until you can make it without a recipe, then use your imagination to create your own favorite miso soup.

2 cups dashi
6 to 8 oz. soft tofu, cut into ⅛-inch cubes
1 oz. reconstituted wakame, cut into ¼-inch pieces
2½ to 3 tbsp. red (aka) or shiro (white) miso
1 tbsp. green onion, very finely chopped

In a small pot, combine dashi and tofu, bring to a boil, then add wakame. Cook over medium heat for 30 seconds. Using a ladle, remove ½ cup of hot soup and add miso into the ladle. Stir to dissolve, return to the pot, and stir. Taste your soup and add more miso if needed. Wait until just before the soup starts to boil, then remove from heat and serve immediately in individual soup bowls with a sprinkle of green onion on top.

Yield: 2 servings
Preparation Time: 2 minutes

ALFALFA SPROUT MISO SOUP

8 oz. tofu, cut into ⅛-inch cubes
2 cups dashi stock
1½ tbsp. red miso
½ cup alfalfa sprouts

In a pot, combine tofu and dashi and bring to a boil. Add miso, stir to dissolve, and wait until stock starts to boil again. Remove soup from heat, and pour into individual serving bowls. Place alfalfa on top and serve immediately.

Yield: 2 servings
Preparation Time: 2 minutes

Chilled Soups

CHILLED YOGURT AND RAISIN SOUP

Soy yogurt is available at selected health food stores. This is a basic chilled soup recipe. You can easily add or alter ingredients to create your own recipe.

2 tbsp. golden raisins
1 cucumber, peeled, seeded, and grated
2 cups soy yogurt, plain
¾ tsp. sea salt
⅛ tsp. black pepper
1 cup nut milk for cooking (see index)
2 tbsp. minced scallion
3 tbsp. chopped walnuts
1 tbsp. fresh minced dill

Soak raisins in very hot water for 20 minutes. Drain, discard water, and chop raisins. Mix all the ingredients in a large glass bowl. Chill for at least 2 hours before serving.

Yield: 4 servings
Preparation Time: 2 hours 20 minutes

CHILLED LEMONY AVOCADO TAHINI SOUP

Avocados not only make excellent dips and stuffing for sushi, they are also a good ingredient for cold soup. Try this unusual recipe at least once during the hot summer.

2 tbsp. minced ginger root
½ cup minced onion
4 tbsp. oil
¼ cup flour
2½ cups soy milk or nut milk
2 ripe avocados
½ tsp. salt
2 tbsp. tahini
1 tbsp. grated lemon rind

In a small pot, brown ginger and onion lightly in oil. Add flour then cook for three minutes over low heat. Gradually add 2 cups warm soy milk into the pot, stirring constantly to prevent sticking, and make a smooth paste. Bring to a boil, reduce heat to low, and simmer for 10 more minutes, until the sauce is smooth. Strain; set aside to cool.

Peel and pit avocados, combine with remaining ½ cup of soy milk, salt, and tahini, and process in a blender until completely smooth. Mix with cooled sauce. If lumpy, blend again. Add lemon rind and season to taste. More milk may be needed to adjust the consistency. Chill well and serve.

Yield: 4 servings
Preparation Time: 14 minutes

CHILLED PEACHY STRAWBERRY SOUP

This is a very refreshing soup for hot lazy summer days, and it is not too difficult to prepare, as long as you don't mind washing the food processor afterwards. If it is handy, garden fresh mint is a nice touch to add to the soup.

2 cups strawberries, sliced
2 cups apple juice
1 tbsp. lemon juice
1½ cups canned peach nectar
   (or 1 cup fresh peach pulp with ½ cup juice)
Pinch ground nutmeg
⅛ tsp. salt
½ cup Chablis
4 sprigs fresh mint

Clean strawberries by removing tops and washing well under cold runnig water. Boil strawberries with apple juice in a stainless steel pot until strawberries lose color, about 10 minutes. Add lemon juice and cook for another two minutes. Remove from heat and cool until manageable, about 10 to 15 minutes. Blend strawberries in food processor with peach nectar until completely smooth. Strain through a fine sieve. Mix with remaining ingredients. Chill and serve each bowl topped with a sprig of fresh mint if available.

Yield: 4 servings
Preparation Time: 12 minutes

Miscellaneous Soups

ONION MISO SOUP

This is an adaptation of a famous French soup, using a combination of caramelized onion, garlic, and miso to create a rich flavor. The key to success is not to burn the onion while cooking it, but to brown it with caution and care.

4 to 5 tbsp. oil
6 large onion, sliced thin
2 tbsp. minced garlic
1 leek (white part only), washed well and thinly sliced
8 cups water
Pinch whole thyme
2 bay leaves
4 to 5 tbsp. red miso
Salt and pepper to taste

Heat a large, heavy pot, add oil, and sauté onion, garlic, and leek until onions are almost caramelized, about 2 hours. Add water, thyme, and bay leaves, then simmer for one hour, skimming from time to time. Add miso, stir, and cook for another two to three minutes. Season to taste with salt and pepper, remove bay leaves, and serve in individual soup bowls.

HOT AND SOUR SOUP

This is a very popular and easy soup to make at home if you have good stock on hand. This version contains no eggs like the original. If you are adventurous, try adding strips of nori seaweed for the aroma and experience. Be sure not to boil the soup after the vinegar is added.

6 cups basic vegetarian stock
8 oz. medium tofu, cut into matchsticks
3 to 4 shiitake mushrooms, soaked,
    stems removed, and thinly sliced
1 carrot, peeled and cut into julienne
4 black fungus, soaked and cut into julienne
⅔ tsp. sea salt
2 tbsp. sake
½ tbsp. soy sauce
1 tsp. mushroom soy sauce
½ tsp. sesame oil
½ tsp. hot chili oil (see index)
3 to 4 tbsp. arrowroot powder
5 tbsp. water
2 to 3 tbsp. vinegar (rice or brown)
1 tbsp. minced green onion

Combine first eleven ingredients in a pot. Bring to a boil, skim well, and lower the heat. Cook for one minute, then thicken with arrowroot powder and water mixture, adding it slowly to the soup, stirring gently and carefully. Add vinegar, stir to combine and serve hot. Sprinkle with green onion.

Yield: 6 to 7 servings
Preparation Time: 10 minutes

MUSHROOM DUXELLE SOUP

Duxelle is a method of French sauce preparation, using mushrooms, shallots, and a lot of cream and wine. Instead of cream or milk, I have substituted a variety of nondairy ingredients. It's a great soup, and if you like, it can be used as a delicious dip or stuffing by cooling and adjusting the consistency.

 3 tbsp. oil
 ½ cup chopped onion
 1 tbsp. minced green onion (white part only)
 1 tbsp. minced garlic
 2 cups chopped mushrooms
 2 tbsp. dry white wine
 3 cups basic vegetable stock
 2 tbsp. minced parsley
 1 potato, peeled and cut into slices
 1 tbsp. white miso
 ⅓ cup Soy Milk Béchamel sauce (see index)
 1 tbsp. lemon juice

Heat heavy sauce pot, add oil, and sauté onion, green onion, and garlic until transparent. Add mushrooms and sauté for 2 to 3 more minutes or until completely soft. Add wine and reduce to almost no liquid. Add vegetable stock, 1 tablespoon parsley, and potato. Cover and continue to cook for 20 to 30 minutes. Add miso and béchamel sauce to the pot and stir well. Cook for five to ten more minutes. Season if needed, or adjust thickness with more soy milk. Serve hot with sprinkles of parsley on top.

 Yield: 4 servings
 Preparation Time: 45 minutes

CREAM OF VEGETABLE SOUP

The traditional recipe for cream of vegetable soup calls for chopped vegetables sautéed in butter and a cream sauce made with flour, butter, cream, and soup stock. That is a lot of dairy products. This soup uses none of the above. In place of butter, safflower oil is used. In place of cream, cashew butter is added. For wheat flour, brown rice is substituted. This soup is dairy-free, wheat-free, and egg-free.

3 tbsp. olive oil
1 large onion, sliced very thin
1 large bunch broccoli, chopped
2 tbsp. minced garlic
2 bay leaves, crushed
½ tbsp. ground rosemary
¼ tsp. ground thyme
½ tsp. basil
4 cups soup stock or water
2 tsp. cashew butter
Pinch cayenne
Salt or tamari to taste
½ cup cooked brown rice

In a large sauce pot, sauté onion until soft. Add broccoli and garlic, then sauté until broccoli becomes bright green in color. Place crushed bay leaf in cheese cloth, then tie and add to the pot with remaining spices, except salt and cayenne pepper. Add water or stock and bring to a boil. Lower heat to simmer, and cook for 20 minutes. Remove from heat and cool, lifting out bay leaf in cheesecloth. Pour soup into a blender with the rice and process until smooth. When puréed thoroughly, return to pot and reheat gently. Taste for seasoning, add cashew butter, cayenne pepper, and salt or tamari to flavor. Serve hot.

Yield: 4 servings
Preparation Time: 28 minutes

AZUKI BEAN SOUP

The Azuki bean is an important ingredient in basic macrobiotic cooking. In Japan, where I grew up, I occasionally ate *zenzai,* sweet cooked azuki beans in a syrupy soup with mochi. I wasn't crazy about the soup, but many Japanese girls really love it. Of course, I did not know anything about the nutritional value of this highly praised food either. There are many Zenzai specialty shops in Japan, and they are always busy. Salt makes the protein in beans harder, so they take longer to cook. When cooking beans, add salt seasonings at the last minute.

>   **2 tbsp. oil**
>   **1 cup finely minced onion**
>   **1 tsp. minced garlic**
>   **½ tsp. minced ginger roots**
>   **1½ cup azuki beans**
>   **6 cups water or vegetable stock**
>   **1 6 x 6-inch piece dashi kombu**
>   **Pinch sea salt**
>   **5 tbsp. red miso**
>   **1 tbsp. white miso**

In a large pot, sauté onion, garlic, and ginger until soft. Add azuki beans and water. Bring liquid to a boil, skimming constantly. Simmer until beans are completely soft. Add kombu and a pinch of salt, then cook for another 5 minutes. Remove kelp from the pot, add red and white miso, and stir gently to blend miso into soup. Serve very hot.

>   **Yield: 6 servings**
>   **Preparation Time: 1 hour 25 minutes**

LENTIL AND SWISS CHARD SOUP

This soup, packed with quality protein and calcium, is a wonderful combination. Leave it overnight if you can; this will definitely increase the flavor.

3 tbsp. olive oil
1 cup minced onion
1 tbsp. minced garlic
¼ cup minced cilantro
Pinch whole cumin
8 cups vegetable stock
1 potato, peeled, cubed in large chunks
2 blanched Swiss chard, cut crosswise
    into ½-inch slices
½ cups lentils, sorted and washed
½ tbsp. ground coriander
Pinch salt
Pinch pepper
3 to 4 tbsp. lemon juice
2 tbsp. grated lemon peel

In a medium-size saucepan, sauté onion in olive oil until golden. Add garlic, cilantro, and cumin, and sauté for two minutes. Add stock, potato, Swiss chard, and lentils to the pot. Cover and simmer over medium heat until lentils are tender. Add coriander, salt, and pepper, and cook for another five minutes. Taste for seasoning, then add lemon juice and grated lemon peel. Serve hot.

Yield: 6 or 7 servings
Preparation Time: 35 to 45 minutes

PISTOU

A famous French soup, hearty pistou is not so easy to prepare and takes a more time than other soups. If you want to enjoy good food and good company, invite your friends over and prepare a huge pot of soup. I wonder why all the guests, without exception, congregate in the kitchen and prefer to stay there during a party. I guess that people feel more at ease and comfortable being in the kitchen, smelling the food, instead of being in the living room with strangers. It is true that in the atmosphere created by a comfortable kitchen and food, a stranger becomes an old friend in no time. You don't have to spend the whole time in the kitchen. Do something else enjoyable with your friends, but be sure to check your soup once in a while, or send a friend in to stir it. After it is done, enjoy the soup and company. The leftovers can be stored in the freezer for another occasion.

1½ cups navy beans
2 tbsp. olive oil
2 cups minced onion
1 cup minced celery
3 zucchini, thinly sliced
3 carrots, thinly sliced
8 cups vegetable stock
2 bay leaves
¼ tsp. savory
¼ tsp. black pepper
2 tsp. salt
1 12-oz. pkg. frozen lima beans

Pistou Sauce

2 cups fresh basil leaves
3 tbsp. minced garlic
3 tbsp. tahini
½ cup water
½ cup olive oil

Soak navy beans overnight. The next day, drain water and wash well, set aside. In a large heavy pot, heat oil and sauté onion and celery until tender. Add zucchini and carrots, cook another 5 minutes or so, then remove vegetables from pot and set aside. Add navy beans, stock, and seasonings except salt to a pot, then bring to a boil. Simmer over low heat for 45 to 50 minutes, or until navy beans are cooked. Return vegetables to the pot along with lima beans, and simmer for another hour over low heat. Add salt and adjust seasonings.

For pistou, place all the ingredients in a food processor or blender and blend until smooth. Remove to a glass container with a lid. The sauce will keep for quite a while if refrigerated. Use 1 tablespoon of pistou on top of each serving of piping hot soup.

Yield: 8 servings
Preparation Time: 2 hours

FARMER'S HEARTY CHESTNUTS AND BARLEY SOUP

This is an old recipe that I have kept a long time. It came from a Japanese farmer's family, and although it has been altered a bit, it is still a good hearty soup.

> 3 oz. barley
> 2 oz. dried chestnuts, soaked for 3 hours
> 1 oz. millet
> 3 tbsp. olive oil
> ½ tsp. minced garlic
> ¼ carrot, cut into large dice
> 1 stalk celery, cut into large dice
> 1 onion, cut into large dice
> 2 red peppers, seeded and cut into large dice
> 5 cups water
> 2 tomatoes, peeled and diced
> Pinch salt
> Pinch pepper
> 2 tbsp. minced fresh coriander leaves

Boil barley, chestnuts, and millet in hot water separately until tender; drain and set aside. Heat a saucepan, add oil, and sauté garlic and all vegetables except tomatoes until transparent. Add water, chestnuts, barley, and millet, then bring to a boil. Cook for 10 to 12 minutes over medium-low heat, add tomatoes, salt, and pepper, then continue to cook for 5 more minutes. Add more salt and pepper if needed. Sprinkle minced coriander leaves on top of the soup before serving. Serve hot or cold.

> **Yield: 4 servings**
> **Preparation Time: 20 minutes**

NUTTY AND PUNGENT CURRIED PEANUT SOUP

This is a spicy soup already, but you may want to add more chilies. It is up to you. You will enjoy the pungent nutty aroma that fills your whole kitchen when you prepare this soup. If you are tall, be especially careful because the aroma of hot spices rises high in the air, and your nose may get burned. Also, be aware that curry is credited with increasing sex drive in women.

4 tbsp. olive oil
1 onion, chopped
1 carrot, chopped fine
1 stalk celery, chopped fine
½ apple, grated
1 tbsp. minced garlic
1 tsp. grated ginger root
2 large dried chilies
2 tbsp. whole wheat flour
2 tbsp. curry powder or paste
5 cups vegetable stock
½ cup chopped tomato
¼ cup peanut butter
¼ cup cooked brown rice
Salt and pepper to taste
2 tbsp. molasses
4 tbsp. roasted peanuts, chopped
2 tbsp. minced cilantro

Heat oil in a medium-size sauce pan. Sauté onion, carrot, celery, apple, garlic, and ginger for five minutes over high heat until all the vegetables turn light brown. Lower heat to medium, add chilies, and cook for 2 minutes. Add flour and curry powder to the pan. Cook for 2 more minutes, stirring frequently. Next, add stock to the pot, and raise heat to high. Add tomato and peanut butter, and bring to a boil. Lower heat, cover, and simmer for 20 minutes. Add rice and simmer for another five minutes, stirring occasionally. At the last minute, add salt and pepper to taste. If you prefer, blend the soup in processor or blender and adjust consistency with more soup stock. Serve with chopped peanuts and minced cilantro on top.

Yield: 5 to 6 servings
Preparation Time: 35 minutes

Salads and Stewed Dishes

Colorful salad dishes are always welcome and can even distract you from boring company or dull conversation. Salad doesn't give you indigestion, criticism, gossip, or headaches. A well combined and thoughtfully arranged salad is a simple art by itself, and much better for your health than unpleasant company. Stay away from bad thoughts and bad company, and be sure to eat lots of salad. The following pages include nutritional information on salad ingredients and on complementary additions to salad.

Sprouts

Sprouts are rabbit food and much more! There are several kinds of sprouts available in North America: alfalfa, chickpea, buckwheat, wheat, barley, oat, azuki, and many more. Sprouts are easy to cultivate at home if you have time and space. Otherwise, you can purchase them in health food stores or supermarkets. If you are growing sprouts at home, constantly keep all the equipment clean to maintain the excellent nutritional quality of the sprouts. If you are cooking sprouts, be cautious because vitamins C and B1 are water soluble and easily destroyed by heat. To minimize nutrient loss, do not soak sprouts in water for long periods of time and do not overcook them.

When shopping for sprouts, avoid any that are soft, mushy, or smell bad. Choose those with moist and tender tips. If the sprouts are sold in plastic bags or containers, look closely to check for freshness—especially at the tips. The shorter the sprouts, the more tender they will be. There are several kinds of sprouts that you can grow in your home. Some are relatively easy; others take a little longer to grow. These are the sprouts I recommend to grow in your home: alfalfa, land cress, mung bean, sesame, green peas, daikon, soba, buckwheat, soybean, brown lentil, and black chickpeas. All the legumes, seeds, and groats are available at natural food stores.

Benefits of Sprouts

Sprouts are an excellent source of various nutrients, including 1½ times the protein of wheat, vitamins C, A, E, D, B1, and B2, niacin, pantothenic acid, calcium, iron, and chlorophyll. High alkaline foods counteract acids produced by acidic foods and toxins created by stresses and worries of everyday life. Sprouts are very alkaline, which is good news for those who consume acidic foods such as meat, cheese, eggs, and sugar. Sprouts work to relieve fatigue and constipation; help to grow strong healthy hair and nails; and have a calming effect on the nerves.

MIXED SPROUT SALAD

Spouts are an almost perfect food, yet they are reasonable to purchase. If you can find fresh sprouts, make a habit of eating them every day. For a complete meal, add your favorite seeds and nuts on top of the salad, and serve with good whole wheat bread and cashew or almond butter.

½ apple
1 cup alfalfa sprouts
1 cup mung bean sprouts
1 cup soybean sprouts
2 oz. mushrooms, sliced thin
1 head butter lettuce
3 tbsp. plain soy yogurt
1 tbsp. grated onion
½ tsp. prepared mustard
½ tsp. lemon juice
Pinch salt
Pinch pepper to taste

Core apple, slice thin, and soak in water with lemon juice until just before serving. Wash and drain sprouts, mushrooms, and lettuce. Mix all remaining ingredients together, then toss with salad ingredients.

Yield: 4 servings
Preparation Time: 10 minutes

SAUTEED SPROUT SALAD

A variety of sprouts are recommended for those who have weak nails or hair, constipation problems, nutritional deficiencies, or a nervous and jumpy constitution. This unusual type of salad can be prepared ahead of time and is very tasty.

1 cup soybean sprouts
1½ tbsp. oil
1 tsp. minced ginger
2 fresh large shiitake, sliced thin
1 tbsp. soy sauce
¼ small onion, cut paper thin
1 small cucumber, cut into matchsticks
1 small carrot, cut into julienne
½ tsp. sesame oil
1 tbsp. brown rice vinegar
1 tbsp. soy sauce
1 tsp. prepared English mustard

Boil bean sprouts, then cool and drain and set aside. Heat a frying pan, then sauté ginger with ½ tablespoon oil until aroma is released. Add shiitake and sauté quickly, seasoning with soy sauce. Set aside. In the same pan, add 1 tablespoon of oil, onion, cucumber, and carrot. Sauté quickly over high heat. Set aside to cool. Mix all the remaining ingredients together. Make a dressing by combining sesame oil, brown rice vinegar, soy sauce, and mustard. Toss the cooked salad ingredients with the salad dressing.

Yield: 2 servings
Preparation Time: 10 minutes

PUNGENT DAIKON SPROUTS ROLLED IN NORI

Daikon or *lo bok* radish sprouts are rolled in a roasted sheet of nori and eaten with a dipping sauce. This way, you can eat a lot of sprouts in one meal. It is easy, simple, and nutritious; but most importantly, it's delicious. Daikon sprouts (*kaiware daikon*) are available in Japanese grocery stores in clear plastic, and have a slightly bitter taste similar to the western type of radish. I recommend this dish along with a high protein meal such as tofu with grains and seeds or nuts on top. The enzymes in the sprouts will help digest the protein in tofu and grains.

2 oz. daikon sprouts
3 1 x 3-inch pieces roasted nori
1 tbsp. tamari
1 tbsp. brown rice vinegar

Remove the roots of the sprouts (about ½-inch), then wash and dry with paper towels. Divide into three bunches. Roll nori around the stems of sprouts, and place on a plate. Combine tamari and brown rice vinegar to make dipping sauce. Serve dipping sauce on the side, and dip the ends of the sprouts rolls into the sauce before eating.

Yield: 3 rolls
Preparation Time: 5 minutes

KOREAN-STYLE SPROUTS SALAD

Koreans eat a lot of garlic and chilies. This dish combines spicy, pungent, bitter, sour, nutty, salty, and sweet flavors to make a well-balanced sauce to accompany plain sprouts. When a recipe suggests grating an ingredient, don't chop it or use a food processor. Grating foods like ginger, garlic, or green onion increases their pungency or bitterness.

1 cup soybean sprouts
1 small carrot, cut into julienne
½ small cucumber, cut into julienne
½ tbsp. tamari
1 tsp. raw natural sweetener or other sweetener
1 tbsp. brown rice vinegar
¼ tsp. grated ginger
1 tbsp. sesame oil
1 tbsp. grated onion
¼ tsp. grated garlic
½ tbsp. lemon juice
Dash hot chili oil

Blanch soybean sprouts quickly; remove and cool. Mix with carrot and cucumber and set aside. Combine remaining ingredients, then toss all vegetables with sauce. Chill for 1 hour before serving.

> **Yield: 2 servings**
> **Preparation Time: 1 hour 10 minutes (including chilling time)**

ALFALFA OHITASHI

Ohitashi means "dipped things" in Japanese, and are foods generally dipped in a soy and dashi-based sauce just before serving. Spinach ohitashi is a popular dish in Japan. Spinach and sesame seeds are an excellent combination, not only for their nutritional combination, but for the nutty rich flavor that sesame seeds add to the rather plain taste of spinach. This dish, which uses alfalfa sprouts instead of spinach, takes only about thirty seconds to prepare. If you wish, present it in your favorite serving dish to make it more elaborate.

> **1 cup alfalfa sprouts**
> **2 tbsp. roasted white sesame seeds**
> **1 tbsp. tamari**
> **1 tbsp. brown rice vinegar**
> **1 tbsp. dashi**

Wash sprouts well, then drain and place in bowl. Sprinkle with sesame seeds. Just before serving, mix tamari, vinegar, and dashi and pour over the alfalfa sprouts.

> **Yield: 1 serving**
> **Preparation Time: 2 minutes**

Other Salad Ideas

MOROCCAN SALAD

This elaborate salad needs a little bit of attention and preparation, but the result is well worth the effort. Sprinkle with minced parsley, or if you have fresh mint leaves handy, use them to decorate the top of the dish.

2 whole green peppers
2 whole red peppers
6 whole large ripe tomatoes
½ cup olive oil
4 to 5 tbsp. lemon juice
1 tbsp. minced garlic
3 tbsp. minced parsley
½ tsp. ground cumin
1 tsp. natural sweetener
Salt and fresh ground pepper to taste
4 whole Japanese eggplants
½ red onion, sliced thin
10 black olives, sliced
2 tbsp. minced parsley or fresh mint leaves
1 tsp. ground coriander
½ tsp. paprika
Pinch cayenne pepper

Roast both red and green peppers whole in a hot oven until dark brown. Remove, then place in a paper bag to cool. Shake well, then remove from the bag. Peel off skins, remove seeds, and cut into strips. Peel tomatoes, remove seeds, and cut into chunks. Combine tomatoes with oil, lemon juice, garlic, 3 tablespoons parsley, cumin, natural sweetener, and salt and pepper to taste. Leave for one hour.

Cook eggplants in 375-degree oven until soft, approximately 10 to 12 minutes. Cut lengthwise into slices, then season the eggplant with coriander, paprika, and cayenne pepper. Arrange eggplant on a platter, then cover with dressing and pepper strips. Decorate with very thinly sliced red onion and black olives, and top with minced parsley or mint leaves.

Yield: 5 to 6 servings
Preparation Time: 1 hour

MARINATED GREEN BEANS

2 lb. green beans, trimmed and cut into 2-inch lengths
1 tsp. minced garlic
½ tsp. salt
2 whole fresh lemons, juice only
¼ cup olive oil
Black pepper to taste
1 medium tomato, chopped

Cook beans in boiling water until tender but still crisp. In a salad bowl, combine remaining ingredients, except tomatoes. Pour over the warm green beans and toss gently. Refrigerate until cold. Toss tomatoes in just before serving.

Yield: 4 servings
Preparation Time: 5 minutes

WAKAME AND CUCUMBER SALAD

Wakame and cucumbers are a refreshing combination that appears on most Japanese tables nearly every day during the long, hot summer.

½ small Japanese cucumber
½ tsp. salt
½ oz. dried wakame (or 1 oz. salted seaweed)
3 tbsp. brown rice vinegar
3 tbsp. soy sauce
1 tsp. natural sweetener or other sweetener
1 tsp. mirin or sake

Remove the ends of the cucumber, and slice paper thin. Put in a bowl, sprinkle with salt and rub in lightly. Add water to cover, and set aside for 20 minutes. Soak the wakame in lukewarm water for 10 minutes. Drain and squeeze out the water, then chop coarsely. Drain the cucumber and pat dry. Combine the remaining ingredients in a small saucepan, heat to dissolve natural sweetener, then remove from heat and chill. Combine cucumber and wakame with the cold dressing just before serving. Toss gently and serve in individual bowls.

Yield: 1 serving
Preparation Time: 25 minutes

ZUCCHINI AND WAKAME SALAD

Wakame means "young shoots" in Japanese. It is the most used seaweed, and it is wonderful in soup for breakfast, in salad at lunch, or sautéed or cooked in different styles. It is an excellent source of calcium, iron, iodine, and other important minerals. In Japan, we have a saying: "Black hair is the origin of all beauty and health." To have beautiful hair and a good complexion, eat seaweed every day.

½ oz. dried wakame
2 tbsp. sea salt
1 lb. zucchini, thinly sliced into circles
2 tbsp. brown rice vinegar
2 tbsp. soy sauce
1 tsp. natural sweetener or other sweetener
2 tbsp. white roasted sesame seeds, chopped
Pinch sea salt

Soak wakame until soft, then drain, removing excess water by squeezing. Remove core and chop into ⅓-inch lengths. Set aside. Sprinkle salt over sliced zucchini, rub lightly, and leave for 30 minutes. Wash zucchini well under cold water to remove salt, drain, and squeeze out excess water. Combine all remaining ingredients and mix well. Toss thoroughly with zucchini and wakame. Chill for 10 minutes and serve.

Yield: 2 servings
Preparation Time: 40 minutes

GREEN PAPAYA SALAD

If you can get fresh cilantro leaves, mince them and add them to your salad. They will bring out the refreshing exotic flavor of this dish.

1 tbsp. tamari
1 tbsp. natural sweetener
2 cloves garlic, minced
Pinch cayenne pepper
1 tsp. lemon or lime juice
2 tomatoes, diced
1 green papaya, peeled and shredded
¼ tsp. salt

In a mixing bowl, combine tamari, natural sweetener, garlic, cayenne pepper, and lemon juice to make a sauce. Stir in tomatoes and salt, then toss very lightly. Add papaya, toss, and serve.

Yield: 2 servings
Preparation Time: 5 minutes

AVOCADO, TOMATO, AND TOFU SALAD

2 tbsp. wine vinegar
¼ tsp. sea salt
Fresh ground pepper to taste
8 tbsp. olive oil
1 tsp. minced garlic
½ tsp. chili powder
2 ripe avocados, peeled, pitted, and diced
8 oz. firm tofu, diced
2 large tomatoes, diced
1 small onion, minced
10 stuffed pimento olives
½ head lettuce, separated into leaves

Combine first six ingredients, then toss with remaining salad ingredients except lettuce. Chill for 30 minutes. Serve over lettuce leaves.

Yield: 3 servings
Preparation Time: 30 minutes

UDON OR SOBA SALAD

Usually Asians eat cold noodles with cold dipping sauce regardless of the season. You can pinpoint the Asians in a large restaurant by listening for the slurping noise when they eat their noodles, even though there may be many other people on the premises. It is considered impolite for a westerner to slurp noodles or to make noise while eating them, but it is not for Asians. There are two good reasons for slurping: slurping cools off the hot soup faster than blowing on it; and noodles must be eaten while they still have "teeth bite," which translates to *al dente*. Overcooked noodles and cold soup that is supposed to be hot are considered worthless to an Asian. They can often finish a whole bowl of noodles, slurping and blowing on the hot soup, in couple of minutes flat, and they are on their way out. They eat very, very quickly.

> 1½ cups green beans or broccoli,
>   cut into small dice
> ¼ cup white miso
> 4 tbsp. dashi or water
> 3 tbsp. brown rice vinegar
> 8 oz. dried udon or soba, parboiled and drained
> 1 small cucumber, peeled and sliced
> 1 scallion, finely minced
> 1 sheet nori, shredded
> 2 tbsp. roasted sesame seeds, chopped

Steam or blanch green beans or broccoli until tender, set aside to cool. Combine miso, dashi, and vinegar to make a sauce. Cut noodles into 3-inch lengths, then toss in with sauce and green beans or broccoli, cucumber, and scallion. Chill and garnish with nori and sesame seeds, then serve.

> **Yield: 4 servings**
> **Preparation Time: 10 minutes**

ARMENIAN SALAD

2 tbsp. minced fresh mint
½ tsp. ground cumin
3 tbsp. olive oil
2 tbsp. lemon juice
Salt and freshly ground black pepper to taste
2 tomatoes, seeded and diced
1 green pepper, seeded and diced
1 medium cucumber, peeled and diced
½ cup sliced celery
2 scallions, minced
½ cup parsley, minced
½ head Romaine lettuce, separated into leaves

Combine mint, cumin, oil, lemon juice, salt, and pepper. Combine all the vegetables, except lettuce, and gently toss with dressing. Serve on lettuce leaves.

Yield: 4 servings
Preparation Time: 5 minutes

CUCUMBER AND ALMOND SALAD

1 English or 3 medium Japanese cucumbers,
    peeled, seeded, and diced
½ cup ground toasted slivered almonds
¼ cup olive oil
1 tbsp. lemon juice
1 tsp. minced garlic
Salt and freshly ground pepper to taste
2 tbsp. minced parsley
½ head lettuce, separated into leaves

Combine all ingredients together, except lettuce, toss thoroughly. Cover and refrigerate until well chilled. Serve on lettuce leaves.

Yield: 3 servings
Preparation Time: 5 minutes

Nonfat Dressings

PON-ZU DRESSING (CITRUS DRESSING)

½ cup dashi
1 tbsp. lemon juice or brown rice vinegar
1½ tbsp. soy sauce
1 3 x 3-inch piece kombu

Mix all ingredients in a glass jar. Allow to sit overnight, then remove kombu.

Yield: ½ cup

SOY VINEGAR DRESSING

2 tbsp. dashi
2 tsp. vinegar
1½ tbsp. soy sauce

Combine all ingredients. Store in an airtight container.

Yield: ¼ cup

NI-HAIZU DRESSING

½ cup rice vinegar
2 tbsp. thin soy sauce
2 tsp. mirin

Combine all ingredients. Store in an airtight jar.

Yield: Almost ¾ cup

SU-NO-MONO VINEGAR DRESSING

2 tbsp. rice vinegar
2 tsp. boiled mirin
⅕ tsp. sea salt
1 tsp. soy sauce
2 tsp. dashi

Mix all ingredients together well.

Yield: 5 tablespoons

GREEN VINEGAR DRESSING

1 very small Japanese cucumber
1½ tbsp. rice vinegar
½ tbsp. lemon juice
2 tsp. natural sweetener
¼ tsp. salt
¼ tsp. lemon rind, grated

Grate cucumber, squeeze out juice. Combine and mix all ingredients.

Yield: ½ cup

UME-SU DRESSING
(PLUM VINEGAR DRESSING)

2 tbsp. umeboshi vinegar
1 tbsp. soy sauce
1 tbsp. dashi
1 tsp. natural sweetener or maple syrup

Mix all ingredients together well.

Yield: 5 tablespoons

AMAZU (SWEET VINEGAR) DRESSING

½ cup rice vinegar
2 tbsp. natural sweetener
½ cups mirin

Combine all ingredients. Store in an airtight jar.

Yield: 1 cup

KOMBU DRESSING

½ cup soaking liquid of kombu
¼ cup soy sauce
½ tsp. salt
¼ cup lemon juice
¼ cup green onion, chopped

Combine all ingredients in a bowl and chill for 30 minutes.

Yield: 1¼ cup

SESAME VINEGAR DRESSING

2 tbsp. roasted sesame seeds
⅓ tsp. sea salt
1 tsp. natural sweetener
1 tsp. soy sauce
1 tbsp. rice vinegar
1 tbsp. dashi

Grind the sesame with sea salt in a Japanese mortar. Combine with all remaining ingredients and mix well. Use immediately or store in an airtight container.

Yield: 5 tablespoons

NAN-BAN-ZU (FOREIGNER) DRESSING

In Japan, this dressing is used for marinating vegetables.

½ whole dried chili
1½ tbsp. mirin
1½ tbsp. brown rice vinegar
⅕ tsp. sea salt
1 tsp. dashi

Remove seeds from chili, then cut into very fine strips. Heat all remaining ingredients. Pour mixture into bowl to cool. Mix with chili. Allow to sit at room temperature in a glass container for 2 to 3 hours.

Yield: 3 tablespoons

SANBAI-ZU DRESSING

½ cup rice vinegar
1½ tbsp. natural sweetener
½ tsp. soy sauce
½ tsp. sea salt

Combine all ingredients. Store in an airtight jar.

Yield: ½ cup

GOMA-SU (SESAME VINEGAR) DRESSING

3 tbsp. roasted sesame seeds
⅓ cup Sanbai-Zu Dressing
4 tbsp. mirin

Chop sesame seeds with a knife until fine. Mix with other ingredients.

Yield: ½ cup

Stewed Dishes

Because stewing is considered an advanced technique in a professional kitchen, I have separated stewed dishes into this section. Stews are a hearty warm idea in the cold winter, and are also amazingly good in hot weather.

NISHIME

Nishime is a typical Japanese-style braised vegetable stew. For best flavor, try to cook it a day in advance and reheat it just before serving. Substitute other fresh root vegetables if the listed ingredients are not available at the market. Other seasonings should remain more or less the same.

> 2 burdock root
> 5 cups water
> 1 tbsp. vinegar
> 1 large carrot
> 1 small section lotus root
> 4 small taro roots
> 2 oz. boiled bamboo shoots
> 3 dried shiitake, soaked for 2 hours
> 5 to 6 snow peas
> 1 cup dashi
> 2 tbsp. mirin
> ¼ cup soy sauce
> 1 tbsp. sake

Peel burdock root, cut into 1-inch lengths, and place in water with vinegar for 30 minutes. Boil burdock root for 2 to 3 minutes, drain, and set aside for later use. Cut carrot lengthwise in half, then into ½-inch slices across. Cut lotus root into ½-inch-thick half-moon shapes. Peel taro root, blanch, drain, and set aside. Cut bamboo shoots into bite-size pieces; set aside. Remove stems from shiitake and discard. Blanch snow peas, then cut in half.

Place all the prepared vegetables, except snow peas, in a pot. Add dashi, mirin, soy sauce, and sake. Boil ingredients with a dropped lid. Simmer for 30 minutes over low heat. Toss snow peas in at last minute, just before serving.

Yield: 5 servings
Preparation Time: 1 hour

VEGETABLE STEW WITH DUMPLINGS

The term *dumpling* is not an attractive expression when you pay attention to the sound of the word; but most people know how dumplings taste, so here you are.

Stew

2 tbsp. oil
½ onion, diced
5 to 6 oz. mushrooms, cut in half
2 small potatoes, peeled and cut in half
3 cups vegetable stock
1½ cups soy milk
1 tsp. lemon juice
2 tbsp. white wine
1 bay leaf

Dumplings

1½ cups all-purpose flour
¾ tsp. baking powder
1 cup or more soy milk
¼ tsp. salt
¼ tsp. pepper
1 tbsp. oil
½ tbsp. parsley, minced

Heat a saucepan, add oil, and sauté onions until soft and transparent. Add mushrooms and potatoes, and sauté for 1 more minute. Add vegetable stock to pot, then bring to a boil. Lower heat, add remaining stew ingredients, and cook until potatoes are soft.

While stew is beginning to cook, make the dumplings. Sift flour and baking powder together. In a bowl, combine soy milk, salt, pepper, oil, and parsley. Add flour mix to the bowl. Stir vigorously to make dough. Adjust consistency by adding more soy milk if required. Roll into bite-size balls. Bring water to a boil, then add dumplings. When dumplings rise to the surface, immediately remove from water and cool. Add dumplings to boiling stew in the pot, stir, cook for 4 minutes, then serve.

Yield: 4 servings
Preparation Time: 30 minutes

VEGETABLE TAGINE

The famous Moroccan meat dish *tagine* is one that I have altered to make a vegetarian meal. If you think the spices are overpowering, use less or none at all. Again, this dish is better eaten the next day.

3 tbsp. olive oil
2 onions, cut into chunks
1 tbsp. minced garlic
4 carrots, peeled and cut into chunks
2 cups vegetable stock or water
3 celery sticks, cut into large chunks
1 cucumber, cut into chunks
10 peppercorns, crushed lightly
5 whole cloves
1 cinnamon sticks
½ tsp. whole cumin
1½ tsp. sea salt
4 ripe tomatoes, cut into large pieces
1 lb. zucchini, cut into large chunks
1 tbsp. couserie d'harrisa

Couserie D'harrisa

> 2 tbsp. cayenne pepper
> 1 tbsp. cumin
> 2 tbsp. minced garlic
> ½ tsp. sea salt
> 1 cup olive oil

First make the couserie d'harrisa by grinding its ingredients, except olive oil, in a mortar until a smooth paste is formed. Then add olive oil and cook for five minutes, stirring constantly. Keep refrigerated in an airtight container.

Heat a large pot, add oil, and sauté onion, garlic, and carrots for 2 minutes. Add stock and celery; cook for 10 more minutes. Add remaining ingredients and cook an additional 20 minutes, skimming often. Remove cinnamon sticks, then serve with steamed rice or couscous.

> **Yield: 6 to 8 servings**
> **Preparation Time: 45 minutes**

ARMENIAN VEGETABLE CASSEROLE

> ½ cup olive oil
> 1 cup parsley, chopped
> ½ cup fresh basil, chopped
> Pinch salt
> Pinch pepper
> 3 Japanese eggplants, sliced into ½-inch rounds
> 3 zucchini, sliced into ½-inch rounds
> 3 carrots, sliced lengthwise
> 1 green pepper, cut in julienne
> 4 large tomatoes, sliced
> 3 tbsp. minced garlic

Brush a shallow baking pan with oil. Mix remaining oil with chopped parsley, basil, salt, and pepper. Layer vegetables in any order, finishing with sliced tomatoes on top. Drizzle oil mixture over them. Bake in preheated 375-degree oven for 40 minutes. Sprinkle with more chopped parsley and basil. Serve hot.

> **Yield: 6 to 8 servings**
> **Preparation Time: 50 minutes**

VEGETABLES IN RED CURRY AND COCONUT SAUCE

4 tbsp. vegetable oil
2 tsp. minced garlic
1 onion, diced
1 cup cabbage, cut into 1-inch chunks
2 carrots, diced into ½-inch pieces
1 cup firm tofu, cut into 1-inch cubes
2 tbsp. red curry paste
4 cups canned coconut milk
1 cup cauliflower florets
½ cup frozen peas, thawed
1 tsp. salt
½ tsp. natural sweetener or other sweetener
1 tsp. dried sweet basil

Heat a large skillet until hot, add oil, garlic, and onion, and sauté until brown. Add cabbage, carrots, and tofu, stirring constantly, still over high heat. After 5 to 6 minutes, add curry paste and milk to make a sauce. Bring to a boil, add remaining ingredients, lower heat, and simmer until vegetables are crisp-tender and have absorbed curry flavor. Serve with steamed rice or pasta.

Yield: 4 servings
Preparation Time: 15 minutes

BRAISED SAUTEED EGGPLANT AND GREEN BEANS

2 Japanese eggplants
½ lb. green beans
3 tbsp. sesame oil
⅓ cup dashi
2 tbsp. sake
2 tbsp. natural sweetener
1 tbsp. mirin
3 tbsp. soy sauce

Cut eggplant into ½-inch-thick half-moon shapes. Put eggplant slices in cold water. Trim the ends from green beans and cut into 1-inch lengths. Drain the water from eggplant and pat dry. Sauté eggplant in sesame oil over high heat for 1 minute, add green beans, and sauté for another minute. Add all the remaining seasoning ingredients, and braise until the sauce is almost completely reduced. Serve at once.

Yield: 4 servings
Preparation Time: 10 minutes

BRAISED SAUTEED SPINACH

This is a simple, tasty, yet nutritious dish. It takes only a few minutes to cook, so try to master its preparation and include it in your daily menus.

2 tbsp. mirin
2 tbsp. sake
2 tbsp. soy sauce
2 tbsp. sesame seeds
1 bunch spinach, washed then blanched
2 sheets tofu pouches, cut into strings
2 tbsp. oil

Combine mirin, sake, soy sauce, and sesame seeds. Set aside. Cut spinach into 1-inch pieces, separating stems and leaves. Blanch tofu pouches in hot water to remove excess oil, drain, then set aside. Heat a saucepan, then quickly sauté the spinach stems first, then add tofu and leaves. Still over high heat, sauté for 20 seconds, then add sauce mixture. Braise for another 2 minutes, then serve.

Yield: 2 servings
Preparation Time: 5 minutes

Sea Vegetables

Most sea vegetables can be found in natural food stores, Oriental food markets, and some supermarkets.

Benefits of Sea Vegetables

Sea vegetables are rich in essential minerals, vitamins, protein, and trace elements that today are often lacking in our land vegetables because of soil demineralization. Sea vegetables contain more minerals than any other kind of food, with an extremely wide range of minerals accounting for from 7 to 38 percent of their dry weight. All of the minerals required by human beings—including calcium, sodium, magnesium, potassium, iodine, iron, and zinc—are present in sufficient amounts. For example, one-fourth cup of cooked hijiki contains over half the calcium found in a cup of milk and more iron than an egg. Although iodine is, by nature, highly volatile and thus somewhat difficult to obtain, sea vegetables contain complex natural sugars that stabilize their iodine, making them an excellent source of this essential mineral.

In addition to being a rich source of minerals, sea vegetables contain an abundance of vitamins, including vitamins A (in the form of beta carotene), B1, B2, B6, B12, niacin, vitamin C, pantothenic acid, and folic acid. Along with some fermented soy foods such as tempeh, sea vegetables are one of the few vegetarian sources of vitamin B12. Amino acids found in sea vegetables help lower cholesterol and relieve water retention.

Hijiki and Arame

Hijiki and arame are both seaweeds harvested in deeper water than wakame, nori, or kombu. Hijiki is a thick, coarse sea grass that grows in rather deep water compared to other sea vegetables. Hijiki's shimmering black color adds vivid contrast and beauty to any meal.

Arame is the shredded form of a wide leaf sea vegetable and has a milder taste and aroma than hijiki. Arame has a color similar to hijiki, but is much finer.

To prepare, soak arame or hijiki in cold water—15 minutes for arame and 30 minutes for hijiki. Remove and wash carefully to remove foreign matter, then drain. It is then ready to use. Usually both sea vegetables are sautéed in quality oil first, then braised with seasonings until tender.

Both are available in small packages at natural food stores or Japanese food stores.

Benefits of Hijiki and Arame

Sea vegetables have a balancing effect on blood sugar levels. Most North Americans have a tendency toward acidic blood, which is caused by stress and a meat-based diet. Sea vegetables, which are weakly alkaline, balance acidic blood and encourage good facial coloring and healthy, thick hair. Like most other seaweeds, hijiki contains all the nutritional minerals and is especially high in calcium, iodine, and iron.

Another astonishing discovery by a Japanese scientist is a most promising compound found in sea vegetables called fucoidan. It helps prevent breast cancer in women and boosts the immune system to fight off colon cancer.

SIMMERED HIJIKI WITH TOFU

In this dish, hijiki is first sautéed and combined with tofu and vegetables, then simmered in soy sauce, giving it a rich flavor.

¼ cup dried hijiki
1 small leek
2 carrots, cut into matchsticks
16 oz. medium tofu, drained
2 tbsp. vegetable oil
2 tbsp. light soy sauce
2 tbsp. sake

Soak hijiki in enough cold water to cover it for 15 to 30 minutes. Drain, reserving the soaking water for another purpose. Cut hijiki into 2-inch lengths. Slice the leek finely across the grain, and wash carefully to remove grit. Cut the tofu into small cubes. Heat a saucepan over medium heat, add oil, and sauté leek and carrots for 2 to 3 minutes. Add hijiki and tofu and continue to sauté, stirring carefully so as not to break up the tofu. Add soy sauce and sake, bring to a simmer. Continue cooking over medium heat until all the sauce is absorbed. Serve in individual bowls, hot or at room temperature.

Yield: 4 servings
Preparation Time: 36 minutes

Kanten

Kanten, also known as agar-agar, is a sea vegetable gelatin made from several varieties of seaweed, kanten comes prepackaged as bars, flakes, or powder. To use kanten bars, tear off a piece of the desired size, then soak in water for 30 minutes to 1 hour. Drain and squeeze out excess water and use as recipe instructs. Texture will be best if it is simmered for not more than 3 to 4 minutes.

Kombu

Kombu is the Japanese name for seaweed. *Laminaria,* the long ribbonlike seaweed, is a staple food for the Japanese. It is eaten in salads and entrees, as a vegetable, as the traditional seasoning in dashi, and as the basic stock for miso soup, sauce, and other preparations. See the soup and salad sections of this book for numerous recipes that include kombu. The Japanese consider kombu to be one of the most celebrated foods that was bestowed by *Kami* (god of the ocean). On happy occasions, kombu is presented to bless the event and to augur well for the future.

Unless otherwise recommended, do not soak, wash, or rinse kombu before using. (Washing kelp removes the minerals and vitamins from the surface of the kelp.) Simply wipe with a clean, dry cloth to remove sand or grit. Do not remove white crystals or grayish dust from the surface of the kombu.

Benefits of Kombu

Kombu is valued for its medicinal properties as well as its culinary uses. Kombu extract, powder, or tea was often prescribed by folk healers in cases of hypertension, due to an amino acid (laminine) found in the seaweed. Kombu is also recommended to reduce high blood pressure, lower cholesterol, and relieve water retention. Its high nutritional content includes iron, iodine, calcium, protein, and other important vitamins and minerals. It is good for high blood pressure, hardening of the arteries, asthma, and arthritis. However, it must be used with caution by those who must avoid salt.

Nori

Nori is a Japanese seaweed laver that has been harvested, placed over the rice straw mat, pressed, then dried into very thin slices. In Korea, laver is called *kim*. Versatile and easy to use, nori is most commonly used to wrap rice balls, the most popular snack in Japanese lunch boxes and picnic baskets. Nori is also used to wrap foods in sushi restaurants, such as *nori-maki sushi, tekka sushi, kappa sushi,* and *temaki sushi. Yaki nori,* or roasted nori, is used mainly to wrap foods.

Once nori is roasted quickly over a direct fire, the natural aroma of seaweed is accentuated and becomes more crunchy and brittle. Another variety of nori is a seasoned crunchy sweet nori called *ajituke nori.* It is sweetened with sugar or mirin then salted and roasted. Customarily, it is served with rice, miso soup, and some pickles for a traditional Japanese breakfast.

High-quality nori is greenish black and has a natural vibrant luster. Usually sushi-nori is preroasted. Another type of nori, *aonori* or green nori, is available in flake form and used as a garnish or sprinkled over rice as a condiment.

To store nori properly requires extra care because once it is opened, nori must be kept dry in an airtight container. Nori is available at Japanese, Korean, or natural food stores.

Wakame

This dark green seaweed grows at depths of about 6 to 8 feet in cold strong ocean currents. To prepare dried wakame, soak it in water for 10 to 15 minutes. Drain and remove the excess water by squeezing. Wakame can be used for stew or in vegetable or bean dishes. It is especially good in soups and salads.

WAKAME AND CUCUMBER SU-NO-MONO WITH GINGER VINAIGRETTE

1 small Japanese cucumber,
    sliced very thin across the grain
2 cups water
Pinch salt
1 oz. salted wakame
1 tbsp. grated ginger
1½ tbsp. brown vinegar
1 tbsp. thin soy sauce
1½ tbsp. dashi stock
1 tsp. ginger root, cut into very fine julienne

Soak cucumber in water with salt for 10 minutes. Boil wakame in hot water for 2 seconds, then submerge in cold water. Squeeze out water, then cut into bite-size pieces. Quickly mix all ingredients together except julienned ginger. Transfer to a serving dish. Garnish top with ginger and serve.

Yield: 3 servings
Preparation Time: 15 minutes

WAKAME WITH SU-MISO

It is handy to know a simple dish like this one, which adds a personal touch to your cooking. This dish is easy, simple, and very nutritious. Best of all, even if you know you are eating seaweed, it tastes good! For best results, make the sauce a day in advance. Add the prepared mustard at the last minute—just before serving—to make a pungent sauce.

> 1 tbsp. brown rice vinegar
> 4 to 5 tbsp. red miso
> 1 tbsp. natural sweetener
> 2 tbsp. dashi
> 1 tbsp. sake
> 1 tsp. English mustard
> 1 oz. dried wakame, reconstituted
>   and cut into bite-size pieces

Combine the first six ingredients together, chill. Place wakame in a serving bowl, and serve Su-Miso sauce on the side for dipping.

> **Yield: 2 servings**
> **Preparation Time: 10 minutes**

Oriental Noodles

North Americans love noodles and pasta. Children's favorite foods often include spaghetti, macaroni, lasagna, and other types of noodles. Asia is no different: everybody, young and old, loves to eat noodles. If you learn about the various other kinds of noodles besides pasta, and their methods of preparation, it will be a big addition to your vegetarian cooking skills, allowing for greater variety in everyday cooking.

There are many kinds of Oriental noodles. Different cultures have special ingredients and cooking methods which make their noodle dishes unique. Oriental noodles are usually more economical than pasta and are just as easy to digest. All Oriental noodles supply plenty of carbohydrates and fair amounts of protein. Most Oriental noodles do not contain eggs or dairy products. To be sure, read the label carefully before purchasing. To provide a complete, balanced meal using pasta or noodles, combine them with plenty of leafy green and yellow vegetables, seeds, and nuts.

Asians take noodles seriously; from flavor, clarity, and color of the broth to the texture of the noodles and selection of the condiments. It can almost become a philosophy. In Japan, there is an actor who describes himself as a philosopher of noodles. He wrote a book called *The Philosophy of Ramen Noodles*.

It is exciting to learn how to cook something completely new and to experience new taste sensations. Take your time to read and pay careful attention to all the details before you dash out to buy new ingredients. The following recipes are for all types of cooks— from beginners to intermediates—with a few difficult dishes thrown in. All you need to do is to practice, practice, and practice some more.

Non-Wheat Noodles

These noodles do not contain any eggs, dairy products, or wheat. They are ideal for those who are allergic to wheat.

Bean Threads or Vermicelli Noodles

These extra-thin transparent noodles are made from either mung bean starch or other kinds of starch, and resemble semitransparent cotton threads. There are several kinds of bean threads on the market. Korean mung bean noodles are pale green in color and are thicker than Chinese vermicelli. Japanese vermicelli (*harusame,* or "spring rain") is almost transparent and very fragile when cooked. Chinese vermicelli is very fine and retains its form even after soaking and cooking. All types of Oriental vermicelli are sold in dried form in individual clear packages. Don't forget, rice vermicelli is different than bean threads.

Some bean threads, Korean and Chinese, are very rigid and hard to handle when breaking them. After opening the package, place them in a bowl and add boiling water. When soft, drain, and rinse in cold water, then proceed to the next step of your recipe.

Japanese harusame are rather fragile compared to the others, and they require special attention. Read instructions on the package or soak them in hot water for 1 to 2 minutes, then drain and wash with cold water and proceed to the next step of your recipe.

Rice Vermicelli

Dry rice vermicelli, *be-fun* or *mai-fun,* are made from fresh ground rice and water, which is made into a dough, shredded into very fine noodles, steamed or boiled, and dried. They are also called cellophane noodles or rice sticks, depending on the shapes. Do not confuse rice vermicelli with bean threads; this product is made from rice, not bean starch. You can find rice vermicelli in almost all supermarkets and Asian food stores.

When preparing rice noodles, be careful not to overcook them. Otherwise, they will end up in a total mess. Open the package, put the noodles in a bowl, and pour boiling water over them. Soak for 2 minutes and not more, drain, and rinse with cold water. Another helpful hint: sprinkle a small amount of oil over noodles and toss to prevent them from sticking and drying. The soaking time varies according to the size of the noodles; judge by sampling the noodles because the package instructions may not always be correct.

Rice Noodles or Rice Sticks

Rice sticks are made using the same method as dry rice vermicelli, but they are flatter and thicker in shape and come in different sizes. There are two kinds of rice noodles: dried and fresh.

Dried noodles need a brief presoaking in hot water. Remove the noodles from the soaking liquid when they are not quite done. Use caution not to oversoak the dried rice noodles; if they are cooked after being oversoaked, the result will be a glutinous mass disaster. If the noodles are not used immediately, sprinkle with oil to prevent from sticking.

Fresh rice noodles need no precooking or parboiling. They come in three different forms: spaghetti, long flat rice noodles, and folded whole rice dough sheets. Fresh rice noodles are pre-steamed and very delicate. You can stir-fry them or drop them into soups and serve immediately. Overcooking either turns them into a paste like oversoaked dried noodles, or into shredded pieces that are very difficult to eat (even for a chopsticks master), or it may cause the noodles to disintegrate into pieces.

Fresh rice noodles can be found in the refrigerated section of Oriental grocery stores. Dried rice noodles are available in most supermarkets; look for a clear package indicating rice noodles, rice sticks, or rice vermicelli.

Yam Noodles (Shirataki)

Shirataki means "white waterfall" in Japanese. These almost transparent noodles can be found in the refrigerated section of Japanese grocery stores. They are usually packaged in water and come in different shapes. They are made from *konnyaku,* or yam powder, and water. When prepared, they are clear and have a chewy texture. Before using these noodles, be sure to parboil them in hot water to remove any unpleasant smells, then rinse well under cold running water.

RICE VERMICELLI AND SHIITAKE WITH SESAME VINAIGRETTE

The key to success with this dish is timing and heat. If the wok is too hot, the vermicelli will stick to the wok. If the wok is too cold, you will have a soggy mess.

½ lb. dry rice vermicelli
2 tbsp. oil
1 tbsp. minced garlic
1 tbsp. minced ginger
½ cup mixed shredded carrot, cabbage, and bamboo shoots
½ tsp. salt
2 tbsp. light soy sauce
5 to 6 shiitake mushrooms, reconstituted
1 tbsp. roasted sesame seeds, chopped
½ cup mung bean sprouts
½ cup bean sprouts
1 tsp. sesame oil
1 tbsp. brown rice vinegar
3 tbsp. green onion, cut into fine rings

Soak dry rice vermicelli noodles in boiling water for 2 or more minutes. Drain, coat with 1 tablespoon of oil and set aside. Heat wok until hot, then add remaining oil. Sauté garlic and ginger until aroma is released. Add shredded vegetables; sauté over high heat until slightly limp. Add shiitake and cook for 30 seconds. Add vermicelli noodles, stirring very quickly. Add salt and soy sauce; toss to coat noodles. Continue to cook until noodles are completely heated throughout. Sprinkle with sesame seeds and bean sprouts, and toss very quickly. At last minute, add sesame oil and vinegar, toss, then serve very hot with green onion sprinkled on top as a garnish.

Yield: 4 servings
Preparation Time: 7 minutes

SINGAPORE-STYLE RICE VERMICELLI

1 pkg. (8 oz.) rice vermicelli
3 tbsp. oil
1 tsp. minced ginger root
1 tbsp. finely minced garlic
6 stalks green onion, chopped
½ cup mixed shredded green cabbage,
    carrots, and onions
½ cup mung bean sprouts
2 pouches (2 oz.) usu-age (deep-fried tofu),
    sliced thin
1 tbsp. roasted sesame seeds
1 tsp. sesame oil
1 tbsp. brown rice vinegar
2 tbsp. soy sauce
1 tsp. curry powder
½ tsp. sea salt
1 tbsp. natural sweetener

Prepare rice vermicelli noodles until soft but not overcooked, about 2 minutes. Drain, cut into 10-inch lengths, then sprinkle with 1 tablespoon of oil. Toss and set aside. Heat wok. Add remaining oil and sauté ginger and garlic over very high heat until aroma is released. Add vegetables, except bean sprouts and tofu. Stir constantly until vegetables are soft. Add noodles, soy sauce, curry powder, sea salt, and sweetener. Stir and toss very quickly until noodles are hot. Add bean sprouts and tofu, then cover and steam for 1 minute. Sprinkle with sesame seeds, toss, and add sesame oil and vinegar. Stir well and serve immediately.

Yield: 4 servings
Preparation Time: 8 minutes

STIR-FRIED FRESH RICE NOODLES
WITH HOT BEAN SAUCE

In this dish, you may choose to use other types of salt seasonings rather than soy sauce and bean paste, such as fermented black beans, black bean sauce, mushroom soy sauce, or any other of your favorite alternatives. Be sure to heat the wok to high heat. Once the noodles are added, stir gently and quickly. Coat the noodles with oil to prevent them from sticking together before cooking. Again, fresh rice noodles are very fragile and delicate, so be careful not to overstir them. If you want to substitute dried noodles, par-boil them first.

3 tbsp. oil
1 tsp. shredded fresh ginger root
1 tsp. minced garlic
1 tbsp. hot bean paste
½ small carrot, cut into thin slices
6 to 7 stalks green onion, cut into 1-inch pieces
4 to 5 fresh mushrooms, sliced thin
1 sheet tofu pouch, sliced thin
½ lb. fresh rice noodles
1 tbsp. soy sauce (optional)
¼ cup bean sprouts
Pinch white pepper

Heat wok until hot, add oil, then sauté ginger and garlic for 10 seconds. Add hot bean paste. Sauté for another 10 seconds. Add carrot, stir fry, then add green onion, mushrooms, and tofu. Fry for 1 minute. Add noodles, stir, and season with soy sauce. Add bean sprouts, tossing quickly over high heat. Add pepper to taste. Serve at once.

Yield: 2 servings
Preparation Time: 5 minutes

STIR-FRIED SLIPPERY FRESH RICE NOODLES

3 tbsp. olive oil
1 tsp. shredded ginger root
1 tbsp. minced garlic
½ cup shredded bok choy or sue choy
6 stalks green onion, cut into 1-inch lengths
Pinch salt
Pinch pepper
½ lb. cut rice noodles, fresh
1 tsp. sesame oil
2 tbsp. soy sauce
½ cup bean sprouts
2 tbsp. sesame seeds, unhulled and toasted
2 tbsp. very finely chopped green onion

Heat wok until hot, add oil, and sauté ginger and garlic until oil starts to release their aroma. Add bok choy and green onion. Stir-fry quickly over high heat, until vegetables become soft; then season with salt and pepper to taste. Add noodles, stirring very carefully. Add sesame oil and soy sauce, stir, then add bean sprouts. Cook for 30 seconds. Serve at once, garnished with sesame seeds and green onion.

Yield: 2 servings
Preparation Time: 5 minutes

FRESH RICE NOODLES PRIMAVERA

I started to prepare this dish because I had a special client who was allergic to wheat, and all I had in the kitchen was fresh rice noodles instead of the dry vermicelli. She loved it. Ever since then, I have been serving this type of noodle on a regular basis.

4 tbsp. olive oil
1 tsp. minced garlic
¼ cup broccoli florets
¼ cup cauliflower florets
10 fresh green beans, cut into 2-inch lengths and blanched
¼ cup sliced mushrooms
Pinch sea salt
Freshly ground pepper
8 oz. fresh rice noodles
⅛ tsp. oregano
⅛ tsp. basil
2 tbsp. minced parsley
1 medium tomato, chopped
2 tbsp. roasted pine nuts

Heat a large frying pan until medium hot. Add oil, then garlic, and sauté until aroma is released. Add broccoli and cauliflower, then stir-fry very quickly over high heat. Add remaining vegetables and cook until tender. Season with salt and pepper. Add rice noodles, toss, then add spices and tomato. Cover and steam for 1 minute, or until noodles are hot. Sprinkle with pine nuts, and serve at once.

Yield: 4 servings
Preparation Time: 5 minutes

FRESH RICE NOODLES AL PESTO

This unusual version of noodles uses miso instead of parmesan cheese, making the recipe free of dairy products. *Pesto* means "pounded" in Italian and refers to a pounded mixture of herbs and oils that coat the hot noodles. This particular dish was designed as part of a no-wheat cooking class for people who cannot tolerate wheat gluten. Instead of using basil, this recipe uses a combination of spinach and parsley. Rice noodles take only a few seconds to cook, so be careful not to overcook them. Use soba, udon, or spaghetti noodles as a substitute for the rice noodles if you wish.

½ cup chopped parsley
½ cup chopped fresh spinach leaves
1 tbsp. minced garlic
2 tbsp. olive oil
1 tbsp. white miso
¼ cup pine nuts, finely chopped
1 lb. fresh rice noodles or Italian pasta

Blend parsley, spinach, garlic, and oil in a food processor for 10 seconds at high speed. Add miso, blend for 2 or 3 more seconds. Add pine nuts, process until a thick paste forms. Heat rice noodle by adding to boiling water for 2 seconds, stir, then drain. If using pasta, cook until *al dente,* then toss with pesto sauce.

Yield: 4 servings
Preparation Time: 10 minutes

SPICY BRAISED YAM NOODLES

3 medium dry shiitake
2 tbsp. vegetable oil
1 whole dry chili, seeds removed
1 pkg. (8 oz.) shirataki (yam) noodles
¼ cup dashi or water
3½ tbsp. soy sauce
1 tsp. natural sweetener or sweetener
1 tbsp. sake
1 tbsp. mirin
1 tbsp. roasted white sesame seeds, chopped

Soak shiitake in hot water for 30 minutes. Remove stems, and slice into very thin slices. Heat a flat skillet, then add oil and sauté chili until lightly browned. Add prepared shirataki; sauté over high heat until noodles are well coated with oil. Add shiitake and stir for 2 seconds. Add remaining ingredients, except sesame seeds, and bring to a boil. Lower heat and simmer until liquid is almost completely reduced. Sprinkle with sesame seeds. Serve at room temperature on a flat platter.

Yield: 2 servings
Preparation Time: 40 minutes (including soaking time)

Wheat Noodles

The following types of noodles are made with wheat or a mixture of wheat and other grain flours. Recently, noodles and pastas made from non-wheat grains have become available in many health food stores. Some wheat-based noodles are dried and others are fresh. Some are deep-fried and dried, and others are steamed and dried. How you prepare various noodles will vary according to the manufacturing method.

Deep-fried noodles should have an expiration date or production date on the package. Some countries require expiration dates on their products and others do not, and if the dates are on the packages, they may be in a foreign language. The best way to avoid bad noodles is to read the translated ingredients. If they contain oil and they are dried, you may want to avoid them. The chances are high that the oil used in the noodles is rancid or the noodles contain chemical preservatives. In Japan, all deep-fried noodles are required to be removed from the store shelves one year after their production date.

Somen

These are fine Japanese noodles made from wheat, salt, and water.

Kishimen

Kishimen are flat-looking Japanese-style noodles which come from the Gifu area in Japan. They are similar to linguine and can be prepared the same as udon or dry linguine. Kishimen is available at select Japanese and Korean food stores.

Steamed Chow Mien Noodles

This thin yellow noodle is made with wheat flour, water, and salt. Sometimes eggs are added, but true steamed noodles do not contain eggs. To be sure, read the label carefully. The noodles are steamed in a very hot closed steamer for a short period of time. They are then cooled and packaged. This type of noodle is available fresh in most supermarkets, Oriental grocery stores, and some health food stores. Steaming makes this noodle unique compared to other types of noodles. Pre-steaming cooks both the carbohydrates and proteins; hence the noodles don't absorb as much cooking oil as other noodles do when fried. Deep-frying or frying makes these noodles crispy and crunchy. You can make your own steamed noodles by placing a small amount of fresh noodles in the top of a very hot steamer. Cover for 4 to 5 minutes, remove, and cool.

To prepare fresh steamed noodles, place dry noodles in a large bowl. Pour boiling water over the noodles. Let stand for 2 or 3 minutes. Drain by pouring the noodles into a colander. Rinse well under cold running water. Drain excess water and pat dry with a paper towel. They are now ready to cook.

Soba

Japanese people have a serious love affair with noodles, and soba and udon are the most popular authentic noodles. Soba noodles, or buckwheat noodles, are usually eaten on New Year's Eve or on happy occasions such as weddings because they signify long-lasting relationships and longevity. The soup stock, dipping sauce, and quality of the noodles will determine the success of soba noodle dishes.

Soba are a fine spaghetti-shaped noodles—tan in color with brown specks—and are packaged in dried form only. They are made of either 100 percent buckwheat or a mixture of buckwheat and unbleached flour with flavorings. There are several types of soba available. These include *cha-soba* (buckwheat noodles flavored with tea), *ito-soba* (fine thin buckwheat noodles), *yomogi soba* (soba seasoned with mugwort), and *jinenjo soba* (buckwheat noodles with mountain potato as a binder).

To prepare these noodles, place them in plenty of boiling water. Wait until the water returns to a boil, then stir well to separate the noodles. Lower heat to medium high, and cook until the desired texture is obtained. If they are for immediate use, do not rinse the noodles, just place them in a soup bowl with hot broth or toss them with cooked vegetables. To serve them cold or to save for later use, rinse the noodles under cold running water to remove the excess starch, then chill. When making salads, toss the noodles with salad dressing just before serving to prevent them from becoming soggy.

Udon Noodles

Soba and udon are the most popular snack foods in Japan, and are eaten as an early snack in the subway station, for lunch at a soba counter, or for dinner in a favorite restaurant. Both soba and udon are eaten cold in the summer time, usually served with a dipping sauce made from dashi and soy sauce, and accompanied by the pungent condiments, wasabi and ginger.

Udon resembles linguini's flat narrow shape and is light beige in color. In North America, both fresh and dried udon noodles are available in most Oriental grocery stores and health food stores. Select udon noodles that are made with unbleached flour and have no preservatives. Udon is usually served in a large bowl with plenty of broth made from kelp and bonito flakes, seasoned with tamari and mirin, and topped with various prepared vegetables.

Prepare dried udon noodles in the same way as soba noodles. Reheat fresh udon noodles by adding them to your favorite hot soup stock.

Thin Wheat Noodles

These popular thin noodles, also known as *so-men* or *si-mien,* are mainly eaten cold during the summertime in Japan. When dried, they are finer than vermicelli; and they are made using only wheat flour, salt, and water. They come in dried form only, therefore before preparation they will need to be parboiled.

Wanton

Wanton noodles are made with wheat flour, salt, water, and baking soda. Authentic wanton noodles do not contain egg. They are sold fresh in Oriental grocery stores. Wanton noodles must be cooked very fast and removed with a large net, then dipped in very cold water to "tighten" the noodles. Then they are returned to the boiling water and cooked again briefly. Toss them with oil, soy sauce, and seasonings; and serve on bed of blanched iceberg lettuce.

Other types of noodles, such as Shanghai ton mien or plain ton-mien, are mostly served with or in a soup stock with a vegetable on top. They are just like fresh pastas. Purchase and experiment by using various cooking and seasoning methods. It is not like cooking lobster or abalone for the first time. Noodles are usually cheap compared to expensive rare materials. So enjoy, and eat more noodles.

Gyoza

Gyoza, wonton, egg roll, and other kinds of wrappers are considered *mien* noodles in Chinese, so I have categorized them here with the wheat noodles. There are quite a few varieties of wrappers available in most North American Oriental food markets and some supermarkets. Cooking methods vary, so it is important to read the cooking instructions on the package.

Gyoza and ramen shops can be found on every corner in Japanese cities. These shops are easily recognized by the large red Japanese lanterns hanging in front. Both gyoza and ramen (which come from Chinese word *lai-mien*) are popular among the Japanese, young and old. They are inexpensive and are served surprisingly quickly. Usually, gyoza are eaten by dipping them into a mixture of half soy sauce and half vinegar with a drop of *ra-yu* (hot chili oil).

If you have used wheat tortillas before, you can experiment by substituting them for regular egg roll wrappers for spring rolls.

CRISPY CANTONESE-STYLE CHOW MIEN

Chow means "sauté" or "fry," and *mien* means "noodle" in Chinese. This is a popular dish among the Chinese, but you need a little speed and practice to make it successful. Good Cantonese-style chow mien should be crispy when served, and the sauce on top should have the right consistency. You can toss the noodles and vegetables together with the sauce at the table to let the noodles soak up all the flavors before they are eaten. Yes, it is tricky, but it is well worth the effort. Follow the recipe carefully until you succeed. Again, in a good chow mien dish, the sauce texture needs to be just thick enough to cling to the crispy noodles in order to allow them to absorb the sauce—not too thick and not too thin.

4 dried mushrooms
1 lb. steamed fresh chow mien noodles
6 tbsp. oil
1 tsp. minced ginger
1 small carrot, peeled and sliced
½ cup broccoli tops, separated
2 stalks green onion, cut into 2-inch lengths
1 small bamboo shoot, sliced
15 sugar peas, trimmed
2 Chinese cabbage leaves, cut into bite-size pieces
3 tbsp. arrowroot powder
4 tbsp. water
2 cups soup stock
1 tbsp. soy sauce
2 tbsp. white cooking wine or sake
½ tsp. salt

Soak dried mushrooms in hot water for 1 hour; remove stems. Cut mushrooms into shreds, and set aside. Boil noodles in plenty of water for 30 seconds; drain and pat dry. Heat wok, add 2 tablespoons oil, and pan-fry prepared noodles until gold on one side—just like making pancakes. Move them constantly to prevent them from burning, and flip to the other side, add 2 more tablespoons of oil and cook in the same manner until gold and crisp. Remove and keep warm on a platter in the oven until the sauce is prepared.

Reheat the wok. Add 2 tablespoons of oil. Over high heat, sauté ginger until aroma is released. Add carrot and broccoli, then stir-fry quickly for 15 to 30 seconds. Add the remaining vegetables. Stir-fry until carrots are almost tender. Add the remaining ingredients except arrowroot powder and water; then bring to a boil. Add arrowroot powder mixed with water, stir gently to thicken, then pour the sauce over the warm noodles and serve immediately

Yield: 4 servings
Preparation Time: 1 hour 10 minutes (including soaking time)

MEGA-HEALTHY PUNGENT
SOBA NOODLES

Over the past several years, I have collected valuable information on important foods that are beneficial to your health. All of the ingredients listed here are reported to improve your health in various ways. This dish is easily prepared and very spicy; if you don't care for hot foods simply omit the chilies.

10 black fungus (mok-yhee)
3 tbsp. olive oil
2 fresh jalapeño peppers, seeded and chopped
3 cloves fresh garlic, minced
1 onion, cut into very fine slices
4 shiitake mushrooms, soaked and sliced
2 stalks green onion, cut into 2-inch lengths
8 oz. dry soba noodles, cooked then rinsed
Sea salt or tamari to taste
½ cup mung bean sprouts

Soak black fungus in warm water for 30 minutes, then drain. Heat a large skillet until hot. Add olive oil. Cook jalapeño peppers and garlic for 10 seconds. Add onion, continuing to cook until onion is soft. Add both mushrooms and green onion; sauté for another 30 seconds. Add noodles and toss very quickly until warm. Season with sea salt or good-quality tamari sauce. At the last minute, toss in mung bean sprouts; cover and steam for 1 minute. Toss again and serve.

Yield: 3 to 4 servings
Preparation Time: 40 minutes (including soaking time)

SOBA SOUP NOODLES
WITH SHIITAKE AND VEGETABLES

Soup noodles are popular in Asia; everyone loves them. Japan, Korea, China, Vietnam, Indonesia, and other countries have their own special kinds of soup noodles. The secrets of good soup noodles are to create your own quality basic stock (see index for Vegetarian Stock), to not overcook the noodles, and to serve them piping hot. You can substitute wanton noodles (not a wanton wrapper), rice sticks, rice vermicelli, ramen, fresh rice noodles, ton-mien, or whatever you would like to put into the stock. In this dish, the noodles should absorb a little bit of the soup while it is being served. Using dried spaghetti or linguine really doesn't give the same results as Oriental noodles.

4 shiitake mushrooms
1 lb. udon or soba noodles
2 tbsp. oil
2 slices ginger root
2 green onions, cut into 2-inch lengths
2 small bamboo shoots, sliced
1 small Chinese cabbage leaf, cut into 2 x 1-inch pieces
1 tbsp. soy sauce
2 tbsp. cooking wine (sake)
8 cups vegetable stock
3 tbsp. soy sauce
1 tsp. salt
⅛ tsp. ground white pepper

Soak shiitake mushrooms in warm water for about 1 hour. Remove stems. Boil noodles in a large pot with plenty of water until soft. Drain and rinse under cold running water. Set aside. Heat wok and add oil, then stir-fry ginger and green onion for 10 seconds. Add bamboo and cabbage; stir quickly. Add mushrooms and remaining ingredients. Bring to a boil, then add noodles and simmer over medium heat until noodles are reheated. Serve piping hot in individual bowls. Garnish with minced green onion or roasted sesame oil and nori.

Yield: 4 to 5 servings
Preparation Time: 1 hour (including soaking time)

CHINESE-STYLE THICK SOUP NOODLES WITH VEGETABLES

The following dish is unique because the soup stock is thickened with starch. It clings to the noodles, and when you taste the noodle, piping hot sauce will find its way into your mouth. Don't make the sauce too thick or too thin. This dish contains two kinds of Chinese mushrooms, both of which are excellent blood purifiers and good sources of minerals.

1 lb. dry soba or udon noodles, cooked
4 dried mushrooms
10 dried black fungus or wooden ear mushrooms
2 tbsp. oil
1 stalk celery, shredded
1 small bamboo shoot, shredded
½ block deep-fried tofu, shredded
4 cups vegetable stock
2 tbsp. cooking wine
1 tsp. salt
3 tbsp. arrowroot powder
4 tbsp. water
⅓ cup bean sprouts
1 tbsp. sesame oil
2 tbsp. shredded green onion
1 tbsp. roasted sesame seeds

Soak dried mushrooms and black fungus in warm water for 30 minutes. Wash and drain, then cut into thin slices. To a heated wok, add oil, celery, bamboo shoot, tofu, and mushrooms. Stir-fry for 1 minute. Add stock, wine, and salt. Bring to a boil, then continue cooking over medium heat for 2 minutes, skimming top. Thicken with arrowroot powder mixed with water. Add bean sprouts and sesame oil. Cook for 30 seconds. Serve over hot noodles in individual deep soup bowls. Garnish with shredded green onion and roasted sesame seeds.

Yield: 4 servings
Preparation Time: 40 minutes

QUICK SIMPLE SAUTEED SOBA NOODLES WITH GARLIC OIL AND HERBS

Soba noodles can be interchanged with linguine, fettuccine, or other Italian pasta. If you prefer, you can create a cheesy taste by adding two tablespoons of nutritional yeast with the salt and pepper.

>**8 oz. dry soba noodles**
>**6 tbsp. cooking liquid**
>**4 tbsp. olive oil**
>**3 cloves garlic, sliced**
>**1 whole dried chili**
>**3 tbsp. minced parsley**
>**Salt and pepper to taste**

Cook noodles, reserving cooking liquid. Set aside. Heat a flat skillet. When hot, add oil, garlic, and chili. Sauté until garlic is gold in color. Add cooking liquid, bring to a boil, then remove from the heat. Toss hot noodles very quickly. Add parsley, salt, and pepper to season. Toss and serve.

>**Yield: 2 servings**
>**Preparation Time: 10 minutes**

SOBA SUSHI

Unlike other types of sushi, this is a whole new experience for sushi lovers. Cooked soba noodles, together with seasoned shiitake, carrot, and green beans, are wrapped in a sheet of nori, then cut into bite-size pieces. It makes an exceptionally healthy snack for people who want to stay away from junk food. It is as nutritious as it is filling.

>**4 dried shiitake mushrooms**
>**1 pkg. (6 oz.) dried soba**
>**1 small carrot**
>**6 to 8 green beans**
>**1 cup dashi**
>**2 tbsp. mirin**
>**2 tbsp. shoyu (soy sauce)**
>**2 sheets nori**

Soak shiitake mushrooms in warm water for 1 hour. Remove stems. Boil soba noodles until *al dente*. Drain in a colander. Rinse well under cold running water. Set noodles aside to drain.

Cut carrot and green beans into large matchsticks. In a large pot, combine shiitake, carrot, green beans, dashi, mirin, and shoyu. Bring the sauce to a boil, then lower heat to medium low. Cook until the sauce is mostly absorbed. Remove sauce mixture from heat, then cool. Drain the remaining sauce, saving it for a later use. Shred shiitake into fine strips.

Spread cooked soba noodles evenly on nori sheets. Place carrot, green beans, and shiitake mix on soba near the edge closest to you. Roll tightly and evenly by lifting the closest edge over the vegetables, and continuing until the opposite edge is reached. Just before serving, cut into 6 pieces with a very sharp knife. Serve soy sauce and prepared wasabi on a side. To prevent nori from becoming soggy, plan to make this dish just before serving.

Yield: 2 rolls or 4 servings
Preparation Time: 1 hour

YAKI-UDON, STIR-FRIED
THICK JAPANESE NOODLES

3 to 4 black fungus (mok-yheer)
5 tbsp. oil
1 tbsp. finely minced ginger
1 oz. cooked prepared seitan, sliced thin
10 snow peas, cleaned
¼ cup mixed vegetables, cut into shreds
8 oz. dried udon, boiled then drained
2 tbsp. soy sauce
2 tbsp. sake
½ tsp. natural sweetener or mirin

Soak black fungus in warm water for 30 minutes; drain, then shred into fine strips and set aside. Heat wok, add oil, and stir-fry ginger until aroma is released. Add seitan, then stir-fry over very high heat until color of seitan starts to change to light brown. Add snow peas, black fungus, and mixed vegetables. Sauté until vegetables are tender-crispy, then add udon noodles. Still over high heat, add soy sauce, sake, and sweetener around the edge of the wok, continuing to stir-fry to add almost a burnt flavor of soy sauce to the dish. Serve piping hot.

Yield: 2 servings
Preparation Time: 35 minutes

UDON IN PLAIN DASHI SOUP

3 to 4 dried shiitake mushrooms
1 pkg. (8 oz.) dry udon
1 6 x 6-inch piece kombu
3 cups water
4 to 5 scallions, cut into ¾-inch lengths
1 carrot, sliced thin
¼ tsp. sea salt
3 tbsp. shoyu (soy sauce)
2 tbsp. mirin
1 scallion, finely minced
1 small piece ginger, grated
¼ tsp. Japanese shichimi chili pepper

Soak shiitake for 1 hour in warm water, then remove, reserving liquid for later use. Boil udon noodles until just tender. Drain and rinse under cold running water. Wipe kombu with a damp cloth. Combine water and kombu in a saucepan. Bring to a boil and cook for 5 minutes. Remove kombu and save for later use. Combine enough kombu and shiitake soaking liquids to make 4 cups dashi. Add scallions, carrot, and shiitake mushrooms to dashi. Bring to a boil, and cook over medium heat until tender. Season with salt, soy sauce, and mirin. Pour over hot noodles in deep individual serving bowls. Garnish with minced scallion on top of the noodles. Serve ginger and Japanese shichimi chili pepper on the side.

Yield: 3 servings
Preparation Time: 1 hour 15 minutes (including soaking time)

VEGETARIAN GYOZA
(JAPANESE POT STICKERS)

You can substitute minced seitan, textured vegetable protein (T.V.P.), or other chewy vegetables for the filling in this recipe. Here, I have used shiitake mushrooms to give a distinctive aroma and flavor to the dish. It is tricky to master wrapping gyoza, but it is worth the effort. Have fun by practicing with them before serving your guests. Make sure you wrap any remaining dough tightly and refrigerate it until next time.

Gyoza

5 dried shiitake mushrooms
1 carrot, minced fine
4 tbsp. minced water chestnuts
½ lb. firm tofu, drained and crumbled
1 tsp. sesame oil
2 green onions, finely chopped
1 tbsp. finely minced garlic
1 cup finely chopped Chinese cabbage
1 tbsp. soy sauce
1 tbsp. dry sherry
1 tbsp. arrowroot powder
1 tsp. minced fresh ginger root
½ tsp. natural sweetener (optional)
½ tsp. salt
2 doz. ready-made pot-sticker wrappers
2 tbsp. oil
½ to ⅔ cup water

Dipping Sauce

3 tbsp. soy sauce
1 tbsp. brown rice vinegar
¼ tsp. hot chili oil
½ tsp. shredded ginger root

For filling, soak shiitake mushrooms in enough warm water to cover for 30 minutes. Drain. Cut off and discard stems, and chop mushroom caps. In a bowl, mix chopped mushrooms with remaining gyoza ingredients, except wrappers, oil, and water.

Place 1 tablespoon of filling in center of each circular wrapper. Lightly moisten edges of circle with water. Fold circle in half over filling to form a semicircle. Starting at one end, pinch curved edges together to make 4 to 6 pleats along the facing edge, pressing the edges to seal securely.

Place filled wrappers on a platter. Heat a flat, wide skillet over medium high heat until hot. Add ½ tablespoon oil, then set half the pot-stickers, seam side up, in frying pan. Cook for 2 to 3 minutes, or until bottoms are golden brown. Add remaining oil to cook remaining pot-stickers. Drain excess oil and reduce heat to medium low. Pour in ¼ cup of water; cover and steam cook until liquid has completely evaporated, swirling pan occasionally. Transfer cooked pot stickers to a serving platter, and keep warm in a 200-degree oven. Add another tablespoon of oil to the pan and repeat the process to cook the remaining pot-stickers. Combine the dipping sauce ingredients in a bowl, and serve dipping sauce on the side.

Yield: 2 dozen Gyoza
Preparation Time: 45 minutes (including soaking time)

Other Pasta and Noodle Ideas

SPAGHETTI WITH EGGPLANT GARLIC SAUCE

Eggplant gives a rich and flavorful touch to any vegetarian dish. By changing spices and herbs, I have created a Mediterranean pasta dish from a Japanese eggplant dish.

½ cup olive oil
2 onions, minced
2 tbsp. minced garlic
1 eggplant, cut in ½-inch cubes
1 green pepper, seeded and diced
2 whole ripe tomatoes, diced
1 tbsp. natural sweetener (optional)
¼ tbsp. dry basil
½ cup fresh minced parsley
4 tbsp. sliced pitted black olives
Salt to taste
Pepper to taste
1 lb. spaghetti, macaroni, or shell pasta, cooked

Heat a heavy flat saucepan. Add oil, then sauté onion and garlic until transparent. Add eggplant. Stir and cook until eggplant is very soft and lightly browned. Add green pepper and sauté for another 3 minutes, or until peppers are soft. Add remaining ingredients and cook until thickened, about 30 to 35 minutes. Spoon over freshly cooked hot pasta just before serving.

Yield: 4 servings
Preparation Time: 50 minutes

NOODLES WITH MOCK MEAT SAUCE

This is a noodle dish resembling spaghetti with meat sauce, but it originated in Shang-hai, China. It has the slightly sweet and salty taste of yellow bean paste blended with pungent flavors and the mild flavor of mushrooms. Yellow bean paste is available in Chinese grocery stores, or hoisin sauce may be substituted. This dish can be served hot or cold. If a spicy sauce is preferred, just add a drop of hot chili oil to the sauce. A small amount of vinegar may also be added to the sauce if desired.

5 to 6 Chinese mushrooms
4 tbsp. soy sauce
6 tbsp. yellow (sweet) bean paste
½ cup water
4 tbsp. oil
½ tsp. minced ginger
1 tbsp. minced garlic
2 sheets (2 oz.) usu-age (tofu skin), minced
2 stalks green onion, minced
1 to 1½ lb. plain fresh noodles
½ lb. bean sprouts, parboiled
2 small cucumbers, shredded

Soak Chinese mushrooms for 1 hour in warm water. Drain, reserving liquid for later use. Chop mushrooms and set aside. In a small bowl, mix soy sauce, yellow bean paste, and water together to make a sauce. Set aside. Heat wok, then add oil and sauté ginger and garlic until aroma is released. Add minced mushrooms and tofu skin. Sauté for 1 minute, then add the sauce mixture and half the minced green onion. Bring to a boil, then reduce heat to medium. Cook for 2 minutes, then cool.

Boil noodles until done to your liking. Drain and place in individual bowls. Arrange the top with parboiled bean sprouts, shredded cucumber, and 3 tablespoons sauce per serving. Sprinkle with remaining minced green onion and serve.

Yield: 4 servings
Preparation Time: 1 hour (including soaking time)

CHILLED NOODLES WITH PEANUT AND SESAME SAUCE

This is a very popular noodle dish in both Japan and China for hot summer days. The sauce consistency may need adjusting according to your preference. If you want to add other vegetables such as snow peas, asparagus, green beans, or others to give more color and flavor, go right ahead; but remember, you are making noodle dish with vegetables, not the other way around. Peanuts and sesame seeds are high in calcium, protein, and trace minerals. In the hot summer or after a heavy workout, this dish is guaranteed to give you energy and vitality.

4 dried Chinese mushrooms
1 lb. fresh noodles
1 tbsp. sesame oil
2 tbsp. soy sauce
½ cup bean sprouts
1 small cucumber, shredded
2½ tbsp. natural sweetener
½ cup sesame oil
¼ cup soy sauce
½ cup vinegar
1 tbsp. minced fresh ginger root
2 tbsp. sesame paste (tahini)
3 stalks green onion, minced
2 tbsp. peanut butter

Soak Chinese mushrooms in warm water for 30 minutes. Remove stems and shred the caps; set aside. Cook noodles in plenty of boiling water until soft. Drain and rinse with very cold running water. Toss with 1 tablespoon sesame oil and chill. Marinate Chinese mushrooms in soy sauce for 10 minutes. Blanch bean sprouts, then chill. Place chilled noodles on a platter or on individual plates. Arrange cucumber, sprouts, and mushrooms on top. Combine the remaining ingredients, adjusting the sauce consistency with water. Serve sauce in small sauce dishes on the side. Leftover sauce should be stored in an airtight container in the refrigerator.

Yield: 4 servings
Preparation Time: 40 minutes

Grains

Whole grains are perfect low-fat foods that are packed with protein and contain a wide range of B vitamins and traces of numerous minerals. One cup of cooked grains averages about 220 calories and contains less than two grams of fat. Eating legumes along with grains provides a complete balanced source of protein. Various cultures have interesting combinations of grains and legumes cooked together in a one-dish meal. I will include some of their recipes here, but do not hesitate to experiment by adding a small amount of legumes to your grain dishes.

Grains contain sulfur-containing amino acids, methionine and cystine, which bean products lack. By combining grains and beans in the correct ratio, you can obtain much more usable protein than either served separately. For example, when you serve 3½ ounces tofu with 1¼ cup rice, you can obtain 32% more protein than the same amounts eaten separately. When you prepare grain dishes, always remember to include beans.

Cooking Grains

The method of cooking grains is simple. Clean the grains first by rinsing them well in a fine sieve under cold running water. Presteamed or rolled grains do not require rinsing. Add a measured amount of water, and cook. After the grain is cooked, stir well to give some room for the grains to expand or fluff. Sometimes a grain is older and therefore drier. Older grains absorb more liquid than new, so adjust the amount of liquid accordingly.

To give an extra nutty aroma, grains can be toasted in a dry or lightly oiled skillet before cooking, just until the grain turns a little darker. Add the required amount of water, and bring to a boil in a heavy saucepan. Stir in the grain. Return it to a boil, lower the heat to medium, and simmer, covered, until the water is completely absorbed by the grain. Do not stir while the grain is cooking. The Japanese say, "Never remove the lid while cooking rice, even if lightning strikes, the baby cries, or the turtle bites your finger." If the grain is too chewy at the end of the cooking time, add another ¼ cup of water for every cup of raw grain used, cover, and simmer until the water is absorbed. Stir to fluff the grain, then cover to steam for 5 to 10 more minutes.

Amaranth

Amaranth was a staple crop of the ancient Aztec culture. It is high in protein, iron, calcium, and trace minerals. Amaranth is a newly available grainlike food that is of special value to people who are allergic to wheat and grains. Cooked brown lentils and split lentils (red or yellow) go well with this grain. Just add cooked lentils to the amaranth after fluffing.

To prepare amaranth, rinse it, then use a ratio of 2½ to 3 parts water to 1 part amaranth. Cover and cook for 20 to 25 minutes.

Amaranth flour shares many of wheat's excellent cooking properties and is widely available at bulk health food stores. Amaranth flour has a nutty flavor that blends nicely with other foods, such as spices, nuts, seeds, and dried fruits. Once it gets old, the flavor of amaranth becomes stronger. It browns more quickly than regular wheat flour, and is good for baking, cooking, breading, and as a thickening agent.

When baking, use 25 to 30 percent amaranth flour and use brown rice or oat flour for the remainder. For grain-free baked goods, use 75 to 80 percent amaranth flour and tapioca, arrowroot, lotus root, water chestnut, potato starch, or potato flour for the remainder.

Because this flour oxidizes fast, it should be kept in the refrigerator or freezer.

Barley

Barley is commonly available as either pearl or pot barley. Pearl barley is refined and has fewer vitamins and minerals than pot barley. Use it for soups, salads, or as a substitute for the usual grains. To prepare barley, rinse it, then use 3½ cups of water to 1 cup of pot barley or 2½ cups water to 1 cup of pearl barley. Cook for 40 to 50 minutes.

Benefits of Barley

In some middle Eastern countries, barley is a staple as a cereal and is considered a medicine for the heart. Research shows eating barley interferes with the liver's production of LDL cholesterol, which leads to heart attacks and circulatory problems. It is preferable to eat less processed barley such as whole grain flour, cracked barley, and barley flakes.

Pressed Barley

I remember a long time ago, when the prime minister of Japan, Mr. Ikeda, made a strong controversial statement: "Polished rice is for the rich, poor people should eat barley." The media picked this up as big news, and all the Japanese were furious, including the rich. He was later assassinated.

Pressed barley, or *oshi-mugi,* cooks just like rice. Some Japanese add pressed barley to their everyday rice preparation. People are now talking about how good barley really is, thirty-five years after the prime minister's statement. Pressed barley is available in Japanese or Korean food stores.

Buckwheat Groats and Flour

Buckwheat is not a grain, it is a seed and is unrelated to wheat, so it is suitable for wheat-free diets. Roasted buckwheat, called *kasha,* and buckwheat are available in bulk health food stores. Buckwheat is high in iron and calcium and easy to prepare. Noodles that are made with buckwheat and wheat flour are called *soba*.

To prepare buckwheat, wash it, then use 2 cups of water to 1 cup of buckwheat and bring to a boil. Lower the heat to low, and cook for 15 to 20 minutes. Fluff and serve.

Buckwheat flour usually comes in two different colors, white and dark. The dark flour is roasted buckwheat flour. Dark roasted flour is not suitable for baking or as a thickening agent—it has a strong taste and flavor. White buckwheat flour is suitable for breading, thickening, and baking. Buckwheat flour contains gluten, which can be a problem for those with gluten intolerance.

When purchasing buckwheat, make sure that the groats are not rancid. If they are sold in bulk, smell them. If they have a slightly rancid odor, do not purchase them. Store buckwheat groats in an airtight container in the refrigerator.

Store buckwheat or kasha in an airtight container in the refrigerator. It will last for up to one year in good condition. To roast buckwheat, place 1 cup in a cast iron pan over meduim heat until sightly brown and aromatic, about 3 to 4 minutes. Remove from heat and cool or cook immediately.

Benefits of Buckwheat

According to a study conducted over several months at the All-India Institute of Medical Science in New Dehli, eating chapati (Indian flat bread) with cooked potato improved glucose tolerance and lowered blood cholesterol levels.

SAUTEED EGGPLANT WITH RED PEPPER AND KASHA

2 tbsp. olive oil
2 small Japanese eggplant (about ¾ lb.),
   cut into ½-inch slices
½ cup minced onion
1 red pepper, cored and cut in ½-inch dice
2 tbsp. natural sweetener
2 tbsp. soy sauce
2¼ cups water
6 new potatoes, cut in ¼-inch slices
5 stalks green onion, coarsley chopped
1 cup kasha
1 bay leaf
Grated rind of 1 lemon
Juice of 1 lemon

Heat a large, flat skillet until hot. Add oil and sauté eggplant until brown on all sides. Add onion and red pepper and cook for 2 more minutes. Add sweetener and soy sauce with ¼ cup water. Bring to a boil and add new potatoes, cover and cook until potatoes are tender, about 6 to 7 minutes. Sprinkle with green onion, and cook for 1 more minute.

While cooking eggplant, combine kasha, remaining water, and bay leaf in another skillet. Bring to a boil, then lower heat, cover with a tight-fitting lid, and cook until all the liquid is absorbed, about 6 to 7 minutes. Add lemon peel and lemon juice, stir, and place cooked kasha in the middle of a large serving platter. Flatten kasha, then place eggplant in the middle and serve.

Yield: 4 servings
Preparation Time: 20 minutes

Bulgur

Bulgur is wheat that has been boiled, dried, and cracked. It makes excellent pilafs, stuffings, salads, and soups. Bulgur is firmer and nuttier than rice when it is cooked, and it comes in fine, medium, and coarse forms. Fine bulgur is used mainly for salads that need no cooking. Medium and coarse bulgur are used in salads, soups, and pilaf. Bulgur and legumes combine well (i.e., bulgur with red lentils is a common middle eastern dish, and bulgur and chickpeas is a Syrian dish). To prepare bulgur, use 1½ cups of water to 1 cup of medium or coarse bulgur. Cook for 30 to 35 minutes.

BULGUR AND YELLOW LENTIL PILAF

5 tbsp. olive oil
1 cup onion, minced
1 tbsp. minced garlic
½ cup yellow lentils
1 cup bulgur wheat
½ tsp. allspice
Pinch ground cinnamon
1 tsp. salt
3 tbsp. minced parsley
Freshly ground pepper
½ cup pine nuts

Clean yellow lentils and soak for 6 hours. Sauté onion in oil in a frying pan with a tight-fitting lid over medium heat until soft and transparent. Add garlic and cook for 1 minute. Add lentils and bulgur. Cook until bulgur is lightly toasted. Add 1½ cups of water and bring to a boil. Add allspice, cinnamon, salt, and parsley. Stir, then lower the heat to low. Cook covered for 30 to 35 minutes. Turn off heat, then leave the pot covered and untouched for 20 more minutes. Add pepper to taste. Place on a serving platter. Sauté pine nuts until light brown, then sprinkle on top of the dish and serve.

Yield: 3 cups or 4 servings
Preparation Time: 1 hour (plus 6 hours soaking time)

TABBOULEH

This healthy exotic salad comes from the Middle East—some say it belongs to the Syrians, and others say it belongs to the Lebanese. In any case, I cannot deny that it is an excellent combination of ingredients that is ideal for anyone to eat at least once a week.

1 cup fine grain bulgur
½ tsp. salt
4 tbsp. finely chopped onion
2 cups finely chopped parsley
⅓ cup freshly chopped mint leaves
4 tbsp. lemon juice
½ tsp. allspice
¼ tsp. freshly ground pepper
4 tbsp. olive oil
3 ripe tomatoes, peeled and chopped
Heart of romaine lettuce, washed

Cover bulgur wheat with cold water for 1 hour. Sprinkle salt over chopped onion, then set aside for 1 hour. Add onion to bulgur, stir well, and drain. Place in a cloth napkin and squeeze out as much of the water as you can. Combine with all the ingredients except oil, tomatoes, and lettuce. Set aside for one-half hour to allow the flavors to blend. Toss with the oil and tomato just before serving. Adjust seasonings if desired. Serve on a platter surrounded by romaine lettuce to serve as a scoop for the tabbouleh.

Yield: 4 servings
Preparation Time: 1½ hours

Couscous

Couscous is the steamed kernel of wheat. It is an excellent substitute for rice or other grains. To prepare couscous, use 2 cups of boiling water to 1 cup of couscous. Cover for 10 minutes, then fluff. It is then ready to use in recipes. Couscous is light and has a very distinctive flavor once cooked. It goes well with sauces.

SAFFRON COUSCOUS

⅛ tsp. saffron, dry roasted and crumbled
½ cup chopped onion
3 to 4 tbsp. olive oil
1½ cups couscous
2 cups boiling water
¼ tsp. coarsely chopped coriander
⅛ tsp. cloves, ground
⅛ tsp. cumin, ground
4 whole cardamom pods
½ cup golden raisins
¼ cup black olives, chopped
Salt and ground black pepper
1 tbsp. fresh lemon juice

Dissolve roasted crumbled saffron in 2 tablespoons of hot water and set aside for 1 hour. Sauté onion in oil in a heavy skillet until transparent. Add couscous and sauté for a few more minutes. Add saffron water and remaining ingredients to the pot, except lemon juice. When water begins to boil, lower the heat and cover. Cook couscous for 5 minutes, or until the water is absorbed. Season with additional salt and pepper to taste and lemon juice.

Yield: 5 to 6 servings
Preparation Time: 12 minutes (plus 1 hour soaking time)

Millet

This small yellow round seed is high in minerals and is both nourishing and versatile. It is excellent for a pilaf or stuffing, and it makes a delicious hot cereal when served with chopped nuts, dried fruit, and soy milk. Once millet is cooked, it has a nutty flavor and a grainy texture. Kasha, which is available at some health bulk food stores, is also sometimes made from millet.

To prepare millet, combine 1 cup of hulled millet and 1¾ to 2 cups of water, and cook for 30 to 45 minutes. Or, toast millet over medium heat until a nutty aroma begins to be released. Add water and bring to a boil. Lower the heat, then cover with a lid. Simmer for 30 minutes, add ¼ cup of hot water, and stir vigorously. Cover and simmer over very low heat for 10 minutes. Turn off the heat and leave, covered and untouched, for another 10 minutes.

Benefits of Millet

In India, millet, tapioca, and rye are used in treating overeating disorders by substituting these grains for existing staples. Unless millet is eaten in excess, it will not increase weight.

NUTTY MILLET AND LENTIL PILAF WITH SPINACH

½ cup minced onion
1 tbsp. minced garlic
3 tbsp. olive oil
1 cup hulled millet
½ cup brown lentils
2 cups water
1 tsp. salt
2 bunches cooked spinach, cut into ½-inch lengths
Freshly ground black pepper
4 tbsp. chopped hazelnuts, toasted
1 tbsp. minced parsley

Sauté onion and garlic in oil in a flat skillet with a tight-fitting lid until tender and transparent. Add millet, and cook until light gold in color. Add lentils, water, and salt. Bring liquid to a boil. Cover and cook for 30 minutes, then stir and add spinach. Cover and cook for another 10 minutes over very low heat. Add black pepper to taste and stir gently. Sprinkle with chopped nuts and toss. Serve hot with minced parsley on top.

Yield: 4 servings
Preparation Time: 45 minutes

NUTTY MILLET AND BASMATI PILAF

2 tbsp. olive oil
1 medium onion, minced
1 cup basmati rice, rinsed
½ cup hulled millet
1¾ cups water
⅓ cup boiling water
½ cup green peas
½ cup walnut pieces

Heat a medium-size saucepan, add oil, and sauté onion until soft and transparent, about 2 minutes. Add basmati rice and millet; stir until lightly toasted and golden in color. Add 1¾ cups water and bring to a boil. Lower heat, cover, and cook for 30 minutes. Stir, then add ⅓ cup of boiling water. Cover and cook over very low heat for 15 more minutes. Remove from heat, add green peas, then stir well. Return pan to stove, and cook for another 5 minutes over low heat, add nuts, toss, and serve.

Yield: 4 servings
Preparation Time: 50 to 60 minutes

Oats

Oats are not refined of their bran and germ, and are therefore considered a better grain. Whole oat groats are the whole grain with only the hull removed. Steel cut oats are sliced whole groats. Use them for cooked cereal and for thickening soups.

Oat Flour

Oats make an excellent flour that can be used for baking, cooking, and for thickening purposes.

For baking or cooking, substitute oat flour for 80 to 100 percent of the wheat flour in your recipe. To make homemade stone-ground pat flour, blend ¾ cup of rolled oats in a blender until finely ground into 1 cup of flour.

Rolled Oats

Rolled oats are steamed, flattened whole oats that are often referred to as old-fashioned oats or oatmeal. To prepare rolled oats, use 1½ cups water to 1 cup of oats. Cook for 10 minutes. For whole and steel cut oats, use 3½ to 4 cups water to 1 cup of oats, then cook until tender, about 45 to 60 minutes.

Benefits of Oats

The latest research indicates that eating oats or oat bran can prevent various diseases. A recent study done at the University of Kentucky College of Medicine reported that eating oat bran helped to drastically lower participants' total cholesterol counts. Oats are also high in protease inhibitors, chemicals that fight cancer-causing viruses in the intestinal tract. Oat bran is rich in insoluble fiber, which is known to relieve constipation and help reduce intestinal problems.

In China, oat tea was used to break the opium habit and to reduce tobacco cravings.

HOMEMADE GRANOLA

For a non-wheat recipe, use rice flour or other types of flour instead of wheat flour.

3 cups rolled oats
½ cup wheat germ or bran
1 cup sunflower seeds
1 cup crushed nuts
½ cup flour or rice flour
1 tsp. cinnamon
¼ cup oil
1 cup natural sweetener
1 tsp. vanilla
¼ tsp. salt
⅛ cup water
½ cup corn meal
½ cup sesame seeds, unhulled
½ cup shredded coconut
½ cup raisins (optional)

Preheat oven to 275 degrees. In a large bowl, combine all liquid ingredients. In a separate bowl, combine all dry ingredients. Add dry ingredients to liquid ingredients; mix well. Place the mixture on a cookie sheet and spread out evenly. Bake for 20 minutes, stir, then bake until golden. Remove and cool. Store in an airtight container.

Yield: about 10 cups
Preparation Time: 25 minutes

MUSELI

2 cups uncooked oatmeal
1 cup plain soy milk
2 apples, cored and chopped
¼ cup whole almonds
¼ cup raw sunflower seeds
¼ cup dried pitted dates, chopped
¼ cup golden raisins
¼ cup sorghum syrup or rice syrup
2 tbsp. wheat germ
Pinch cinnamon

Place oatmeal and soy milk in a bowl. Mix, cover, and place in the refrigerator overnight.

Place all ingredients together in a large bowl, stir well, and season with cinnamon.

Yield: about 6 cups
Preparation Time: overnight

Quinoa

Quinoa, pronounced *keenwa,* is called the grain of the future. It is now grown organically by North American farmers, and is available in most natural food stores. It originated in the Inca civilization, and was known as the "mother grain." The protein content is the highest—16 percent—of grains such as wheat and rice, and it has complete essential amino acids like soy beans. It is a balanced source of nutrients, complex carbohydrates, natural sugars, essential fatty acids, B vitamins, and trace minerals.

Quinoa is excellent as a staple grain, for stuffings, desserts, and with bean dishes. Before cooking quinoa, it is essential to rinse it to remove the bitterness. To prepare, use twice the amount of water as quinoa, bring to a boil, and cook for 15 to 20 minutes. Stir from the bottom to fluff, and leave in the pot for 10 minutes before serving.

QUINOA AND SHIITAKE STIR-FRY

½ lb. fresh shiitake mushrooms,
    stems removed and sliced
2 tbsp. oil
1 tbsp. minced garlic
1 whole jalapeño pepper,
    seeds removed and chopped
⅓ cup slivered almonds
2 cups cooked quinoa
2 tbsp soy sauce
1 tbsp. fresh lemon juice
1 tbsp. finely minced ginger
3 tbsp. minced green onion

Heat a wok until hot. Add oil and cook garlic until golden. Add shiitake and cook for 2 minutes over high heat. Remove shiitake to a plate using a slotted spoon, leaving the wok over the heat. Add almonds to wok with remaining oil. Cook until lightly toasted, return shiitake, and add quinoa. Stir-fry over high heat until quinoa is heated, about 1 minute. Add soy sauce and stir vigorously for 30 seconds, then add lemon juice and toss quickly. Sprinkle with very finely minced ginger and green onion mixture.

Yield: 4 servings
Preparation Time: 20 minutes

Rye

Rye has a higher concentration of minerals than wheat, with a faintly sour flavor and chewy texture. It is used primarily as a bread flour, but there are a few other forms. Rye berries are narrow whole grains, which are excellent combined with other grains like rice or quinoa or with noodles. Rye flakes are steamed, flattened rye berries, and are commonly used for hot cereals and casseroles. Cracked rye berries are used for specialty loaves, croquettes, and hot cereals.

To prepare rye, use 1 cup of rye to 3 cups of water for whole or cracked rye, then cook for 45 to 60 minutes. For rolled rye, use 2 cups of water for 1 cup of rye, and cook for 15 to 20 minutes.

Wheat

Wheat is the grain crop most widely cultivated in the world. It comes in several varieties, including soft red spring wheat, hard red winter wheat, and durum wheat. Whole wheat contains large amounts of protein, essential nutrients, and almost the full range of B vitamins.

Cracked Wheat

Cracked wheat is similar to bulgur. It is not precooked, so it takes longer to cook. To prepare cracked wheat, use 1 cup of wheat to 3 cups of water, then cook for 35 to 40 minutes.

Wheat Berries

Cooked wheat berries are beneficial for strong teeth and gums, beautiful skin, and for preventing stomach problems. Wheat berries have a slightly chewy, sweet flavor. To prepare them, use 1 cup wheat berries to 3½ cups water. Cook for 50 minutes.

Wheat Bran

Wheat bran is high in lime, iron, vitamin B-complex, and potash. When shopping for bran, there are three kinds to look for: coarse, medium, and fine. All three are interchangeable in recipes, so take your pick. Look for a package with a nutty aroma and no mustiness. Always store wheat bran in the refrigerator in an airtight container to protect it from becoming rancid. Bran absorbs more liquid than flour, so adjusting liquid is necessary if replacing flour with bran in a baked recipe.

Wheat Flakes

Wheat flakes, or rolled wheat, are steamed and flattened wheat berries. To prepare them, combine 1 part wheat berries with 2 parts water, and cook for 15 to 20 minutes.

Chappati Flour

Chappati flour, also called ata flour, is a fine ground whole wheat flour. It is used to make various breads in East Indian cuisines and is available at Indian grocery stores.

Wheat Germ

Wheat germ is the part of the wheat that contains the richest concentration of B and E vitamins and protein. When shopping for wheat germ, buy it in small quantities, and try to use it as soon as possible. Store it in the freezer. If a recipe calls for toasted wheat germ, place it on a flat cookie sheet in a 325-degree oven to toast for 12 to 15 minutes. Stir every 5 minutes. Remove and cool, then store in the freezer.

BLUEBERRY WHEAT BRAN PANCAKES

½ cup wheat bran
¾ cup whole wheat pastry flour
1 tsp. baking powder
½ tsp. baking soda
1 tsp. arrowroot powder
½ cup frozen blueberries
2 tbsp. frozen orange juice concentrate
¾ cup soy milk
1 tsp. lemon juice
3 tsp. oil

In a large bowl, combine all the dry ingredients and the blueberries. Stir well. In a separate bowl, combine the orange juice concentrate, soy milk, and 2 teaspoons oil. Add the wet mixture into the dry mixture, and stir to combine. Heat a cast iron skillet over medium heat, rub a small amount of oil on the skillet, and ladle 2 tablespoons of batter onto the skillet. Cook until small bubbles form on the surface, then flip to the other side and cook until done (the cooking time varies with the type of skillet you use), about 2 minutes on each side. Repeat the process with the remaining batter.

Yield: 4 servings
Preparation Time: 10 minutes

CHAPPATI

**2 cups chappati flour (or mixture of 1 cup each
  whole wheat flour and cake flour)**
2 cups less 2½ tbsp. water
flour (for dusting)

Place flour in a large bowl and gradually add enough water to make a soft dough. If cooking in a hot climate, the amount of water may have to be adjusted. Knead dough for 8 to 10 minutes, until smooth and elastic. Place dough in a bowl and cover with a damp cloth. Set aside for 1 hour.

Form dough into 12 balls. Dust balls with flour and keep them covered. Heat a large, flat, heavy cast iron skillet over medium heat. While skillet is heating, roll out one ball, thinly and evenly, to about 5½ inches round, dusting both sides with flour. Place it onto the skillet and cook until it bubbles, about 30 seconds. Turn and cook the other side for 30 more seconds. Remove and place on a plate. Cover with a clean dry cloth. Repeat the process with remaining dough balls.

Yield: 12 chappati
Preparation Time: 1½ hours

Rice

Rice is the staple grain for half of the world's population. Westerners wake up in the morning to the smell of coffee and baked bread or toast. As a child, I woke to the smell of miso soup and steaming hot rice. Three decades later, I still eat rice three times a day. Rice is prepared by either boiling or steaming. When properly cooked, its grains remain firm and separate from one another. Rice should have body. It should not be lumpy, sticky, mushy, or wet (with some exceptions). According to personal preference, rice should not be too hard or too soft.

When a recipe indicates an amount of water for cooking rice, it is just a guideline. All rice is not the same. Some rice is older than others, depending on how long the rice has been sitting on the shelves, and older rice requires more water. One of the reasons that I recommend choosing a busy store to purchase rice is that it is more likely to have newer rice. Newer rice is more chewy and seems to me to have a superior taste. Adjust the water ratio according to your own liking.

Cooking Rice

Combine water and rice together in a pot. Bring rice to a boil over medium high heat. Cover and boil for 3 minutes, then reduce heat to medium low. Without removing the cover, boil for 7 to 8 more minutes, then lower the heat to the minimum. Cook for 5 to 6 minutes or more. Do not lift the lid at this point. Turn off the heat. When the cooking is done, lift the lid and stir the rice, loosening it gently with a lifting motion, then cover with the lid and let stand for 8 to 10 minutes.

Storing Cooked Rice

Before storing leftover rice, let the rice cool completely, then place it in a covered container or wrap it in plastic. It should keep for about a week in the refrigerator. To reheat rice, place the rice in a pan and add 1 tablespoon of water for each cup of rice. Cover tightly, then heat over very low heat for 5 to 6 minutes.

Seasoning Rice

Use a liquid that is already flavored, or use water with seasonings instead of just plain water. Simply replace the water in the ingredient list with soup stock, flavored liquids, or fruit juice. Sauté the rice with a small amount of oil, or dry-toast the rice before adding the liquid, then proceed with cooking, using the water or stock called for in the recipe, to give a nutty aroma to the dish.

Prepared rice may be seasoned with herbs and spices, depending on your preference. For making sautéed rice dishes or rice salads, see the index for Seven Flavorings section.

Cooking Polished Rice

Rinse rice under cold running water. Rub the grains together in a fine sieve or colander until the water runs fairly clear. Drain and set aside for 1 hour before cooking. For long grain, use 1 cup rice to 1½ cups water; for steamed long grain, use 1 cup rice to 3 cups water. For medium grain, use 1 cup rice to 1 cup water; and for steamed short grain, use 1 cup rice to 2 cups water.

Benefits of Rice

Walter Kemper, M.D., of the Duke University Medical Center, validated in the 1940s that eating rice with fruits works to lower blood pressure and reduce kidney problems. Rice contains protease inhibitors that are believed to prevent cancer, and a Japanese scientist showed that phytic acid or phytates in rice bran block the absorption of unwanted calcium in the intestinal tract, resulting in less calcium in the urine to form kidney stones.

Brown Rice

Brown rice contains three times the vitamins, fiber, and minerals of refined polished rice. It contains high concentrations of vitamins E and B and protein. You can purchase various kinds of brown rice in natural food stores or regular supermarkets. Choose the rice according to your recipe. Long grain rice becomes separated when cooked and is light, not gluey. It is suitable for pilaf, rice salads, fried rice, and casseroles. Medium grain can be used interchangeably with long grain, but is slightly stickier. Most of the medium grain rice requires less water than long grain, but this again depends on brand, humidity, age, and cooking temperature.

For long, medium, and short grain, and for wild rice, use 1 cup rice to 2½ cups water. Combine water and rice together in a pot. Bring rice to a boil over medium high heat, then boil covered for 3 minutes. Reduce heat to medium low. Cook for 35 to 45 minutes, or until done.

SESAME BROWN RICE

2 cups medium grain brown rice
4 cups water
Pinch sea salt
½ cup toasted sesame seeds

Wash rice well by rinsing until the water runs clear. Drain well, combine with the measured amount of water and salt in a heavy pot. Bring to a boil over medium heat, then reduce heat to low and cook for 50 to 60 minutes, covered with a tight-fitting lid. Remove the lid, fluff, allow to rest for 10 minutes. Add freshly toasted sesame seeds to rice, then serve hot.

Yield: 4 cups
Preparation Time: 1 hour 10 minutes

BROWN RICE FORESTIERE

6 dried shiitake, soaked and sliced thin
2 oz. shimeji mushrooms, ½-inch bottoms
    removed and separated into small pieces
2 tbsp. soy sauce
2 tbsp. sake
2 tbsp. dashi
Salt to taste
2 cups freshly cooked brown rice

Combine mushrooms with soy sauce, sake, dashi, and salt in a cooking pot, then bring to a boil. Cook for two minutes. Mix with freshly cooked brown rice, stir well. Cover and steam for 4 more minutes, until the aroma of mushrooms is absorbed into the rice.

Yield: 4 servings
Preparation Time: 7 minutes

Basmati Rice (Brown and White)

Basmati is produced mainly in India. Nutty and aromatic, it is a superb grain for both nutrition and taste. You can buy it in busy Indian or health food stores in the bulk food section, or in your local supermarket.

To cook basmati, use 2 cups polished basmati to 2½ cups water, or 2 cups brown basmati to 3½ cups or more of water.

SAFFRON AND ORANGE BASMATI PILAF

This dish was created by one of the students from my cooking class. I altered the recipe a bit to allow for easier access to ingredients. It is exotic because of the orange juice and saffron. Once you start to cook it, you will enjoy the aroma of brown basmati and the mixture of fragrances from various ingredients that fill your kitchen.

I use Mexican or American saffron instead of Spanish for reasons of price and availability. To dry-roast saffron, spread it in a dry cast-iron frying pan and stir over medium low heat until slightly brown. Store in an airtight container for easy access.

⅛ tsp. saffron
1½ cups boiling water
¼ tsp. sea salt
¼ cup shredded coconut
1 cup white basmati rice
1 tbsp. olive oil
½ cup fresh orange juice
½ tsp. orange rind, grated
¼ tsp. ground coriander
¼ tsp. nutmeg
4 whole cardamom pods, pounded
⅓ cup walnuts, chopped
½ cup golden raisins

Crumble saffron and mix with 3 tablespoons of water. Set aside for 1 hour. Combine hot water, saffron liquid, sea salt, and coconut. Bring to a boil, then add rice and cover. Simmer over low heat for 30 minutes. Remove the lid and stir well, then cover and set aside for 5 minutes. Coat a baking dish with olive oil, and set oven at 350 degrees. Transfer the rice to the baking dish; add orange juice, rind, spices, nuts, and raisins. Cover tightly and bake in preheated oven for 35 minutes.

Yield: 4 to 5 servings
Preparation Time: 1 hour 10 minutes

Wahini Rice

Wahini or wehani rice is a short grain brown rice with huge amber grains. When this rice is cooking, the kitchen fills with the aroma of popcorn. It is available in some natural food stores, but it is more difficult to find than other types of rice. When purchasing this and any other type of rice, be sure that it is fresh. Even packaged rice may become rancid. Avoid any rice that smells musty or any packaged rice in which the grains are clumped together. Wahini rice is prepared the same way that short grain brown rice is cooked.

One-Pot Rice Cookery

The goal of this method is to have only one pot or pan to wash—and maybe a lid and some dishes. You can learn one-pot cookery here and now, or you can become an expert in washing multiple pots and pans. This method is detailed in the following recipes. Some ingredients are added to the rice in the beginning and some are added later for particular reasons.

One-pot cookery is simple, creates no mess, and combines all the flavor into one dish that you can bring right to the table. You can then maintain the temperature of the dish and the wonderful fragrance of the foods.

CHESTNUT RICE

This traditional dish is normally prepared in late autumn in Japan. Sweet fragile chestnuts are a good accompaniment to chewy rice. If fresh chestnuts are not available, use dried chestnuts, which are available in Chinese food stores.

1 lb. chestnuts in the shell (or ½ lb. dried)
2½ cups medium grain polished rice
½ cup sweet glutinous rice
4½ cups water
2 tbsp. sake
½ tsp. sea salt

Soak chestnuts in cold water for 2 to 3 hours, or boil for 10 to 20 minutes. Peel and soak in cold water for 20 to 30 minutes to remove bitterness. Rinse both kinds of rice well, add water, and bring to a boil. Cover and reduce heat to medium low. When rice is almost cooked (after about 15 minutes), add chestnuts, sake, and salt. Stir and cook rice for 15 more minutes over very low heat. Remove from heat. Fluff, cover, and steam for 5 more minutes, then serve.

Yield: 7 tp 8 servings
Preparation Time: 40 minutes

FRIED BROWN RICE AND WAKAME IN LETTUCE WRAP

This is a very economical and fast way to make a meal. Leftover brown rice is sautéed with tofu, various seasonings, and wakame seaweed, then it is served with lettuce leaves on the side. Guests can serve themselves by wrapping the filling in the lettuce leaves.

1½ tbsp. soy sauce
1½ tbsp. red miso
1 block medium firm tofu, pressed for 1 hour
3 tbsp. oil
1 tsp. ginger root, very finely minced
1 tbsp. garlic, minced
1½ cup cooked brown rice
1 oz. dried wakame seaweed
Salt and white pepper top taste
3 scallions, finely chopped
2 tbsp. white roasted sesame seeds
12 red or iceberg lettuce leaves

Mix soy sauce and miso; set aside. Place crumbled tofu in a wok, then heat over medium heat until water is released. Reduce heat to low, and continue to cook for another 3 minutes. Remove tofu from the pan and drain to remove liquid. Heat the wok until hot, add oil, and sauté garlic and ginger for 10 seconds, then add brown rice and tofu to the wok. Stir quickly over high heat, then add wakame. Toss and season with salt and pepper. Continue to stir-fry rice, still over high heat, pouring soy sauce and miso mixture around the edges of the wok. Toss quickly to combine, and remove from wok to a serving platter. Sprinkle scallions and white roasted sesame seeds on top. Serve lettuce leaves on the side for your guests to use to wrap their rolls.

Yield: 6 to 7 servings
Preparation Time: 30 minutes

KAYAKU RICE

1 cup polished short grain rice
2 dried shiitake
1 sheet age (deep-fried tofu pouch)
1¼ cups dashi stock
1 burdock root, peeled and cut into julienne
1 small carrot, cut into julienne
2 tbsp. soy sauce
3 tbsp. sake
⅓ tsp. sea salt
4 tbsp. green peas, fresh or frozen

Wash rice and soak for 30 minutes. Drain and set aside. Soak shiitake for one hour, remove stems, and slice into thin strips. Pour boiling water over the tofu pouch to remove the oil; drain and cut into julienne. Combine rice, tofu, and shiitake with dashi, burdock root, carrot, soy sauce, sake, and salt in a cooking pot. Place over medium heat. When it starts to boil, lower heat to simmer. Cook until almost all the water is absorbed, about 10 to 12 minutes. Remove lid and fluff. When done, stir well to allow the rice room to expand. Add green peas, then stir, cover, and steam for 5 more minutes.

Yield: 2 to 3 servings
Preparation Time: 50 minutes

Rice Flour, Brown and Polished

Rice flour is a powder made from rice that has been put through a mill. Rice contains no gluten or the allergen that affects people who are sensitive to wheat. In cooking, it is dryer than wheat, so cakes are more crumbly and muffins are more dense. When using rice flour, compensate by adding more baking powder.

To make your own rice flour, grind raw rice in ¼-cup batches in a blender, then strain through a very fine sieve. Substitute ⅞ cup (1 cup less 2 tablespoons) of rice flour for 1 cup of wheat flour.

Brown rice flour makes an excellent substitute for wheat flour when making cookies and pie crust, but it has a tendency to get dry very quickly. To prevent it from drying, substitute ground nuts or seeds for 25 percent of the flour, or add plumped dried fruits, stewed fruits, or vegetables such as zucchini and carrots. When combining with oat flour, use an equal amount of rice flour as a substitute for wheat flour. Brown rice flour is not recommended for breading or thickening.

HOMEMADE BAKING POWDER

2 tbsp. baking soda
4 tbsp. rice flour
4 tbsp. cream of tartar

Mix ingredients together. Keep in an airtight container.

Yield: less than ⅓ cup

Rice Paper

This unique product of Southeast Asia comes in a variety of shapes and a variety of sizes. They are usually sold dried in Oriental food stores and markets, and they are also called rice crêpes or cellophane sheets. Once you know how they are made, they are easy to use in your creations.

Rice paper is made from ground rice and water, which is blended to make a syrupy liquid, then poured thinly over either a bamboo mat or a cheese cloth before it is steamed. Once cooked, they are removed and sun dried. This is a versatile ingredient. Because rice paper does not contain any gluten, it can be a substitute for wheat-based wrappers.

To prepare rice paper, remove one sheet carefully from the package without breaking or cracking it. Dip the rice paper into lukewarm water to wet and soften it, then remove it immediately and place it on a working surface. When it is pliable, fill it with your favorite fillings that do not contain too much liquid. For example, fill it with noodle salad, broiled tempeh with nuts, or a leftover bean dish. Fold the paper to make a cylinder shape, and seal the food inside by wrapping the ends, preventing the food from drying out.

Rice paper is used mostly in Vietnamese, Thai, and Southeast Asian cuisine. It is versatile and serves many purposes as a non-wheat wrapping material; but it is an extremely fragile material to handle. Many meals can be created by using different filling combinations. Once it is wrapped, it can be served cold or cooked in a hot oven for a crispy, crunchy wrapper.

SALAD ROLL WITH TAHINI MISO SAUCE

This is a handy dish that you can prepare ahead of time for lunch or for a delicious refreshing snack. If the roll is wrapped properly, the contents will keep for up to twenty-four hours or more. You can roll up almost anything that is edible, but avoid high water-content foods to prevent the paper from getting soggy. Serve the sauce in a separate small container as a dip for the rolls. Choose any type of dressing that is thick enough to cling to the roll.

In Vietnamese cuisine, a light peanut sauce or sweet vinegar sauce is served with the roll for dipping. Don't limit yourself. Create your own sauce by using your imagination and blending your favorite ingredients. For a creative stuffing, try a combination of avocado and cucumber with fresh mint leaves, spicy tofu, and peanuts or tomato, or seitan and spinach with chickpea spread, and so on. Just have fun using whatever you like as filling.

> 1 cup shredded lettuce
> 1 cup grated carrot
> 1 cup cooked rice noodles
> ½ cup shredded bamboo shoots
> 1 cup pressed tofu, julienne (optional)
> 8 sheets rice paper, 8 inches in diameter

Hot Tahini Miso Sauce

¼ tsp. hot chili oil
3 tbsp. tahini
6 tbsp. warm water
2 tbsp. white miso
1 tsp. minced ginger
2 tbsp. soy sauce
2 tbsp. natural sweetener
1 tbsp. lemon juice

Combine lettuce, carrot, noodles, bamboo shoots, and tofu; set aside. Combine Tahini Miso Sauce ingredients; set aside. Soften rice paper by dipping it very briefly in warm water; place on a working counter. When rice paper is pliable, place a small amount of stuffing ingredients in the center, and spoon 1 tablespoon of sauce over top. Fold both ends over, then roll the rice paper to make a cylinder shape. If these are to be stored, wrap in plastic wrap or brush with vegetable oil.

Yield: 8 rolls
Preparation Time: 10 minutes

SPINACH-FILLED CRISPY RICE PAPER ROLL

4 tbsp. oil
1 tbsp. minced garlic
½ small onion, minced
8 oz. medium soft tofu, pressed
1 bunch spinach, washed, cut into ½-inch lengths,
   and blanched
2 tbsp. tamari or soy sauce
1 tbsp. nutritional yeast
4 tbsp. minced scallion
5 6-inch sheets rice paper

Heat wok until hot, then add 3 tablespoons of the oil. Sauté garlic and onion until soft and transparent. Add tofu and scramble into small pieces. Continue to cook until the tofu's water is almost evaporated. Add spinach and toss with soy sauce and nutritional yeast. Cook for another minute, then add scallion. Remove from the heat and cool, then set aside.

Dip rice paper in warm water, then place it on a counter top. Divide the filling into 5 portions. Arrange a portion on each sheet of rice paper, then roll it by folding both ends first then making a cylinder. Place rolls on a baking pan, seam side down, and brush surface lightly with remaining oil. Bake in a preheated 400-degree oven for 5 minutes or more, until golden crisp on the outside. Serve hot.

Yield: 5 rolls
Preparation Time: 10 minutes

Zo-Sui

Zo-sui is a not pretty expression for any dish as far as the direct translation is concerned. But for the Japanese, especially for men, it is a must. After Japanese men have been out drinking heavily, they usually cap the evening by eating *ocha-zuke* or *zo-sui* to settle their stomachs before they go to bed. Ocha-zuke is a dish of rice with condiments on top and piping hot green tea poured over all. The condiment could be pickled daikon or some dried salted salmon with seaweed. Customarily, wasabi is served on the side.

Zo-sui is a dish that can consist of almost anything that you find in the kitchen, but it is primarily rice. *Zo* means "mixed, nothing in particular, or miscellaneous." *Sui* means "braised or cooked." I use leftover rice and basic soup stock with various vegetables to make a fabulous meal. You can serve it in a large bowl as a main course.

MINESTRONE-STYLE ZO-SUI

1 cup leftover rice
1 oz. salted or dried wakame
1 thumb-size piece fresh ginger root
5 cups dashi or other vegetable stock
2 tbsp. sake
½ tsp. sea salt
1 tsp. mirin
1 tbsp. soy sauce
1 to 2 oz. enoki mushrooms,
    ½-inch bottom removed

Wash rice, drain in a sieve, and set aside. Wash wakame in a colander, cut into bite-size pieces, then pour hot water over wakame. Drain and set aside. Peel ginger, grate, and set aside. Put dashi in a ceramic or stainless pot, and bring to a boil. Add sake, salt, mirin, soy sauce, and enoki mushrooms. Add rice and bring to a boil, then reduce heat and simmer for 10 minutes. Add wakame just before serving, stir. Garnish with grated ginger on top of the soup.

Yield: 4 servings
Preparation Time: 20 minutes

Various Rice Main Dishes

NASI-GOREN

This is a popular spicy Indonesian rice dish that is very simple to make. Use leftover long grain or basmati rice for the best results. It is better to make your own sambal sauce and always keep it handy. Sambal sauce is an excellent seasoning and appetite enhancer. Remember that it is hot, and use it sparingly.

2 tbsp. salad oil
½ onion, chopped fine
1 cup cooked brown long grain rice
1 to 2 tsp. sambal sauce
2 oz. cucumber, sliced thin
1 lemon, sliced

Sambal Sauce

1 tsp. chili powder
1½ oz. red dried chili
½ cup water
1 tbsp. oil
½ onion, minced
1 tsp. minced garlic
1 stalk lemon grass
½ tsp. salt
½ tsp. pepper

Make Sambal Sauce first. Blend chili powder, chilies, and water in a blender. Heat a flat skillet, then add oil. Sauté onion until transparent. Add remaining sauce ingredients. Cook over low heat for one hour, then remove and cool. Keep in an airtight container.

In a frying pan, sauté other half onion in oil until transparent. Add brown rice and stir-fry for 1 minute, tossing frequently to separate rice. Add 1 to 2 teaspoons sauce according to your taste. Toss quickly to prevent sambal sauce from sticking. Serve garnished with cucumber and lemon slices.

Yield: 2 servings
Preparation Time: 3 to 4 minutes

WILD AND BROWN RICE PILAF WITH CASHEW CREAM SAUCE

2 tbsp. oil
½ cup onion, minced
2¼ cups brown rice
¼ cup wild rice
2 stalks celery, chopped
1 tbsp. garlic, minced
¼ tsp. thyme
¼ tsp. sage
1 tsp. soy sauce
2½ cups stock or water

Cashew Cream Sauce

1 cup cashew pieces, lightly toasted
2½ cups water
1½ tbsp. safflower oil
2 tbsp. rice flour
1 tsp. ginger, minced
2 tsp. soy sauce or tamari
1 tbsp. parsley, minced
1 tbsp. white miso

In a heavy skillet, heat oil and sauté onion, stirring until limp and transparent. Add rice, celery, and garlic. Stir-fry for 2 to 3 minutes. Add thyme, sage, soy sauce, and stock. Bring to a boil and simmer over medium heat for 15 minutes. Cover and reduce heat to low; then cook covered until rice is tender, about 30 minutes. Stir to fluff, cover, and leave to steam for 10 minutes, so rice can expand.

To make Cashew Cream Sauce, blend cashews and water in a blender to form cashew milk. Strain through a fine sieve. Set aside. Heat oil in a saucepan over medium heat. Mix in flour, reduce heat to low, and cook for 2 to 3 minutes, stirring to prevent burning. Slowly add cashew milk to pan, whisking constantly until it becomes smooth. Add ginger, soy sauce or tamari, parsley, and miso; then simmer for 3 to 4 minutes. Strain through a fine sieve and adjust thickness by adding more water if desired. Pour cashew sauce over rice or serve on the side.

Yield: 5 to 6 servings
Preparation Time: 1 hour

BLACK SESAME RISOTTO
WITH BRAISED BURDOCK ROOT

6 tbsp. olive oil
½ onion, minced
2 cups cooked brown rice
1 tbsp. black sesame seed paste
2 tbsp. lemon juice
Pinch salt
Pinch pepper
½ burdock root, cut into julienne
1 cup dry red wine

Sauté onion in 2 tablespoons oil until transparent. Cool. Mix onion with brown rice. Combine rice mixture, black sesame paste, and lemon juice together, and season with salt and pepper.

Heat a flat skillet until hot, then add 4 tablespoons oil. Sauté burdock root over high heat for one to two minutes. Add red wine, and reduce until almost completely gone. Season with additional salt. Serve rice at room temperature on a platter surrounded by burdock root.

Note: If black sesame seed paste is not available, chop 2 tablespoons of black sesame seeds until a very fine paste is formed. Add ½ teaspoon of sesame oil to the mixture, then use 1 tablespoon of the paste in the recipe.

Yield: 4 or 5 servings
Preparation Time: 20 minutes

Legumes

Legumes are high in protein and fiber. Cooked legumes have less than two grams of fat per cup and contain a rich amount of the B vitamins, thiamin, riboflavin, niacin, complex carbohydrates, and minerals including iron, calcium, potassium, and phosphorus. The amino acids in beans complement those in grains; when eaten together, they provide an abundance of high-quality protein in proper proportion ready for assimilation.

In general, sweet foods and beans are a bad digestive combination. Eat dessert or fruit at least an hour or two after a bean dish. Legumes build up the hemoglobin content of the blood. They prevent cardiovascular disease and lower cholesterol and triglyceride levels.

Cooking Legumes

To prepare beans (except azuki, lentil, black-eyed peas, and mung beans) for cooking, soak them for at least several hours or overnight. Use four times as much water as beans because they will expand considerably. You can also bring liquid with beans to a boil, turn off the heat, cover, and leave for two hours. Add a piece of kombu to shorten their cooking time and help soften them. When using this method, discard the soaking water and wash the beans well, changing the water frequently because the substance in beans that gives you gas is water soluble. To finish cooking the beans, bring the beans to a boil uncovered for 10 minutes. Skim off any foam or skin that rises to the surface, cover, and continue to cook until the beans are tender. Never add any salt seasonings until the beans are tender—they slow down the cooking process considerably.

Azuki Beans

This highly prized Japanese bean is used in desserts, soups, and folk remedies.

Benefits of Azuki Beans

Azuki beans are high in phosphorus, calcium, vitamin A, and protein. Traditional medicine recommends azuki beans cooked with pumpkin or squash to help restore and maintain proper blood sugar balance. The high content of sapponin in azuki beans aids constipation, helps digest fatty acids, and lowers cholesterol and blood pressure. These beans also help with the production of a nursing mother's milk. For centuries, azuki beans have been used in the Orient as a folk remedy for kidney problems.

For constipation, cook 1 cup of azuki beans with 5 cups of water until tender. Eat ½ cup of cooked azuki beans every day or prepare meals with a 3 x 3-inch piece of kombu together with azuki beans. For kidney and water retention problems, eat ½ cup of azuki beans with the same amount of bean cooking liquid with each meal. For low blood pressure and cold fingers (poor circulation), eat 1 cup of cooked azuki beans every day.

Black Beans

Various traditional foods, each symbolizing a hope for the new year, are always included in the first meal of the year in Japan. Black beans symbolize longevity and wealth, and they are eaten at traditional celebrations and happy occasions such as the New Year's holiday, birthdays, and weddings to wish longevity and long happiness.

Boiled and braised black beans, which represent health, are an important part of this special and elaborate dinner. To prepare black beans, soak them for at least 10 to 12 hours before boiling. Boil them because the skins loosen easily and can clog pressure cooker valves. Cook for 1 to 1½ hours.

Benefits of Black Beans

Also known as "meat of the field," black soybeans are almost identical in nutritional composition to yellow soybeans, but are easier to digest and more flavorful. Black beans are an excellent legume noted for their various medicinal advantages. They are thought to help cure a cough, throat pain, and eliminate poison from the kidney. The Japanese, Chinese, and Koreans use it to prevent or relieve water retention, arthritis, rheumatism, and asthma.

As a folk remedy for small intestine and stomach weakness or disorders, boil 3 cups of water and 5 ounces of black beans for 20 minutes. Drain, preserving the liquid, and drink 1 cup of the cooking liquid between each meal.

To prevent arthritis, detoxify beri-beri, and relieve acute nephritis, boil 2 cups black beans with plenty of water until tender. Add 1½ cups of raw natural sweetener and 4 tablespoons tamari before eating.

For asthma and bronchitis, boil ¾ ounce black beans with ¾ cup water for 20 minutes, then drain and drink the liquid slowly.

To relieve water retention, boil 1 tablespoon of both black beans and dried corn for 10 to 15 minutes. Drain the liquid and drink as a tea every 6 hours.

For another Japanese longevity drink, roast ⅓ cup each of dried black beans and azuki beans in a pan over heat for 15 minutes. Remove and cool. Roast ⅓ cup of black sesame seeds over low heat in a pan until they start to pop, then remove and cool. Blend beans and sesame seeds in a blender separately until very fine. Combine together and keep in an airtight container. Make one serving by mixing 1 tablespoon bean and seed powder, sweetener, and 1 cup of water. Boil, then thicken with a kudzu and water mixture.

BLACK BEAN SOUP

1½ cups dried black beans
4 tbsp. olive oil
2 cups finely minced onion
1 tbsp. minced garlic
2 stalks celery, finely minced
6 cups water
2 bay leaves
½ tsp. ground cumin
2 tbsp. soy sauce
½ tbsp. chili powder
1½ tbsp. celery seed
Pinch ground coriander
¾ tbsp. salt
4 tbsp. red miso

Soak beans in water for 3 to 4 hours; drain and rinse well. Set aside. In a thick stainless steel pot, sauté onion and celery in olive oil until soft. Add garlic, and cook for two minutes. Add black beans, water, and the remaining ingredients, except salt and miso, to the pot. Bring to a boil, then lower the heat to simmer. Cook until beans are completely tender. Test a few beans by mashing them with your finger. If they mash easily, without resistance, then they are ready. Remove from the heat. Remove 2 cups of soup and beans from the pot, and blend until completely smooth. Pour back into the pot. Put the pot back on the heat and season with salt and miso. Cook 5 more minutes and serve.

Yield: 4 to 5 servings
Preparation Time: 1 hour 10 minutes (plus 3 to 4 hours soaking time)

Black-Eyed Peas

These legumes with black "eyes" have a distinctive flavor that is good with rice. Prepare and cook by boiling for 1¼ hours. Do not presoak these beans.

BLACK-EYED PEA STEW WITH CURRY

4 tbsp. oil
1 tbsp. minced garlic
1 tbsp. minced fresh ginger root
1 small onion, chopped
1 small leek, chopped finely (white part only)
1 apple, cored and chopped
1 carrot, chopped
2 tbsp. flour
2 tbsp. curry powder
5 cups vegetable stock or water
½ lb. small mushroom
3 large ripe tomatoes, chopped
1 cup dried black-eyed peas
1 tsp. tamarind concentrate

Heat a large pot. Add oil and sauté garlic and ginger for 5 seconds, or until aroma is released. Add onion, leek, and apple. Cook until transparent. Add carrot to the pot and cook for 1 minute. Lower the heat to medium and sprinkle with flour and curry powder. Cook for 2 more minutes, stirring continuously. Add stock, mushrooms, and tomatoes. Bring to a boil, skimming constantly. Add well-washed peas, and cook over medium low heat until peas are tender, about 35 to 45 minutes. Add tamarind about 10 minutes before the peas are tender. Season with salt if desired.

Yield: 6 servings
Preparation Time: 1 hour

Black Chickpeas

Black chickpeas are smaller version of garbanzo beans with their dark skins still attached. They are a good bean to use to make dahl, curry dishes, or to add to soups. Black chickpeas do not require soaking, but before washing them, check for rocks or other debris.

BLACK CHICKPEAS DAHL

1 cup black chickpeas
4 cups water or vegetable stock
2 to 3 tbsp. vegetable oil
1½ tbsp. minced garlic
1 tbsp. minced ginger
2 cups minced onion
¾ tbsp. whole cumin seeds
¾ tbsp. black mustard seeds
2 tbsp. tomato paste
1 whole cinnamon stick
½ tsp. ground turmeric
1 tbsp. curry powder
4 dry red chilies
½ tsp. ground cloves
1 tsp. ground coriander
1 tsp. ground cardamom
¼ cup cilantro, coarsely chopped

Pick and wash black chickpeas well. Boil in 4 cups of water for 30 minutes, checking the water level constantly. If water level reduces, add more water to maintain the same water level. Heat a heavy pot over high heat, add oil, and sauté garlic, ginger, and onion until tender. Lower heat and add cumin and mustard seeds. Sauté for 20 seconds, then add tomato paste. Cook for 1 minute over medium heat. Add crushed cinnamon stick, then sauté for 3 to 4 minutes. Add remaining ingredients, except chopped cilantro, and bring to a boil. Drain the water from black chickpeas, then add them to the pot. Simmer for 1 hour, stirring occasionally until beans are tender. Season, sprinkle with cilantro, and serve.

Yield: 3 to 4 servings
Preparation Time: 45 minutes

Chana Dal

This small, Indian version of the yellow split pea comes hulled and split. The taste of chana dal is earthy and nutty. Prepare them by themselves or with other grains. Roasted chana dal is eaten as a snack in India. Uncooked chana is available in East Indian grocery stores. Chana dal do not require soaking; just sort, rinse, and add them to the recipe.

Chana Flour

Made from chana dal, this flour is widely used in many Indian dishes. It makes an excellent thickening agent for stews, soups, and some desserts.

Fava Beans

Also known as horse beans or broad beans, these are widely used in both West and East Asia, as well as in the Middle East. Fava beans are used in Asia for making miso-type sauces and they can be roasted and eaten as a snack. They are excellent with soups, stews, and salads. There are few types of fava beans available in North America: dried beans with or without skins and fresh beans hidden inside large pods. Fresh fava beans appear seasonally in some Chinese grocery and specialty stores.

Fresh fava beans are protected with a hard shell in a pod. To remove the hard shell, remove beans from pods and boil in lightly salted water for ten minutes, or until tender. Drain to cool. You may have to bite into one to test for tenderness. Place them in the refrigerator for several hours to firm the inside of the beans for less breakage when peeling. Once peeled, they are ready to sauté or add to soups or salads.

To prepare dried fava beans with shells, boil for 2 to 3 minutes, then remove from heat. Leave beans in the hot water for 1 to 1½ hours, then bring to a boil again. Cook for 45 to 50 minutes, or until tender. Rinse under the cold running water, then peel. One cup of beans makes two cups of peeled fava beans. They are excellent stir-fried, stewed, added to soups, and puréed.

FALAFEL

½ cup fava beans, mashed
½ cup chickpeas, mashed
¼ cup cooked semolina or cooked fine bulgur wheat
1 large onion, minced
1 tbsp. garlic, minced
¼ cup parsley, minced
½ tsp. thyme
¼ tsp. cayenne
1 tbsp. lemon juice
1 tbsp. corn starch
1 cup wheat germ

Mix all ingredients well. Adjust consistency with wheat germ. Form into 1½ to 2-inch balls. Deep-fry in 390-degree oil until crisp.

Yield: 24 to 26 balls
Preparation Time: 15 minutes

Garbanzo Beans or Chickpeas

These beans have a unique nutty taste and are a popular ingredient in the Middle East, India, and the Mediterranean. They are used in stews, dahl, dips, spread, and many other types of dishes.

To prepare chickpeas, add a pinch of baking soda (about ⅛ teaspoon) to 1 cup of chickpeas and 5 cups of water. Soak overnight to help soften their insides nicely. Cook with soaking liquid until tender. Cooking time will vary, depending on the beans, from 1 hour to 3 hours. Beans are like grains—the older the beans, the longer they take to cook.

Chickpea Flour

Chickpea flour is an excellent thickening agent that gives a rich-looking, light yellow color to stews and soups. It is mild and blends well with other types of flour. Substitute chickpea flour for 25 percent of the recipe's flour. Chickpea flour is available at most East Indian stores, and is sold sometimes as "gram" flour. Don't confuse gram flour with graham flour (a wheat flour).

Great Northern Beans

Highly versatile, great northern beans are puréed for dips or spreads, or added to soups, salads, and other dishes. To prepare these beans, soak them overnight, then boil them for ½ to 2 hours.

Kidney Beans

Red kidney beans are a popular bean in many countries. In Mexico, I ate a lot of dishes made from this bean. It is meaty and versatile. It comes in a can, cooked, and is available at all supermarkets. To cook your own kidney beans, wash them well and drain. For each cup of kidney beans, use 6 to 7 cups of water. Bring to a boil, lower heat to low, and cook for 5 minutes, uncovered. Turn off the heat, and leave the beans in the pot for 1 to 2 hours. Heat again, covered this time, for 40 to 45 minutes, or until tender. Add seasonings 5 to 7 minutes before completion.

KIDNEY BEAN SALAD

1 cup dried kidney beans
7 cups water
1 tbsp. minced garlic
½ cup walnut meats
1 tbsp. dijon mustard
1½ tbsp. brown rice vinegar
1 whole chili, seeds removed
3 tbsp. olive oil
2 tbsp. minced green onion
2 tbsp. minced cilantro

Cook kidney beans in water until tender. Drain and reserve ½ cup of liquid to make dressing. In a blender, place garlic and walnuts. Blend until a paste is formed. Add mustard, vinegar, and chili; blend again. Scrape the sides of the blender, then slowly add oil to the mixture. Add reserved liquid from cooked beans to the mixture to make a smooth paste, about 4 to 5 tablespoons. Combine beans and dressing together with green onion and cilantro. Chill overnight, tightly covered.

Yield: 4 to 5 servings
Preparation Time: 1 hour

KIDNEY BEAN STEW

1 onion, finely shredded
1 green pepper, chopped
2 tbsp. olive oil
1 tbsp. oregano
1 tsp. ground cumin
1 tbsp. chopped fresh garlic
1 tsp. chili powder
1 tbsp. fresh coriander leaves
1 cup crushed tomatoes
1 cup cooked kidney bean juice
1 tbsp. vinegar
1 tbsp. barley malt
1 bay leaf
2 cups cooked kidney beans
1 tsp. sea salt

In a large pot, sauté onion and green pepper in olive oil until tender. Add oregano, cumin, garlic, chili powder, and coriander leaves. Sauté for five minutes, then add remaining ingredients, except salt. Bring to a boil, then lower heat to simmer for 50 to 60 minutes, until beans absorb the flavor from the sauce. Season with salt, if desired.

Yield: 6 to 8 servings
Preparation Time: 1 hour 10 minutes

Lentils

Lentils cook quickly, which may be why they are a popular legume in many nations. This bean does not require soaking, so wash and clean them well before adding them to recipes.

LENTILS WITH SPINACH

2 bunches fresh spinach
5 tbsp. olive oil
1 cup minced onion
1 tbsp. minced garlic
1 tsp. whole cumin seeds
1 cup lentils, cleaned and washed
4 cups hot water
1 whole cinnamon stick
Salt and pepper to taste

Wash spinach well, then drain and cut into ½-inch lengths. Set aside. Heat a heavy skillet, add oil, and sauté onion and garlic until transparent. Add cumin, and cook to bring out the aroma, about 10 seconds. Add lentils, and cook for 10 more seconds. Add 4 cups of hot water, and bring to a boil. Cook until lentils are tender, about 25 to 30 minutes. Add spinach, stir well, and cook for another 2 to 3 minutes, or until spinach is cooked. Stir well, and season to taste with salt and freshly ground pepper.

Yield: 4 servings
Preparation Time: 35 minutes

Pea Beans (Ingen Beans)

These beans originated in middle America and spread over most of the world. They are popular and they have more varieties than any other bean, including yankee (navy), kidney, tiger, pinto (partridge with reddish black spots), or lima (butter or ford hooks). To prepare these beans, soak them overnight, then cook for 1 to 2½ hours in 6 to 7 cups of water (per cup of dried beans). The cooking time will vary.

Peanuts

Peanuts originated in South America, and they were imported to China in the middle of the eighteenth century.

Benefits of Peanuts

Peanuts are high in protein (25 percent) and vitamins B1, B2, and E, and contain trace minerals. They are, however, high in fat (45 percent). Whole peanuts are not easily digested. Peanut butter, already ground, is easier to digest.

PEANUT SAUCE

3 tbsp. oil
½ medium onion, minced
1 tbsp. garlic, minced
1 tsp. curry paste (any kind)
1 cup ground roasted peanuts
⅓ cup natural sweetener
½ tsp. cumin powder
1 tsp. coriander powder
½ tsp. Laos (Siamese ginger)
2 tbsp. coconut milk
½ cup water

In a skillet, sauté onion, garlic, and curry paste in oil until brown. Add peanuts, then sauté for another 40 to 50 seconds. Add natural sweetener, cumin, coriander, and Laos, stirring quickly for another 15 to 20 seconds. Add coconut milk and water, thinning the sauce slowly into a thick smooth paste.

Note: If Laos is not available, substitute fresh grated ginger root.

Yield: ½ cup
Preparation Time: 5 minutes

Split Peas

Split peas are an easily digestible legume best known for making thick, hearty soups. There are several types of split peas available in East Indian or Middle Eastern grocery stores. If you have a chance to browse through these stores one day, purchase a small amount of each type to experiment. Some types use various different names, which can be confusing. Every type of split pea has its own unique flavor and character, but it may not be much different than using the regular western type of split peas or lentils.

To prepare split peas, no presoaking is needed. Just sort, rinse, and cook for 1 to 1½ hours.

VARIETIES OF SPLIT PEAS

Chana Dal

Indian version of split yellow peas.

Masoor Dal

A hulled red (salmon) color split pea.

Mung Dal

A hulled and unhulled mung bean.

Toovar Dal or Arhar Dal

A hulled and unhulled dull yellowish split pea.

Urad Dal

A hulled light yellow color split pea.

YELLOW SPLIT PEAS DAHL

1 cup yellow split peas
4 cups water
3 tbsp. oil
⅙ tsp. asafetida (hing)
½ tsp. coriander, crushed
1 tsp. whole black cumin seeds
2 tsp. curry powder
10 peppercorns
½ tsp. ground turmeric
½ tsp. garam masala
1 medium onion, chopped
1 tbsp. garlic, chopped
1 whole tomato, peeled and chopped
2 tbsp. tamarind concentrate
½ tsp. salt
1 tbsp. grated ginger
2 tbsp. minced cilantro

In a pot, boil split peas and water. Lower heat and simmer until the split peas are almost tender, about 1 hour. Heat a small pot, add 1 tablespoon of oil, then add asafetida. A few seconds later, add the coriander, black cumin, curry powder, peppercorns, turmeric, and garam masala. As soon as the spices darken, whcih should be just a few seconds, remove from heat and set aside to cool. Blend the mixture in a blender until a smooth paste is formed, and set aside.

Heat a medium-size saucepan, add remaining oil, and sauté garlic and onion until transparent. Add the spice mixture and cooked split peas with cooking liquid. Bring to a boil, then lower the heat to medium. Add tomatoes and tamarind concentrate. Cook over low heat for 10 to 15 minutes, adding water if necessary to make a soupy consistency. Add salt and sprinkle with minced cilantro and grated ginger root. Cool for another 5 minutes and serve.

Yield: 3 to 4 servings
Preparation Time: 80 minutes

Soybeans and Soy Products

Soybeans

It is believed that the name *soybean* originated from the Swedish word *soya-bone*. It was introduced by the Swedish Doctor Tunenberg in his *Encyclopedia of Japanese Plants,* who visited Japan in the late seventeenth century. In those days, all foreigners were restricted from entering Japan for any reason with the exception of one city. The city that allowed visitors was Nagasaki, located on the northwest peninsula of Kyushu Island. However, they only allowed one type of visitor—doctors.

Tunenberg travelled from Nagasaki to Edo, present-day Tokyo. He picked a curious variety of samples from the roadside along his journey. He noticed one plant that the Japanese were treating as gold. It produced hairy pods with sweet earthy beans called *daizu* in Japanese. It meant "big" or "large." This bean produced a peculiar, wonderful seasoning that the Japanese used for flavor and a preservative, called *shoyu.* He introduced this golden Japanese plant, the soybean plant, as a major ingredient in soy sauce making in his book. I believe from then on, the word *soya-bone* started to spread over Europe and became "soybean."

Soybeans were considered one of the five major grains in Japan. Next to barley, they were the most important staple for Japanese people. Originating in middle northeast China, it is believed that soybeans were introduced to Japan about two thousand years ago, and have since been cultivated widely in China and Japan. After the Second World War, the United States began to produce soybeans in large quantities. Currently, the United States is one of the largest soybean producers in the world.

Soybeans are versatile and can be used in many forms. They are a major ingredient in tofu, tempeh, natto, miso, shoyu (soy sauce), chiang (Chinese miso), tamari, soy milk, soy flour, soy protein, and textured vegetable protein (TVP). Soybeans are used to make soy butter, stews, condiments, and meat substitutes; and they can be used in recipes in place of white beans.

It is a pleasure to see North America accepting the old Oriental methods of using soybeans—especially producing many high-quality soy products locally. In North America, we have the technology and raw materials to produce excellent soy products. Maybe one day, we will be exporting American miso and Canadian tempeh to Asia. You never know.

Cooking Soybeans

Soybeans take long time to cook until tender, which is perhaps the reason many people avoid cooking them. Cooking a small or large amount of beans does not change the cooking time. When you have the time, prepare a large amount of beans, separate them into two or three portions, then freeze them. It saves time, electricity, and most of all, it is very convenient. They are not seasoned, so you can use them for any dish.

Remove any grits or foreign matter from soybeans, and wash them well, changing the water often. Soak the beans in four times the amount of water overnight. Place soybeans with soaking liquid in a pot, and bring to a boil. Lower heat to low, and cook until tender, about 1½ hours. To test for doneness, squeeze one bean between your fingers—it should mash without force.

Storing Cooked Soybeans

Drain the beans well, then place them in a flat container, and cool. After the beans are completely cooled, put in a freezer bag, seal tight, and freeze; or place beans and cooking liquid together in a container, cool off, then place in the refrigerator.

Benefits of Soybeans

Soybeans are also called "meat of the field" because they contain not only a quality economical source of protein, iron, and trace minerals, but also because they have a high content of linoleic acid and vitamin E. These two nutrients help to prevent hardening of arteries and various degenerative diseases. Soybeans have a considerable amount of lecithin, which is considered a worthy cholesterol binder.

The Japanese use yellow and black soybeans for various reasons; the old way of using soybeans as a remedy is unique and quite interesting. These folk remedies have been used for many years, helping to heal or prevent various illnesses and symptoms, without having advanced medical technology.

Yellow soybeans are used to treat slurred speech caused by a stroke. Cook soybeans in water until they become almost syrupy, then cool. Consume a small amount of syrup, just like you do with cough medicine.

For stiff shoulders, migraine headaches, hypertension, and to strengthen the liver, consume ½ cup cooked soybeans twice a day. For insomnia, combine 2 tablespoons each of natural sweetener and roasted ground soybeans (*kinako*) with hot water. Blend well to make a hot drink. Sip slowly just before going to bed.

For inflammation of the skin or a muscle, make a paste with sesame oil and soy flour, spread evenly over cheese cloth, and place over the inflamed area.

BRAISED SOYBEANS AND HIJIKI

Ready food, as the Japanese call this dish, can be prepared when you have time while reading, studying, or watching television. This is an excellent dish alone or combined with grains. It is usually eaten at room temperature.

> ⅓ cup soybeans
> 4 cups boiling water
> ⅛ cup dry hijiki
> 3 tbsp. soy sauce
> 1 tbsp. mirin
> 1 tbsp. sake

Soak soybeans in cold water for 7 to 8 hours; drain and rinse. Add boiling water to soybeans in a pot, bring to a boil, and cook for 10 minutes. Turn off heat, cover, and leave for 2 to 3 hours. After time is up, bring water to a boil, lower heat, cover, and cook until beans are soft, adding water occasionally. Drain and set aside.

Wash hijiki in cold water, soak for 30 minutes, and drain. Combine soybeans and hijiki in a pot. Fill with just enough water to cover the soybeans. Bring to a boil. Add remaining ingredients. Lower heat to medium, cook for 7 to 8 minutes. Remove from heat and leave all ingredients in the sauce overnight. If necessary, add more seasonings to the beans the next day.

> **Yield: 4 servings**
> **Preparation Time: 3 hours (plus 8 hours soaking time)**

SOY BURGER I

This is a large recipe. If you want to freeze the extra patties, place wax paper between them before wrapping.

5 cups pressure cooked soybeans
2 tsp. sea salt
1 cup small rolled oats
½ tsp. ground black pepper
1 tsp. garlic powder
2 tsp. oregano
1 tsp. basil
3 tbsp. soy sauce
½ tsp. pysillium powder
½ cup onion, minced
½ cup green pepper, chopped

In a food processor, blend all ingredients except onion and green pepper until a thick dough is formed. Remove and transfer to a large bowl. Add onion and pepper, combining by hand until well mixed. Make into a patty or sausage shapes, bake or fry, and serve.

Yield: 24 to 28 patties
Preparation Time: 10 minutes

SOY BURGER II

½ lb. dried soybeans
2 tbsp. oil
1 large onion, minced
1 tbsp. garlic, minced
1 carrot, grated
1 green pepper, diced
1 cup cooked millet
2 tbsp. soy sauce
1 tbsp. red miso
1 tbsp. tomato paste
¼ cup wheat germ
1 tbsp. corn starch
¼ cup soy flour
¼ tsp. dry basil
2 tbsp. parsley, chopped
⅛ tsp. ground black pepper

Soak soybeans overnight. Cook soybeans until tender; drain and mash. Set aside. Sauté garlic and ginger in oil in a skillet. Add vegetables, then sauté until tender. In a large bowl, mix remaining ingredients well. Add soybeans and vegetables; combine thoroughly to form a thick, moist dough. Heat a large skillet. Form 4 to 5-ounce patties and fry until one side is brown; flip and fry the other side until brown.

Yield: 14 to 15 patties
Preparation Time: 20 minutes (plus overnight soaking time)

SOYBEAN FRITTERS

1 cup pressure cooked soybeans
1½ cups liquid from cooked soybeans
½ cup corn kernels (frozen)
2 cups whole wheat flour
1½ tsp. baking powder
1 tsp. salt
1½ tsp. garlic powder
1 tbsp. natural sweetener
1 tbsp. soy sauce
1½ cups onion, minced
1 tbsp. nutritional yeast
2 cups oil for deep frying

In a large bowl, mash soybeans. Add soybean liquid until liquid and beans make a thick paste. Add remaining ingredients and mix well. In a wok, heat oil until ½ teaspoon of fritter comes to the surface immediately when dropped. Deep-fry 1-inch diameter (golf ball size) fritters until golden.

Yield: 30 to 34 fritters
Preparation Time: 15 minutes

Soy Milk

Soy milk is extracted from soaked soybeans that have been ground with water, boiled, and strained through a cloth. The straining removes the pulp (*okara*) and most of the solid residue from the beans. The white liquid obtained is the milk. Soy milk has most of the nutrients soybeans have—it is a wonderful soy by-product. It contains high-quality protein, vitamins B1 and E, and fat. One glass of soy milk has the same amount of protein as one egg. It should be stored in the same manner as milk.

SOY BECHAMEL SAUCE

¼ cup flour
4 tbsp. oil
2 cups plain soy milk
Salt and pepper to taste
Pinch nutmeg

Heat ¼ cup of flour together with oil in a pot over medium low heat. Cook for 2 to 3 minutes, stirring constantly. Add 1 cup of warmed soy milk, and stir slowly until milk starts to boil again. Add remaining soy milk gradually to thin down the paste. After adding all the milk, cook the sauce over low heat for 10 minutes. Season with salt, pepper, and nutmeg.

Yield: 2 cups
Preparation Time: 13 minutes

Soybean Custard

When a coagulant is added to boiled soy milk, it curdles. Curdled soy custard, or *tofu-fah,* is the most tender form of bean curd, produced before it goes through the straining and pressing process to make tofu. It is sold as soy curd or soy pudding and is eaten hot with good tamari, cold with syrup as a snack, or it can be added to soups. Soybean custard is sold by the pint, mostly packaged in plastic containers. It is available in local Oriental food stores.

Natto

Natto is a Japanese product similar to tempeh, an Indonesian fermented soy food. Authentic natto is made from cooked soybeans wrapped in rice straw. Microorganisms from the straw help digest and ferment the beans. It is believed that natto originated from salt-natto, like chiang, from China. The name *natto* comes from it being made in *natsusho* (a storage room) inside a Buddhist temple.

Some people are offended by this slippery gooey food, and will even refuse to be in the same room with it because of its strong odor. I've seen people refuse to walk with a person who has just eaten natto. Try to remember that the Japanese consider natto to be an excellent food for gaining sexual stamina and vitality for both men and women.

To prepare natto, open the frozen package, thaw, then add ½ tablespoon of soy sauce with finely minced green onion and a touch of fresh ginger juice. Stir vigorously with chopsticks until a bubbly sticky mass is formed. Add a touch of prepared Japanese mustard, stir, and it's ready to eat. Condiments that combine well with natto include miso, grated ginger, minced okura, chopped green shiso leaves, minced green onion, jinenjo potato, minced scallion, umeboshi meat, grated daikon, pickled shallots, roasted sesame seeds, roasted powder nori, and minced takana.

Only frozen natto is available in North American Oriental food stores. Natto is eaten with cooked brown rice, millet, in sushi, and in noodle dishes.

Benefits of Natto

Made of cooked soybeans instead of concentrated soy milk, fermented natto has more nutritional value than regular tofu. It has five times the protein and vitamin B2 of regular soybeans. It is also high in vitamins B1, B6, and B12 and low in cholesterol.

Natto is an excellent source of protein, iron, and calcium. It is low in calories, and hence is recommended to many people who need various nutritional input but have weak digestive systems. Because it is fermented, all the carbohydrates are predigested, so it is easy on your stomach. Natto is an ideal food to eat with grains to give complete essential amino acid intake for a day. The Japanese eat natto on a regular basis to adjust intestinal balance.

Okara

In the process of making tofu, ground soybeans are pressed to make soy milk. The remaining pulp is called *okara*. If you have a tofu manufacturer where you live, phone and ask them where you can get okara. They most likely will be happy to get rid of this leftover because it is usually thrown in the garbage. Once in a while, however, it is available at Japanese food stores for those who know how to prepare it. Okara still contains a high amount of protein, fiber, and other trace minerals. It makes an excellent addition to pancakes, muffins, breads, and many other dishes.

In Japan, a chemical company succeeded in making fertilizer and a mulch for growing certain types of medicinal mushrooms from okara. Okara still is a valuable food with plenty of protein left, if you know what to do with it.

OKARA SPRING ROLL IN RICE PAPER

⅓ cup dried shiitake or regular mushrooms
5 to 6 tbsp. oil
1 tbsp. ginger, minced
1 tbsp. garlic, minced
½ cup green cabbage, cut into matchsticks
¼ cup carrot, cut into very fine julienne
½ cup mung bean thread, boiled, drained,
    and cut into 2-inch lengths
½ cup bean sprouts
2 cups okara
4 tbsp. sunflower seeds
2 tbsp. hot chili sauce
6 stalk green onion, shredded
3 tbsp. raw natural sweetener
2 tbsp. soy sauce
1 tbsp. sesame oil
1 tbsp. sesame seeds
10 10-inch sheets rice paper
3 tbsp. flour
2 tbsp. water

Soak shiitake in warm water for 1 hour; remove and discard stems. Cut mushrooms into very thin slices. Heat a wok until very hot, then add oil and sauté ginger and garlic for 10 to 15 seconds. Add cabbage, carrot, mushrooms, and bean thread; cook until vegetables are tender, about 1 minute. Remove from heat and transfer to a large bowl. Add remaining ingredients except rice paper, flour, and water. Stir well and set aside.

Dip rice paper in lukewarm water for 1 second; remove and place on a cutting board. Place about ⅓ cup of stuffing on each sheet of rice paper, then roll up to make ½-inch cylinder rolls. Mix together flour and water, then use the paste to seal the ends of the rolls. Arrange the rolls on a greased roasting pan. Bake in a preheated 400-degree oven until crispy and golden in color.

Yield: about 10 rolls
Preparation Time: about 12 minutes (plus 1 hour soaking time)

Tempeh

Recently, tempeh has been gaining popularity in the West. It is a staple in Indonesia produced by fermenting cooked soybeans with a starter culture that is grown in hibiscus leaves. Versatile, nutritious, and easy to use, it is available in most natural food stores.

Sometimes gray or black spots appear on the tempeh. These are caused by natural sporulation and should cause no worries. Tempeh can be purchased fresh or frozen, with or without grains. If you have any problem finding tempeh products, ask at your favorite natural food store.

Normally Indonesian deep-fried tempeh is cooked until a chewy crispy skin is formed. With a little imagination, this product can be used in many dishes where you want a meat substitute to obtain enough protein, calcium, and vitamin B12 (e.g., Teriyaki Tempeh or Glazed Tempeh in Madeira Sauce). To prevent tempeh from absorbing large amounts of fat, try sautéing it over high heat with a small amount of oil, or brushing it with a little oil and broiling or baking it in a oven.

Benefits of Tempeh

Tempeh is high in protein, calcium, and vitamin B12.

FRIED SPICY TEMPEH

1 8-oz. pkg. tempeh
1 tsp. salt
1 tbsp. soy sauce
2 tbsp. natural sweetener
3 cups water
3 to 4 tbsp. oil
1 tbsp. minced garlic
1 tbsp. minced ginger
1 tbsp. minced jalapeño pepper
2 tbsp. coarsely chopped cilantro
1 tbsp. lime juice
¼ cup roasted cashews

Mix the first five ingredients except tempeh. Marinate tempeh in brine for 25 to 30 minutes. Remove tempeh from brine, pat dry, and cut into bite-size pieces.

Heat a flat skillet, add oil, and fry tempeh until golden. Add garlic, ginger, and jalapeño pepper, tossing for 10 seconds. Remove from heat and sprinkle with cilantro and lime juice. Toss in cashews and serve immediately.

Yield: 2 servings
Preparation Time: 35 minutes

BARBECUED TEMPEH

2 8-oz. pkg. tempeh, cut into ¾-inch slices
4 tbsp. oil
1 cup barbecue sauce
1 cup sliced mushrooms

Heat a large cast iron skillet. Add oil and fry tempeh until gold and crispy. Remove from the pan and pat dry. Add ½ cup of sauce, place tempeh and mushrooms over the sauce, flatten firmly, then cover with remaining sauce. Place in a preheated 350-degree oven for 15 to 20 minutes, or until the sauce starts to bubble. Remove from oven and serve.

Note: See index for Barbecue Sauce recipe.

Yield: 4 to 5 servings
Preparation Time: 25 minutes

Tofu

Tofu is a well-known Japanese food in the West. It is versatile, nutritious, economical, and available in stores almost everywhere. As most westerners become aware of the health dangers of overeating dairy products, meat, and eggs, they are turning to tofu as an excellent source of easily digestible protein.

Tofu is made from concentrated soy milk and *nigari* (natural sea salt concentrate). There are several kinds of tofu available: soft tofu, firm tofu, pressed tofu, soy milk curd, and several kinds of deep-fried tofu.

I have experienced quite a few amusing incidents relating to tofu over the past several years. Being a cook, many comments about tofu passed by my ears, and most were like "Do you eat that stuff?" or "I don't mind tofu as long as it's cooked with meat," and finally, "You serve those tasteless spongy beige curds with plants (referring to artichokes)?" It seems funny to me to hear comments like these because tofu was a common food to me while in Japan. If I was born in North America and had not had been educated about tofu, I would probably would say the same things about something so strange. To be honest, I think the first person to try beef, sea cucumber, or tofu must have been very brave.

I made edible "human" meat as a prop for the movies *Alive* by Touchstone Pictures and *Arctic Blue*. On both occasions, it seemed that eating tofu was delightfully preferable to eating animal or human flesh.

When using tofu, remember that the tofu's water content will vary depending on the manufacturing procedure used for pressing. The water content will affect the cooking process a great deal.

VARIETIES OF TOFU

Deep-Fried Thick Tofu or Atsu-Age

Unlike *usu-age, atsu-age* has a chewy texture outside yet is still soft and moist inside when eaten fresh from the deep-fryer. It is a perfect material to braise with various sauces. If done properly, the tofu will absorb the sauce, and the hot sauce will burst out when chewed. What a sensation! This product is available under various names such as tofu cutlet and deep-fried tofu.

To make this tofu, the whole piece is usually used, but it may also be cut into various shapes. It is pressed first, then deep-fried in oil at high temperatures until the outside of the tofu becomes crispy and gold in color. Atsu-age is an excellent substitute for meat in many dishes, but be sure to boil it first to remove excess oil before using.

As another type of deep-fried tofu available in various sizes and shapes, it can be found at most Oriental stores and health food stores. It is normally packaged in heavy plastic or sold in bulk.

Deep-Fried Thin Tofu or Usu-Age

Deep-fried thin tofu, tofu puff, tofu pouch, or *usu-age* is a Japanese and Chinese product made from tofu, and is essential to Japanese and Oriental cooking. It is also called *abura-age* in Japanese. When properly fried, tofu should be crisp and golden outside and soft and tender-moist inside. The chewy texture of usu-age makes for an excellent addition to many dishes. Nutritional and versatile, usu-age is commonly added to soups, sautéed with hijiki seaweed or other delicate vegetables, braised in soy sauce and filled with seasoned rice, or cut open at three ends to make a sheet to use as an excellent wrapper.

It is normally cut into rectangular shapes and deep-fried in medium-temperature oil for 20 to 30 minutes. It is then placed in hot oil to complete the cooking process, so the protein of the tofu becomes crisp and chewy and the trapped air inside makes it puffy.

Tofu pouches are made by pressing a firm tofu block, slicing it thin, then slowly deep-frying it at medium heat for 30 to 40 minutes, until it is puffed up to five times its original size. This thin, crispy deep-fried tofu is also used as a filling, sautéed with vegetables, braised with seaweed, or broiled until crisp.

Because it is a deep-fried product, be sure to remove excess oil by boiling it first, then wash under cold running water to remove the excess oil, and squeeze out excess water before using. Usu-age is available in clear packages in most Oriental grocery stores—Japanese ones in particular—in the refrigerated food section. It is usually labeled as "tofu pouch" or "usu-age."

Fermented Tofu

Fermented tofu, or *fu-yu,* is made by fermenting salted tofu at room temperature, then marinating it in Chinese wine or various types of brine. Mainly used as a salty flavoring, it has a very strong and cheesy flavor for most of us, similar to blue cheese or Roquefort cheese.

To use this type of tofu, sauté it with a small amount of oil over medium heat to increase its aroma. If you prefer, add garlic or ginger with fu-yu. Mash with the back of a ladle to make a paste, then add other ingredients. It is an excellent substitute for cheese when blended with different tofu products and other ingredients.

Firm Tofu

The Japanese call firm tofu *momen-dou fu* after the pattern of cotton on the bottom of the tofu. Depending on the manufacturer, the taste and texture of the tofu will vary. Firm tofu is versatile—an excellent addition to many dishes for almost any purpose. If it is packaged or bought in bulk, open the package and place tofu in a glass or ceramic container filled with water. Refrigerate and change the water daily to maintain freshness. It should last for 4 to 5 days. To find the best tofu in your area, make a few phone calls to local markets and inquire about their tofu. They should be more than happy to provide you with information. All tofu products are available at supermarkets and health, ethnic, and Asian food stores.

This type of tofu is excellent for those who want to cut down on eating eggs, but are not sure what to eat for breakfast. It is a good substitute for eggs, as long as you learn to deal with the water in the tofu.

Mock Duck Tofu

Firm tofu is lightly pressed and mashed; shredded black fungus (wooden ear), gingko nuts, and carrots are added; then it is seasoned and deep-fried. Check with your local supplier for this tofu product. The name *ganmodoki* comes from this product's resemblance to duck skin.

Dried Tofu

Dried tofu, *koya dofu*, is frozen and dehydrated naturally, outside the house in cold weather. This product usually comes from the Nagano prefecture, located northeast of Tokyo. Their cold severe winter makes it an ideal place to produce this type of high-protein tofu. It comes in dried form in boxed packages, and can be purchased in Japanese food stores. To reconstitute, soak in warm water for 30 minutes, and squeeze out excess water before braising.

Pressed Tofu

When tofu is pressed and the water removed, it becomes much firmer than regular tofu, like a firm chewy cheese. Pressed bean curd, or *gon dou-fu,* may be bought either plain or seasoned. There are several types of pressed tofu available in most Chinese groceries and Oriental food stores.

Plain pressed tofu is an excellent substitute for dairy products, such as ricotta cheese and cottage cheese, when mixed with nutritional yeast, lemon, or brown rice vinegar. To mix flavorings, open the package and place the tofu in the food processor. Blend on high speed for three seconds, then stop and scrape the sides of the processor. Blend for three more seconds, then remove the dry cottage cheeselike substance to a bowl. Add yeast, pepper, lemon juice, or vinegar according to your taste. It is also excellent sliced thin and marinated in a salad dressing or dip, used as a substitute for noodles, or diced and added to a rice or vegetable dish. Use your creativity.

Flavored pressed tofu has a chewy texture and various tastes from being smoked or marinated with various sauces. It makes excellent mock chicken or mock ham dishes.

Silken Tofu

Soft tofu or silken tofu is translated from *kinu-goshi,* which means "sieved through silk" in Japanese and has nothing to do with the method of production for this tofu. The name comes from the the texture of the cut surface and its resemblance to smooth soft silk. It is used for soups, dressings, and desserts. In hot summer weather, it is served in chilled water with ice, condiments, and a dipping sauce. It has been said that to determine the quality of tofu, it should be served plain. Good tofu does not need assistance. Most silken tofu comes in a package. Keep it in the container until you are ready to use it. It should last 2 to 3 weeks refrigerated.

Benefits of Tofu

Tofu is high in calcium and protein, low in fat, and contains no cholesterol. Tofu is easy to digest and an economical source of protein. It is a particularly important food in a grain-centered diet because it has an abundance of lysine, an essential amino acid present in only small amounts in many grains and grain products. Conversely, tofu is deficient in those amino acids that most grains are high in. This complementary relationship means that tofu and grains eaten together, not necessarily in the same meal, provide considerably more usable protein than they would if eaten alone.

BRAISED TOFU WITH SWEET MISO SAUCE

Add soaked and drained hijiki at the last minute to add a vivid contrast color to this dish.

3 tbsp. oil
1 tbsp. minced ginger
1 tbsp. minced garlic
2 tbsp. red miso
4 tbsp. natural sweetener
7 tbsp. soy sauce
7 tbsp. water
2 lb. deep-fried tofu, cut into bite-size pieces
4 tbsp. arrowroot powder mixed with 4 tbsp. water
1 tsp. sesame oil
4 tbsp. chopped green onion
2 tbsp. roasted white sesame seeds

Heat oil in a wok, then sauté ginger and garlic until aroma is released. Add miso, and sauté for 10 to 15 seconds, then add natural sweetener, soy sauce, and water. Bring to a boil. Reduce heat to simmer, add tofu, then cook for 10 to 12 minutes more, until the sauce is absorbed by the tofu. Thicken the sauce by adding arrowroot powder (starch) and water mixture, while slowly and gently mixing tofu. Add sesame oil and cook for another minute. Sprinkle with green onion and sesame seeds. Serve hot or at room temperature.

Yield: 5 to 6 servings
Preparation Time: 15 minutes

CRISPY TOFU SKIN

This is an excellent material use to wrap rice or other vegetables.

3 3 x 5-inch usu-age pouches
1 tbsp. olive oil
½ tbsp. soy sauce or tamari
½ tbsp. sake

Blanch usu-age in boiling water, then remove and rinse under cold running water. Squeeze out water. Cut ⅛-inch off each side to separate into two sheets. Heat a frying pan, add oil, and fry both sides of tofu sheet until golden. Remove skin from the pan and sprinkle with soy sauce and sake. Serve piping hot.

Yield: 2 servings
Preparation Time: 5 minutes

BRAISED USU-AGE WITH SUE CHOY

To add color, chewy texture, and more food value, add ten pieces of soaked and well-cleaned black fungus with the dashi.

½ cup dashi
3 tbsp. soy sauce or tamari
2 sheets usu-age, prepared as above
    and cut into ½-inch squares
½ tsp. sea salt
½ tbsp. sesame oil
1½ lb. sue choy, washed, cut into ½ x 2-inch pieces
1 tbsp. umeboshi vinegar (optional)

In a medium-sized pot, combine dashi, soy sauce, usu-age, sea salt, and sesame oil. Bring to a boil. When the liquid begins to boil, add sue choy. Cover and cook until sue choy becomes soft. Uncover, reduce heat, and cook over medium heat until the sauce is reduced to 2 to 3 tablespoons. Add umeboshi vinegar, toss, and serve.

Yield: 3 or 4 servings
Preparation Time: 10 minutes

STIR-FRIED SPINACH IN GARLIC AND FU-YU SAUCE

2 tbsp. olive oil
2 cloves garlic, minced
1 small cube fu-yu (fermented tofu)
1 bunch cooked spinach, cut into ½-inch lengths
Pinch pepper
1 tsp. soy sauce
¼ tsp. sesame oil

Heat a wok until hot. Add oil, then add garlic and fu-yu, mashing with back of spatula. Sauté fu-yu until aroma is released. Add spinach and sauté quickly over high heat. Season with pepper and soy sauce. Add sesame oil just before serving.

Yield: 2 servings
Preparation Time: 5 minutes

SAUTEED TOFU PROVENÇAL

16 oz. firm tofu
3 tbsp. olive oil
½ small onion, minced
1 tsp. minced garlic
½ cup bread crumbs
1 tbsp. minced fresh basil
½ tsp. salt
Pinch white pepper
4 tbsp. minced parsley
2 large ripe tomatoes
1 tbsp. olive oil

Wrap tofu in a paper napkin and press for 30 minutes to remove water. Cut in half, then into ¾-inch thicknesses. Heat a skillet until hot, add 1½ tablespoons of oil, and sauté onion and garlic until light gold in color. Add bread crumbs to the skillet, and sauté for one more minute. Add basil, salt, and pepper. Remove the skillet from the heat; set aside.

Heat a larger flat skillet, add remaining oil, and fry tofu until golden brown on both sides. Season with additional salt and pepper, then sprinkle with 2 tablespoons of parsley. Toss gently to coat the tofu evenly. Cut tomatoes into ½-inch slices. Over high heat, quickly sauté tomato slices in a separate skillet with a small amount of oil, then place in a casserole dish. Arrange tofu and crumb mixture on top of the tomato slices, sprinkle with remaining parsley, and bake in preheated 450-degree oven for 3 to 4 minutes, or until golden brown.

Yield: 3 to 4 servings
Preparatation Time: 40 minutes

CURRY-FLAVORED STIR-FRIED TOFU

In this recipe, be sure the tofu is well pressed to remove the water before cooking. If not, the dish will be watery or soggy.

3 tbsp. sesame oil
½ tsp. minced ginger root
1 tbsp. minced garlic
1 small onion, very thinly sliced
1 small green pepper, cut into julienne
2 16-oz. blocks firm tofu, pressed for 1 hour
    and crumbled in large chunks
1 tbsp. curry powder
1½ tbsp. soy sauce
1 tsp. natural sweetener
Pinch white pepper

Heat a wok over high heat, add sesame oil, and sauté ginger and garlic until aroma is released. Add onion and green pepper, and stir-fry until soft. Add tofu, and stir gently. Add curry powder, soy sauce, and natural sweetener. Stir-fry for one more minute, then add pepper, toss, and serve.

Yield: 8 or 9 servings
Preparation Time: 6 minutes

BROILED TWO-TONE TOFU

This dish is known as *dengaku* and is a popular tofu dish in Japan. The tofu is pressed first, then skewered with a flat bamboo fork that resembles a cocktail fork. Sweet miso sauce is then spread over the tofu. Usually it is broiled over hot wooden charcoal. The flavor of miso combined with sweet seasonings increases with broiling and gives the sauce an incredible aroma. It is a tedious recipe, but well worth the effort. To make this in the modern kitchen, I recommend using the oven instead of a broiler or barbecue. Once you master the technique of making this dish, try using other vegetables to make eggplant dengaku, or taro root dengaku. The dengaku miso can be prepared ahead of time, and will keep for up to one month in the refrigerator.

> **2 16-oz. blocks firm tofu**

Spinach Dengaku Miso Sauce
> **5 to 6 leaves spinach**
> **2 tbsp. white miso**
> **1 tbsp. natural sweetener**
> **1½ tbsp. mirin**
> **2 tbsp. dashi**

Red Dengaku Miso Sauce
> **1½ tbsp. natural sweetener**
> **2 tbsp. red miso**
> **1 tbsp. mirin**
> **4 tbsp. dashi**

Press tofu between two plates with a 2-pound weight for one hour; drain and pat dry.

To make Spinach Dengaku Miso Sauce, blanch spinach in boiling water quickly; remove and dip in cold water. Rinse, remove and squeeze out water. Place spinach in a mortar and grind it into a fine paste. Add miso, natural sweetener, mirin, and dashi. Mix well to make a sauce, then set aside.

Place all the Red Dengaku Miso Sauce ingredients in a pot, bring to a boil, and cook over low heat for 15 minutes, stirring continuously to prevent burning; set aside.

Heat oven to 450 degrees for 10 minutes. Cut tofu in half horizontally, then into thirds. Arrange all the tofu pieces on a cookie sheet, leaving a ½-inch space between each piece. Broil for 3 to 5 minutes. Spread miso sauce on top of 6 pieces of tofu and spinach miso on the others; broil for another 3 to 4 minutes, then serve.

> **Yield: 12 pieces**
> **Preparation Time: 20 minutes (plus 1 hour tofu pressing time)**

DEEP-FRIED TOFU
WITH SWEET SOY SAUCE

This is another famous Japanese dish, known as *age-dashi dou-fu* and popular among young and old. My son started eating this dish when he was six months old. It is a simple dish to prepare, but like the Japanese saying, "simple things have depth." Good age-dashi tofu has a chewy skin on the outside, but is soft and watery inside. The sauce is slightly sweet, but not too sweet; and the sauce is warm, but not as hot as the tofu. The tofu must be served extremely hot.

> 1 16-oz. block firm tofu
> 2 tbsp. wheat flour or arrowroot starch
> 3 cups oil
> 1 small thumb-size piece ginger, peeled and grated

Tsuke Dashi (dipping sauce)

> ½ cup dashi
> ½ tbsp. mirin
> 2 tbsp. soy sauce

Press tofu for 20 minutes, drain water, and cut into 8 pieces. Boil tsuke-dashi ingredients for 5 seconds, remove from the stove, cool, and set aside. Dust tofu pieces with flour, removing excess flour by patting between your hands. Deep-fry in hot oil until tofu becomes golden and crisp. Place in a serving bowl, place grated ginger on top and the warm sauce in a bowl just before serving.

> Yield: 2 servings
> Preparation Time: 24 minutes

VEGETARIAN PEPPERY TOFU

This is a famous dish created by an old woman in the Sichuan province. She created this nutritious and tasty meal from simple ingredients. It is known as *ma-po dou-fu,* which translates to "grandmother's tofu." This dish contains all seven seasonings in one, with burning hot chili and piping hot sauce, as well as the slippery tofu and the crunchy texture of za-choy. The water from the tofu will be released into the sauce while cooking, and the sauce will be absorbed into the tofu. Do not overcook the tofu over high heat, or the water trapped in the tofu will expand, ruining the smooth texture of the tofu.

1 tsp. minced ginger
1 tbsp. minced garlic
2 tbsp. oil
1 tbsp. chili bean paste
¼ tsp. salt
7 shiitake mushrooms, reconstituted and minced
2 tbsp. minced Sichuan za-choy
1 tbsp. mushroom soy sauce
2 tbsp. natural sweetener
½ cup vegetable stock
16 oz. medium firm tofu, cut into 1-inch cubes
2 tbsp. dark soy sauce
1½ tbsp. arrowroot powder mixed with 2 tbsp. water
1 tbsp. vinegar
1 tsp. sesame oil
2 tbsp. green onion, minced
Pinch toasted ground Sichuan pepper

Heat wok, then sauté ginger and garlic in oil until light and golden in color. Add bean paste and stir-fry for 10 seconds. Add salt and vegetables; sauté for 30 seconds. Add mushroom soy sauce, natural sweetener, and stock. Bring to a boil. Add tofu and simmer over medium heat for 5 minutes. Add dark soy sauce to adjust color. Thicken with arrowroot powder and water mixture, stirring gently. Cook for 1 more minute. Add vinegar and sesame oil, then toss, being very careful not to break up tofu. Sprinkle green onion and Sichuan pepper on top. Serve piping hot with steamed grains.

Yield: 3 servings
Preparation Time: 10 minutes

PRESSED TOFU SALAD WITH SPINACH

If you wish, sprinkle 1 tablespoon of nutritional yeast on top of the spinach while cooking.

16 oz. pressed tofu, cut into large matchsticks
2 tsp. olive oil
2 tbsp. minced onion
½ tsp. minced garlic
1 whole chili, seeds removed
1 bunch cooked spinach, cut into 1-inch lengths
1 tbsp. wine or brown rice vinegar
2 tbsp. minced capers
Salt and pepper to taste

Arrange cut tofu on top of the serving plate. Heat a skillet, add oil, and sauté onion, garlic, and chili until aroma is released. Add spinach, sauté quickly, then add vinegar, capers, salt, and pepper at the last minute. Remove from heat and place on top of the tofu on the serving plate.

Yield: 2 servings
Preparation Time: 4 minutes

MANDARIN CREPES
WITH SPICY SHIITAKE FILLING

I use pressed tofu as a meat substitute in this famous mandarin crêpe dish. You can make your own hard-pressed tofu by pressing tofu between two cutting boards with a two-pound weight (tilted so the water can drain away). For this recipe, press the tofu for 1 hour. Make the crêpes ahead of time, then freeze them in an airtight plastic bag, and reheat in a steamer. Serve sauce, filling, and crêpes separately, so guests can serve themselves. To wrap a crêpe properly, hold it in your left hand, spread one tablespoon of sauce on the crêpe, add some filling on top. Roll it up and eat it quickly before it has a chance to become messy. If you don't have time enough to make crêpes, serve washed and drained iceberg lettuce leaves instead.

Filling

3 tbsp. olive oil
½ cup shredded pressed tofu
½ cup reconstituted shiitake or fresh mushrooms, sliced
½ cup bean sprouts
¼ cup shredded bamboo shoots
Salt and pepper to taste

Sauce

5 tbsp. soy sauce
1 tsp. chili bean paste
1 tsp. sesame oil
1 tbsp. minced garlic
1 tbsp. arrowroot powder
1 tbsp. natural sweetener

Mandarin Crêpes

1½ cups all-purpose flour
¾ cup whole wheat flour
¾ cup boiling water
2 tbsp. oil

Heat a wok over high heat until hot; add olive oil, then stir-fry all the filling ingredients and season with salt and pepper.

For the sauce, combine all ingredients in a small pan. Bring to a boil and stir until thick. To adjust the thickness, add liquid if needed.

For crêpes, combine flours, then add ¾ cup boiling water slowly to the flour mixture, kneading until dough holds together. On a lightly floured board, knead until smooth, about ten minutes. Cover with a damp cloth and leave at room temperature for one hour.

Shape dough into a long log. Cut into 1-inch-thick slices and cover with a damp cloth. With a rolling pin, roll each slice of dough on a floured board to make a crêpe 3 inches in diameter. Lightly brush oil on one side, then cover with another crêpe that has not been brushed with oil. Press firmly together, return to a board and roll again to make 7-inch round crêpes. Heat a flat skillet on medium high, place a crêpe on the skillet, and press with your palm. Cook for 15 seconds on each side until blisters appear on the crêpe surface and it feels dry. Remove from skillet carefully. Pile crêpes together and wrap. Store in an airtight plastic bag until ready to serve. Serve on a large platter with sauce and filling on the side.

Yield: about 24 crêpes
Preparation Time: 1 hour 15 minutes

Tofu Skin

Tofu skin, *yuba* or *fu-pai,* is made from the layer of skin that forms on top of boiling soy milk. The skin is carefully removed in one piece, then dried. It is paper thin and creamy beige in color. Once soaked in water, it becomes almost transparent. In dried form, it is very brittle and must be handled gently. When purchasing tofu skin, make sure to get them intact.

Tofu skin can be used to wrap foods such as meat, vegetables, rice and beans, then steamed, fried, or deep-fried. It can be made into vegetarian mock duck or mock ham by reconstituting it, tying it into various shapes, then cooking it in a seasoned broth. Tofu skin is available in Chinese food markets and some supermarkets.

To prepare tofu skin, simply soak it in warm water, remove it when it is soft, and use it for wrapping purposes. You can also deep-fry the skin first to give it a crunchy, chewy texture before adding it to a dish.

Wheat-Free and Egg-Free Breakfast Ideas

For those who are allergic to wheat products or suspicious that wheat could be aggravating their allergic symptoms, it may be helpful to try the following recipes for breakfast. Perhaps the symptoms will disappear. When substituting with rice flour, it may be necessary to adjust the amount. Try making one waffle or pancake first; if the result is not satisfactory, then add more rice flour or liquid as required. Do not expect the same results as with wheat flour.

There are more than a few varieties of flour available in various health food stores. Some are excellent for this particular use, and some are not. It is not a big investment to purchase these flours, but read about them before experimenting.

Another important hint to remember when substituting for eggs in baking is to use pysillium powder or slippery elm powder; both are useful binders that don't add too much flavor to your foods. Both are available at your nearest health food store.

BREAKFAST SCRAMBLED TOFU

The arrowroot powder in this recipe is not diluted with water—this is the trick. Sprinkling arrowroot powder on top of the tofu while it is being cooked, while not a conventional method, really works to hold the water of the tofu.

> **2 tbsp. olive oil**
> **⅓ cup sliced mushrooms**
> **1 tsp. minced garlic**
> **1 stalk celery, chopped**
> **1 8-oz. block firm tofu, cut into ½-inch cubes**
> **1 tbsp. arrowroot powder**
> **Salt and pepper to taste**
> **2 tbsp. nutritional yeast**
> **Pinch saffron, basil, or turmeric**
> **1 tbsp. minced parsley**

Heat a skillet until hot, add oil, then sauté mushrooms and garlic until garlic browns slightly. Add celery; stir and cook for one minute over high heat. Add tofu, sprinkle with arrowroot powder, and sauté very quickly. Season and toss for half a minute, sprinkle with nutritional yeast and remaining spices, and serve.

Yield: 2 servings
Preparation Time: 3 minutes

SCRAMBLED MOCK EGG

1 block firm tofu, pressed
⅓ tsp. sea salt
1½ tbsp. tamari sauce
2 tbsp. natural sweetener
¼ tsp. turmeric
3 tbsp. oil
1 tbsp. minced garlic
3 tbsp. minced green onion
2 tbsp. hot chili sauce (optional)
3 tbsp. arrowroot powder mixed with 2 tbsp. cold water

Preheat oven to 400 degrees. After pressing tofu for 30 minutes, crumble into large chunks by hand. Place tofu in a roasting pan, season with salt, tamari, and natural sweetener. Sprinkle with turmeric and stir well. Bake in oven for 20 to 30 minutes. Remove pan from the oven, drain the liquid from the pan, and cool tofu; set aside.

Heat oil in a wok, then sauté garlic over very high heat until aroma is released. Add tofu and green onion, then stir-fry very quickly. Add chili sauce, and cook until all the water is reduced. Thicken with starch and water mixture. Serve with stir-fried or steamed vegetables.

Yield: 4 servings
Preparation Time: 25 minutes

SANTA CRUZ SCRAMBLED TOFU

2 tbsp. oil
4 mushrooms, sliced
1 clove garlic, finely chopped
2 green onions, chopped
½ tbsp. minced chili (optional)
16 oz. firm tofu, crumbled
Salt and pepper to taste
½ avocado, cubed
½ tomato, chopped
1 tbsp. minced cilantro

Heat a flat skillet, add oil, and sauté mushrooms, garlic, and green onions until soft, about 1 minute. Add chilies and stir-fry for 10 seconds. Add tofu, and cook until water begins to release. Season with salt and pepper, then toss with avocado and tomato. Sprinkle with cilantro.

Yield: 4 servings
Preparation Time: 10 minutes

TOFU AND BROWN RICE PANCAKES

2 cups firm tofu, boiled and drained
2 cups cooked medium grain brown rice
½ cup walnuts, roasted and chopped
2 tbsp. lemon juice
½ cup mushrooms, coarsely chopped
½ tsp. sea salt
1 to 2 tbsp. whole wheat flour
1 tsp. garlic powder
2 tbsp. tamari
3 to 4 tbsp. oil

Chop tofu into small pieces. Combine all ingredients, except oil, and form into small patties. Heat a flat skillet, add oil, and fry patties until brown on both sides. Serve.

Yield: about 6 to 7 pancakes
Preparation Time: 10 minutes

WHEAT-FREE WAFFLES

To add more flavor, substitute nut or seed flour for up to 20 percent of the flour and use less olive oil.

1 cup oat flour
1 cup white rice flour
2 tsp. baking powder
4 tbsp. olive oil
1 cup water or fruit juice

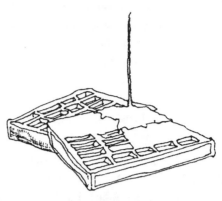

Mix all ingredients to make a thick batter. Let sit for 30 minutes before using. Drop on a hot, lightly oiled waffle iron, and cook as directed.

Yield: 7 to 8 waffles
Preparation Time: 10 minutes

WHEAT-FREE HAZELNUT PANCAKES

You can make your own hazelnut flour, or find it already made at a local health food store.

1¼ cups hazelnut flour
¼ cup tapioca flour
2 tsp. baking powder
1 cup pear or fruit juice
1½ tbsp. oil
Pinch sea salt
2 tbsp. natural sweetener
2 tbsp. tofu, puréed

Mix all ingredients in a blender or food processor to make a thick batter. Chill for 30 minutes. Drop by tablespoonful onto a hot, lightly oiled skillet. Cook one side until gold in color, flip to the other side, then reduce the heat to low and cook for 2 to 3 minutes.

Yield: 12 to 13 pancakes
Preparation Time: 40 minutes

WHEAT-FREE RICE PANCAKES I

1¼ cups brown rice flour
½ cup tapioca flour
¼ cup sweet rice flour
2 cup fruit juice
2 tsp. baking powder
¼ tsp. sea salt
Pinch pepper
2 tbsp. olive oil

Sift all the dry ingredients in a large bowl. Mix wet ingredients. Pour wet mixture into dry mixture slowly, whisking until a smooth batter is formed. Leave at room temperature for one hour. Drop by tablespoonful onto a hot, lightly oiled skillet. Cook until both sides are golden in color. Repeat the process with remaining batter.

Yield: 12 to 13 pancakes
Preparation Time: 1 hour 10 minutes

WHEAT-FREE RICE PANCAKES II

2 cups white rice flour
3 tbsp. baking powder
1 tsp. natural sweetener
¼ tsp. sea salt
¾ cup puréed pears
¼ cup chopped peaches
2 tbsp. olive oil
1 tsp. guar gum
1¼ cup water

Sift all the dry ingredients in a large bowl. Mix wet ingredients. Pour wet ingredients into dry mixture slowly, whisking until a smooth batter is formed. Leave at room temperature for one hour. Drop by tablespoonful onto a hot, lightly oiled skillet. Cook until both sides are golden in color.

Yield: 12 to 13 pancakes
Preparation Time: 1 hour 10 minutes

WHEAT-FREE CRÊPES

For a variation, use 50 to 60 percent chickpea flour (chana) with either oats, brown rice flour, amaranth flour, or sweet rice flour. Chana and amaranth flour are available at local East Indian food stores.

1 cup chana flour
2 to 3 tbsp. oat flour
½ cup or more water or fruit juice
⅛ tsp. sea salt
¼ cup pressed tofu
3 tbsp. plus ½ tsp. olive oil

Blend flours, water, salt, tofu, and 3 tablespoons oil in a food processor or blender until smooth. Heat a large, flat skillet until hot, and spread an additional ½ teaspoon of oil on the bottom with a paper napkin. Pour ¼ cup of batter into skillet, and tilt to cover the bottom of the skillet with batter. When batter starts to bubble and set, flip the crêpe and cook the other side for 3 to 4 seconds. Remove from pan, and repeat the process with the remaining batter.

Yield: about 6 crêpes
Preparation Time:10 minutes

Bibliography

General Nutrition

Composition of Foods; Raw, Processed, Prepared: Agriculture Handbook #8. Washington: U.S. Department of Agriculture, 1963.

Thrash, M.D., Agatha Moody. *Nutrition for Vegetarians.* Thrash Publications.

Lad, Vasant. *Ayurveda: The Science of Self-Healing.* Lotus Press., 1985.

Belleme, Jan and John Belleme. *Cooking with Japanese Foods.* Massachusetts: East West Health Books, 1986.

Carper, Jean. *The Food Pharmacy.* Toronto: Bantam books, 1988.

Dwyer, Johanna T. and Toshio Oiso, M.D. *Changing Food Patterns: Nutrition in Health and Disease and International Development: Symposia From the Xll International Congress of Nutrition.* New York: 1981

Kandans, Ph.D., Joseph M. *Encyclopedia of Fruits, Vegetables, Nuts, and Seeds for Healthful Living.* New York: Prake Publishing Company.

Whitaker, M.D., Julian. *99 Medical Secrets Doctors Won't Tell You.* Phillips Publishing, Inc., 1993.

Kinoshita, Shigetaro . *Kurashi no Naka no Kanpo.* Tokyo: Nicchyu Shuppan Co., Ltd., 1975.

Konishi, Kiyoko. *Japanese Cooking for Health.* Tokyo: Gakken Co. Ltd., 1983.

Smith, M.D., Lendon. *Feed Your Self Right.* New York: Dell Publishing Co., Inc., 1983.

Klaper, M.D., Michael. *Vegan Nutrition: Pure and Simple.* Florida: Gentle World, Inc., 1987.

Muramoto, Noboru. *Healing Ourselves.* New York: Avon Books, 1973.

Nutrition Search, Inc. *Nutrition Almanac.* New York: MacGraw-Hill, 1990.

Hall, Ross Hume. *Food for Naught: The Decline in Nutrition.* Maryland: Harper & Row Publishers, 1984.

National Academy of Sciences. *Recommended Dietary Allowances.* Washington: National Academy Press, 1980.

Apples

Sable-Amplis, R., et al. *Further Studies on the Cholesterol-Lowering Effect of Apple in Humans: Biochemical Mechanism Involved.* 1983.

Apricots

Mahmud, S., et al. "Apricot in the Diet of Hunza Population." *Hamdard* 27 (1984):166

Beans

Beans and Sprouts. Tokyo: Shufu no Tomo. Co., Ltd., 1982.

Troll, W., et al. "Protease Inhibitors: Possible Anticarcinogens in Edible Seeds." *Prostate* 4 (1983): 345-49.

Broccoli

Graham, S., et al. "Diet in the Epidemiology of Cancer of the Colon and Rectum." *Journal of National Cancer Institute* 61 (September 1978): 709-14.

Brussels sprouts

Godlewski, C.E., et al. "Hepatic Glutione S: Transferase Activity and Alfatoxin B1-induced Enzyme Altered Foci in Rats Fed Fraction of Brussels Sprouts." *Cancer Letter* 28 (September 15, 1985): 151-57.

Brown Rice Vinegar

Togo, Kuriwa. *Rice Vinegar: An Oriental Home Remedy.* Tokyo: Kenko Igakusha Co., Ltd., 1977.

Cabbage

Tajima, K., et al. "Dietary Habits and Gastrointestinal Cancers: Comparative Case-Control Study of Stomach and Large Intestinal Cancers in Nagoya, Japan." *Japanese Journal of Cancer Research* 76 (August 1985): 705-16.

Graham, S., et al. "Diet and Colon Cancer." *American Journal of Epidemiology* 109 (January 1979): 1-20.

Carrots

Menkes, M. S., et al. "Serum Beta-Carotene, Vitamins A and E, Selenium, and risk of Lung Cancer." *New England Journal of Medicine* 315 (November 13, 1986): 1250-54.

Norell, S. E., et al. "Diet and Pancreatic Cancer: A Case-Control Study." *American Journal of Epidemiology* 124 (1986): 894-902.

Ziegler, R. G., et al. "Carotenoid Intake, Vegetables, and the Risk of Lung Cancer Among White Men in New Jersey." *American Journal of Epidemiology* 123 (1986):1080-93.

Chili Peppers

Lundberg, J. M., et al. "Cigarette Smoke-Induced Airway Oedema Due to Activation of Capsaicin-Sensitive Vagal Afferents and Substance P Release." *Neuroscience* 10 (December 1983): 1361-68.

Sambaiah, K., et al. "Hypocholesterolemic Effect of Red Pepper & Capsaicin." *Indian Journal of Experimental Biology* 18 (August 1980): 898-99.

Ziment, I., ed. *Practical Pulmonary Disease.* New York: John Wiley and Sons, 1983.

Ziment, I. *Respiratory Pharmacology and Therapeutics.* Philedelphia: W. B. Saunders Company, 1978.

Enzymes

Howell, Edward. *Enzyme Nutrition: The Food Enzyme Concept.* New Jersey: Avery Publishing Group, 1985.

Fats and Oils

Erasumas, Udo. *Fats and oils.* Burnaby, B.C.: Alive Books, 1986.

Free Radicals

Lavine, Stephen A., and Jeffrey H. Reinhardt. "Biochemical Pathology Initiated by Free Radicals, Oxidant Chemicals, and Therapeutic Drugs in the Etiology of Chemical Hypersensitivity Disease" *The Journal of Orthmolecular Psychiatry* 12 (1983).

Eggplant

Ibuki, F., et al. "An Improved Method for the Purification of Eggplant Trypsin Inhibitor." *Journal of Nutritional Science and Vitaminiology* 23 (1977): 133-43.

Garlic

Borida, A. K., et al. "Effect of Garlic on Blood Lipids in Patients with Coronary Heart Disease." *American Journal of Clinical Nutrition* 34 (1981): 2100.

Departments of Neurology and Traditional Chinese Medicine and Pharmacology of the First Affiliated Hospital and Department of Microbiology, Hunan Medical College, Changsa. "Garlic in Cryptococcal Meningitis: A Preliminary Report of 21 Cases." *Chinese Medical Journal* 93 (1980): 123-26.

Lau, B.H.S., et al. "Allium-Satvbum (Garlic) and Atherosclerosis: A Review." *Nutrition Research* 3 (1983): 119-120.

Srivastava, K. C. "Evidence for the Mechanism by Which Garlic Inhibits Platelet Aggregations." *Prostaglandins, Leukotrienes, and Medicine* 22 (1986): 313-21.

Ginger

Giri, J., et al. "Effect of Ginger on Serum Cholesterol Levels." *Ind. J. Nutri. Dietet.* 21 (October 1984): 433-36.

Srivastava, K. C. "Effects of Aqueous Extracts of Onion, Garlic, and Ginger on Platelet Aggregation and Metabolism of Arachidonic Acid in the Blood Vascular System: In Vitro Study." *Prostaglandins, Leukotrienes, and Medicine* 13 (1984): 227-35.

Grape

Shackleton, B. *The Grape Cure: A Living Testament.* London: Thorsons Publishers Limited, 1964.

Kale

Khachik, F., et al. "Separation, Identification, and Quantification of the Major Carotenois and Chlorophyll Constituents in Extracts of Several Green Vegetables by Liquid Chromatography." *Journal of Agricultural & Food Chemistry* 34 (July-August 1986): 603-16.

Lemon

Kroyer, G. "The Antioxidant Activity of Citrus Fruit Peels." *Z. Ernahrungswiss* 25 (March 1986): 63-69.

Miso

Shurtleff, William, and Akiko Aoyagi. *The Book of Miso.* New York: Ballantine Books, 1976.

Mushrooms

"Mushrooms." *American Health Magazine,* (May 1987): 129-34.

Chibata, I., et al. "Lentinan: A New Hypocholesterolemic Substance in Lentinus Edodes." *Experientia* 25 (1969): 1237.

Chihara, G. "Experimental Studies on Growth Inhibition and Regression of Cancer Metastases." *Gan to Kagaku Ryoho.* 12 (June 1985): 1196-1209.

Hammerschmidt, D. E. "Szechuan Purpura." *New England Journal of Medicine* 302 (May 22, 1980): 1191-93.

Takehara, M., et al. "Isolation and Antiviral Activities of the Double-Strained RNA from Lentinus Edodes (Shiitake)." *Kobe Journal of Medical Science* 30 (August 1984): 25-34.

Kabir, Y. "Effect of Shiitake (Lentinus edodes) and Maitake (Grifola frondosa) Mushrooms on Blood Pressure and Plasma Lipids of Sponteneously Hypertensive Rats" *Journal of Nutrition and Vitaminology* 33(October 1987): 341-46.

Bergner, Paul. "Medicinal Mushrooms." *Health World Magazine.* (November/December 1988).

Oats

Degroot, A. P., et al. "Cholesterol-Lowering Effect of Rolled Oats." *Lancet* 2 (1983): 203-4.

Judd, P. A., et al. "The Effect of Rolled Oats on Blood Lipids and Fecal Steroid Excretion in Man." *American Journal of Clinical Nutrition* 34 (1981): 2061.

Olive Oil

Grundy, S. M. "Comparison of Monounsaturated Fatty Acids adn Carbohydrates for Lowering Plasma Cholesterol." *New England Journal of Medicine* 314 (March 20, 1986): 745-48.

Onion

Attrep, K. A., et al. "Separation and Identification of Prostaglandin A1 in Onion." *Lipids* 15 (1980): 292-97.

Bordia, A. K., et al. "Effect of Active Principle of Garlic and Onion on Blood Lipids and Experimental Atherosclerosis in Rabbits and Their Comparison with Clofibrate." *J. Assoc. Phys. Ind.* 25 (1977): 509.

Potato

Kantorovich-Prokudina, E. N., et al. "Effects of Protease Inhibitors on Influenza Virus Reproduction." *Vopr. Virusol* 27 pt. 4 (July/August 1982): 452-56.

Rice

Ohkawa, T., et al. "Rice Bran Treatment for Patients with Hypercalciuric Stones: Experimental and Clinical Studies." *Journal of Urology* 132 (December 1984): 1140-45.

Salt

Adshed, S. A. M. *Salt and Civilization.* London: Macmillan Academic and Professional Ltd., 1984.

Austin, George T. *Shreve's Chemical Process Industries* New York: McGraw-Hill, 1984.

Othmer, Kirk. *Concise Encyclopedia for Chemical Technology.* New York:John Wiley and Sons, 1985.

"Food Processing Top 100 Food Companies." December, 1990.

Seaweed

Fujihara, M., et al. "Purification and Chemical and Physical Characterization of an Antitumor Polysaccharide from the Brown Seaweed Sargassum fulvellum." *Carbohydrate Research* 125 (1984): 97-106.

Funayama, S., et al. "Hypotensive Principle of Laminaria and Allied Seaweeds." *Journal of Medicinal Plant Research* 41 pt. 1 (January 1981): 29-33.

Furusawa, E., et al. "Anticancer Activity of a Natural Product, Viva-Natural, Extracted from Undaria pinnantifida on Intraperitoneally Implanted Lewis Lung Carcinoma." *Oncology* 42 (1985): 364-69.

Iritani, N., et al. "Effect of Spinach and Wakame on Cholesterol Turnover in the Rat." *Atherosclerosis* 15: 87-92.

Shimada, A. "Regional Differences in Gastric Cancer Mortality and Eating Habits of People." *Gan no Rinsho* 32 (May 1986): 692-98.

Teas, J. "The Consumption of Seaweed as a Protective Factor in the Etiology of Breast Cancer." *Medical Hypotheses* 7 (1981): 601-13.

Yamamoto, I., et al. "Antitumor Activity of Edible Marine Algae: Effect of Crude Fucoidan Fractions Prepared from Edible Brown Seaweeds Against L-1210 Leukemia." *Hydrobiologia* 116 (1984): 145-48.

Yamori, Y., et al. "ÒDietary Prevention of Stroke and Its Mechanisms in Stroke-Prone Spontaneously Hypertensive Rats—Preventive Effect of Dietary Fiber and Palmitoleic Acid." *Journal of Hypertension* (Suppl.) 4 (October 1986) S449-52.

Soybeans

Troll, W., et al. "Soybean Diet Lowers Breast Tumor Incidence in Irradiated Rats." *Carcinogenesis* 1 (June 1980): 469-72.

Takeshi, H. "Epidemiology of Human Carcinogenesis: A Review of Food Related Deiseases." *Carcinogens and Mutagens in the Enviroment,* 1 (1982): 13-30.

Spinach

Iritani, N., et al. "Effect of Spinach and Wakame on Cholesterol Turnover in the Rat." *Atherosclerosis* 15: 87-92.

Lai, C. N., et al. "Antimutagenic Activities of Common Vegetables and Their Chlorophyll Content." *Mutation Research* 77 (1980): 245-50.

Squash and Pumpkins

Wieczorek, M., et al. "The Squash Family of Serine Proteinase Inhibitors: Amino Acid Sequences and Association Equilibrium Constants of Inhibitors from Squash, Summer Squash, Zucchini, and Cucumber Seeds." *Biochemical and Biophysical Research Communications* 126 (January 31, 1985): 646-52.

Sugar

Tamura, Toyoyuki. *Considering Foods and Body: When Can We Stop Calcium Ketsubo-sho, Side effects of sugar.* Tokyo: Mebae Sha, 1987.

Schauss, A. *Diet, Crime, and Deliquency.* Berkely: Parker House, 1980.

Tea

Oguni, I. K., et al. "On the Regional Differences in the Mortality of Cancer for Cities, Towns, and Villages of Shizuoka Prefecture (1972-1978)." *Annual Report of Shizuoka Women's College* 29 (1981): 49-93.

Onisi, M., et al. "Epidemiological Evidence about the Cavity Preventive Effect of Drinking Tea." *Journal of Preventive Dentistry* 6 (1980): 321-25.

Stich, H. F., et al. "Inhibitory Effects of Phenolics, Teas, and Saliva on the Formation of Mutagenic Nitrosation Products of Salted Fish." *Int. J. Cancer* 30 (December 15, 1982): 719-24.

Stich, H. F., et al. "Inhibition of Mutagenicity of a Model Nitrosation Reaction by Naturally Occuring Phenolics, Coffee and Tea." *Mutat. Res.* 95 (August 1982): 119-28.

Tanizawa, H., et al. "Natural Antioxidants: Antioxidative Components of Tea Leaf (Thea sinensis L.)" *Chem. Pharm. Bull.* 32 (1984): 2011-14.

Tomato

Taberner, P. V. *Aphridisiacs: The Science and the Myth.* Philadelphia: University of Pennsylvania, 1985.

Umeboshi Plum

Matsumoto II, Kosai. *The Mysterious Japanese Plum.* Santa Barbara: Woodridgepress, 1978.

Water

"Danger in the Water." *Maclean's Magazine* (Jan 15, 1990): 30-39.

Wheat Bran

Burkitt, D. P., et al. "How to Manage Constipation with High-Fiber Diet." *Geriatrics* (February 1979): 33-40.

Cummings, J. H., et al. "Colonic Response to Dietary Fiber from Carrot, Cabbage, Apple, Bran, and Guar Gum." *Lancet* (January 7, 1978): 5-8.

Index

shiitake and, 127; vitamin B5 and, 37; watercress and, 169

Blood purifiers, grapes as, 108; lemon as, 116; lotus root as, 118

Blood sugar, apple and, 52; oats and, 256; onion and, 137; salt and, 43

Blood thinners. *See* Anticoagulants

Bok Choy, 60, Stir-fried Bok Choy, 60-61

Braising and Stewing. *see* Cooking techniques

Bran: wheat bran, 259

Breast cancer, 327

Broccoli, 61-63; benefits of, 61; Broccoli with Deep-fried Tofu, 62; Steamed Broccoli Salad with Mustard Sauce, 63

Bronchial cough, ginger and, 105

Bronchitis, apricot and, 54

Brown Rice, 264-65; Black Sesame Risotto with Braised Burdock Root, 276; Brown Rice Forestiere, 265; Fried Brown Rice and Wakame in Lettuce Wrap, 268-69; Nasi-Goren, 274-75; Tofu and Brown Rice Pancakes, 317; Sesame Brown Rice, 265; Wild and Brown Rice Pilaf with cashew Cream Sauce, 275-76

Brown basmati, 266

Brown Rice Vinegar, 63

Brussels sprouts, 64-65; benefits of, 64; Brussels Sprouts in Sesame Sauce, 64-65; Brussels Sprouts with Walnuts, 65

Buckwheat Groats and Flour, 249-50; Sautéed Eggplant with Red Pepper and Kasha, 250

Bulgur, 251-52; Bulgur and Yellow Lentil Pilaf, 251

Tabbouleh, 252

Burdock Root, 65-68; Black Sesame Risotto with Braised Burdock Root, 276; Burdock in Sesame Vinegar Sauce, 67; Burdock with Nutty Miso Peanut Sauce, 67-68; Glazed Burdock Root, 66

Cabbage, 68-69; Simple Salt-Pickled Cabbage, 69

Cardamom Pods, Green, 69

Caffeic acid, cabbage and, 68

Caffeine, 17, 36, 37, 42, 43

Calcium, chard and, 75; chilies and, 76; cucumber and, 87; dates and, 96; flax seed oil and, 101; in shiitake, 127; lemon and, 116; mandarin oranges and, 119; requirement of, 40; sources of, 41; symptoms of deficiency of, 41

Cancer, shiitake and, 127; tea and, 328; Cancer research, 58

Capsaicin, 26, 324

Carrots, 69-71; Carrot Salad, 71; Orange Snow, 70; Spicy Herbed Chili Carrot, 71

Catarrh, chard and, 75

Cauliflower, 72-73; Cauliflower with Fresh Mint and Lime Dressing, 73; Chilled Cauliflower with Avocado Taratour, 72-73; Steamed Cauliflower with Aromatic Herbs, 113

Celery, 73-74; Sautéed Celery Kimpira, 74

Chana Dahl, 282

Chana Flour, 282

Chanterelle Mushrooms, 125

Chappati Flour, 260, Chappati, 261

Chard, 75; benefits of, 75; Sautéed Swiss Chard with New Potatoes and Rosemary, 75

Chiang, 79; varieties of, 80. *See also* Miso

Chickpeas. *See* Garbanzo Beans

Chickpea Flour, 283

Chilies, 76-79; benefits of, 76; Chili Bean Paste, 78; Hot Chili Oil, 79; Hot and Sour Dressing, 77; Jalapeño Pepper Dip, 78; Sichuan Chili Bean Paste, 77

Chinese broccoli. *See* Gai-lan

Chinese Cabbage (haku-sai or nappa), 79

Chlorine, cucumber and, 87; flax oil and, 101

Chlorophyll, 68, 325, 328; blanching and, 29; cabbage and, 68; spinach and, 150; cauliflower and, 72; oil and, 20

Cholera, garlic and, 104

Cholesterol, apple and, 52; barley and, 249; carrot and, 70; garlic and, 104; lecithin and, 115; manganese and, 43; miso and, 121; natto and, 298; oats and, 256; onion and, 137; sea vegetables and, 215; sesame oil and, 145; shiitake and, 127; soy beans and, 293

Choline, 41

Chow Mien Noodles, 231; Crispy Cantonese-Style Chow Mien, 233-34